Metal Milestones bietet Ihnen praxisorientiertes Fachenglisch für Metallberufe an Berufsschulen, Berufsfachschulen, Fachschulen sowie für technisch ausgerichtete Englischkurse in der Erwachsenenbildung.

Metal Milestones im Überblick:

- Konsequente Berücksichtigung neuester Lehrpläne (Lernfelder) sowie durchgängiges Sprachkompetenztraining nach dem Gemeinsamen Europäischen Referenzrahmen (Sprachstufen A2 – B2).
- 20 kompakte 4-seitige Module: Fachmodule mit Schwerpunkt auf Fachenglisch wechseln sich mit Modulen (A – H) ab, in denen der Schwerpunkt auf der beruflichen Kommunikation liegt.
- Schnelle Orientierung im Buch durch Übersicht der Lernziele jeweils am Modulanfang.
- Die Kompetenzen auf einen Blick: Viele Aufgaben bereiten bereits gezielt auf die Anforderungen des KMK-Zertifikats hin. Diese Aufgaben sind mit den Kürzeln R (Rezeption), P (Produktion), I (Interaktion) und M (Mediation) gekennzeichnet.
- Typische Sprachhandlungssituationen im Berufsalltag werden multimedial mit Audio- und Videounterstützung (u. a. Originalvideos der BBC) trainiert.
- Zahlreiche Partner-, Gruppen- und Internetaufgaben werden durch Texte und Aufgaben zur Arbeitssicherheit *(Safety first)* abgerundet.
- In den Modulen befinden sich hilfreiche Verweise auf die nach beruflichen Situationen geordneten Redewendungen *(Phrases)*.
- Unter der Überschrift *Understanding technical English* befinden sich Hinweise und Aufgaben zum richtigen Umgang mit englischem Fachvokabular.
- Möglichkeit zur Binnendifferenzierung durch anspruchsvollere Aufgaben sowie Aufgaben zur Vorbereitung auf das KMK-Fremdsprachenzertifikat in verschiedenen Stufen.
- Auf den Fachwortschatz in den jeweiligen Modulen kann über die *Word Bank* (auf jeder Doppelseite) direkt zugegriffen werden.
- Online-Grammatiktraining über die Milestones-Codes 🌐 3u5mw9 in den Modulen A – H.
- Vertieftes Grammatik- und Hörverstehenstraining im Workbook mit Prüfungsvorbereitung auf das KMK-Fremdsprachenzertifikat inklusive Audio-CD-ROM mit allen technischen Milestones-Fachbänden- und Workbook-Audios (MP3).

Milestones Workbook für technische Berufe mit Prüfungsvorbereitung KMK-Fremdsprachenzertifikat und Audio-CD-ROM

Lehrerhandbuch für alle technischen Milestones-Fachbände mit 6 Audio-CDs + Digitaler Lehrer-Service (Lehrer-Software mit multimedialen Schülerbüchern, Audios, Videos, Lösungen, Übungsmaterial, Übungsgenerator, Dokumentenpool mit veränderbaren Materialien)

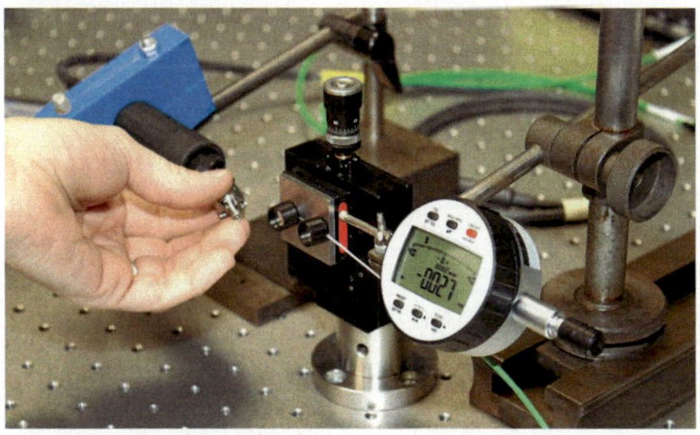

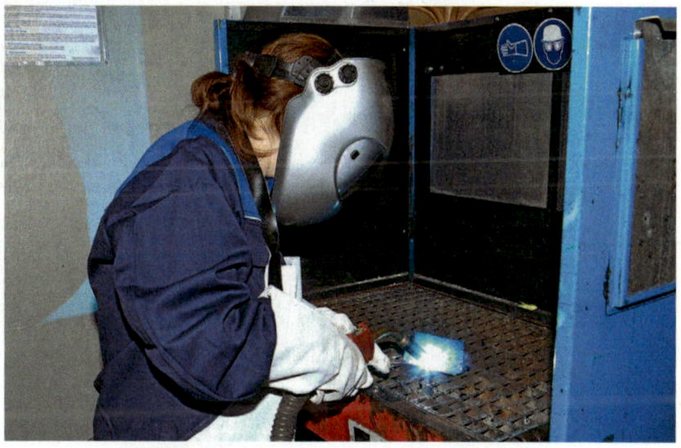

Üben interaktiv: Online Grammatiktraining

Modul A: 3u5mw9	**Modul E:** 5zw8jx
Modul B: gc2x9w	**Modul F:** pf5r3n
Modul C: x3gj95	**Modul G:** 3b9c4h
Modul D: cy8yn5	**Modul H:** 842j42

Die Module A – H legen den Schwerpunkt auf die Skills zu *Business Communication*, die im Workbook intensiv trainiert werden.

V 1 Company tour

V 2 Telephoning

V 3 Job interview

V 4 Technical support

V 5 Waste – the future's most valuable resource

V 6 Pipe inspection

V 7 High voltage work

V 8 Ras Laffan

V 9 Pipelines

V 10 Robots in the hospital

V 11 Portable power stations

V 12 Car speed control

Appendix

Umschlagseiten

Modulelemente	
Nach diesem Modul	Lernziele
WORD BANK	Fachvokabular
UNDERSTANDING TECHNICAL ENGLISH	Hinweise und Aufgaben zu englischem Fachvokabular
SAFETY FIRST ⚠	Aufgaben zur Arbeitssicherheit
Video Lounge	Aufgaben zu authentischen Videos (die Videos und die Videoskripte befinden sich im Lehrerhandbuch)
→ Phrases: Telephoning	Verweis auf Phrases (Telephoning) im Anhang

Symbole	
◎ A 1.27	Audioverweis mit Tracknummer (CD1 – Track 27)
P, M, I, R	Produktion, Mediation, Interaktion, Rezeption
🌐	Aufgabe mit Internetrecherche
▲	Anspruchsvollere Aufgabe (advanced)
👥	Partner- und Gruppenaufgaben
🌐 3u5mw9	Grammatiktraining online über www.klett.de
KMK II	Aufgabe zur Vorbereitung auf die Prüfung des KMK-Fremdsprachenzertifikats (Niveaustufe II)

01

NACH DIESEM MODUL:

- √ kenne ich die englischen Begriffe für gängige Werkstattausstattungen,
- √ kann ich auf Englisch die wichtigste Schutzkleidung benennen,
- √ kann ich die wichtigsten Sicherheitsschilder auf Englisch erklären.

The general workshop

The apprentices who work in machine tool companies learn how state-of-the-art machine tools are manufactured. They are trained in mechanical engineering and learn basic skills in the general workshop. For example, they are shown how to work with hand tools at the work bench. They also use bench vices and work with simple machines such as column drills. After their basic training the apprentices learn to operate centre lathes and milling machines.

R **1** Look at the photo of a general workshop. Which typical workshop tool(s) can you see?

2 Give the English words for the following equipment which you find in a general workshop.

Drehmaschine • Werkbank • Fräsmaschine • Handwerkzeug • Ständerbohrmaschine

3 What tools do the apprentices learn to use in the general workshop?

4 What skills do the apprentices learn after their basic training?

5 Outline which tools you have already worked with in the general workshop.

A | A visit to a machine-tool company

Andreas Baier, the chief executive of WMT, a machine-tool company near Karlsruhe is showing a visitor from England around. After passing through the shop floor, they look at the general workshop where the company's apprentices are trained. This training workshop is well-equipped and even has a CNC machine, which apprentices use when they are more advanced.

R **1** ⓞ A 2.12

Listen to the dialogue and say what the parts of the workshop a – f are.

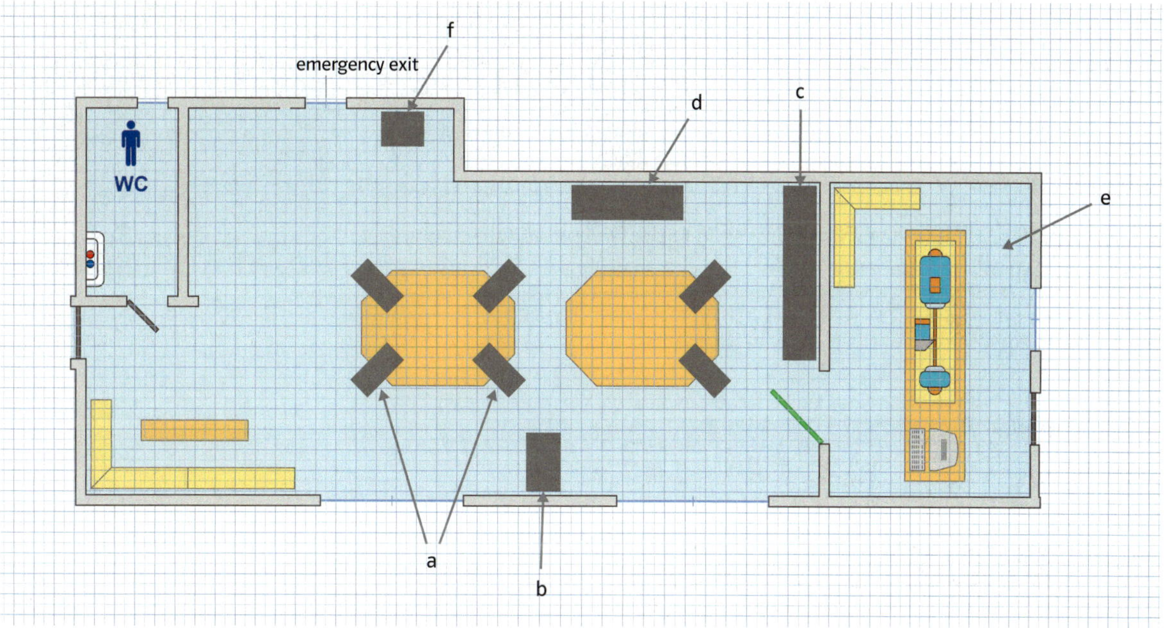

R **2** ⓞ A 2.12

Listen to the dialogue again and complete the sentences.

1. All ? receive their first year of practical training in the general workshop.
2. You find all sorts of ? on the shop floor of a machine tool company.
3. The ? contains a lot of sophisticated machines.
4. The operation of the ? is not taught until the third year.
5. After training for three years, the young people will go on to become ?.
6. There are ? in the workshop showing the way to the first-aid kit.

R **3**

Ask and answer questions about the workshop in the plan above.

Example:

How many … are there?

Where are the benches in relation to the windows?

Which machine is …?

P **4**

Draw and label a plan of the workshop where you do your training. Then explain the plan to your partner.

WORD BANK

CNC (computerized numerical control) – computergesteuert
general workshop – Grundwerkstatt
machine tool – Werkzeugmaschine
manufacture (v) – herstellen, produzieren
mechanical engineering – Maschinenbau
operate (v) – bearbeiten
shop floor – Fabrikhalle, Produktionshalle

B | Protective clothing in the workshop

When you work with tools and machinery in a workshop, you must always be aware of possible danger. For example, you could break or damage something, or even worse, you could injure yourself. Therefore, it is important to wear protective clothing.

I/P **1** **SAFETY FIRST** ⚠

1. Say which protective clothing the machinist is wearing in the photo.

> safety boots • an overall • a hairnet • goggles • safety glasses • ear protection • a safety helmet

2. What other protective clothing do you think she should wear to avoid an accident?

3. Say what task you are going to do in the workshop. Your partner gives you safety instructions. Use the phrases below.

Example:

> I'm going to stop work for today.

> Don't forget to put away all tools after use.

I'm going to … I need to … We want to …	carry heavy metal stock into the milling shop. drill holes in a metal plate. grind the surface of a metal block. *stop work for today.* weld two metal bars. bring in a new column drill.	*Don't forget to …* Keep … Remember to … Use … Wear …	a hairnet a hand shield a mask *all tools after use* goggles safety boots the gangway free

4. ▲ **Explain why the protective clothing in exercise 1 is necessary. Use a dictionary.**

M **2** **UNDERSTANDING TECHNICAL ENGLISH**

1. Use an English-German dictionary to find the general and technical meanings of the words.

> bench • metal stock • design • vice • (milling) shop

2. Translate the sentences.

a. The apprentices learn to work with metal at a bench.
b. Metal stock is a basic material in all mechanical workshops.
c. All jobs in mechanical engineering follow a design.
d. A vice is an important tool in the workshop.
e. All flat material is machined in the milling shop.

C | Safety signs in the workshop

Safety signs warn of possible danger in the workshop. They also show where we can get help in an emergency and tell us what protective clothing we should wear.

R **1** **Match the meanings with the signs (1–15).**

no mobile phones allowed • danger of slipping • wear goggles • first aid • wear a hard hat • wear ear protection • fire extinguisher • emergency phone • no entry • wear safety boots • emergency exit • no cameras allowed • high voltage • no smoking • toxic materials

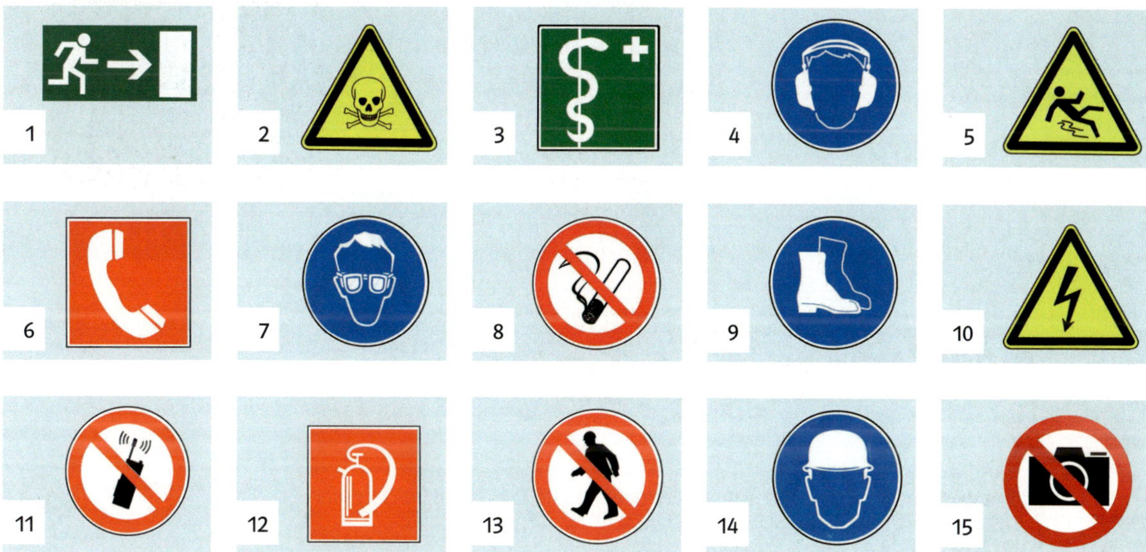

M **2** **Give the German meanings of the signs in exercise 1. You can use an English-German dictionary.**

3 **Which of the signs in exercise 1 do you have in your own workshop? Which one(s) do you not have? Give reasons why this is the case.**

I **4** **Use the Internet to find out about the safety signs used in industry in Britain. Outline how they are different to signs in Germany. Discuss your results in class.**

P **5** **Think of situations where the following are forbidden in industry:**

1. the use of a camera,
2. the use of a mobile phone.

P **6** KMK I **Die Auszubildenden der englischen Niederlassung Ihrer Firma besuchen Ihre Ausbildungswerkstatt. Sie erhalten den Auftrag, dem Besuch die erforderlichen Sicherheitsvorkehrungen in der Grundwerkstatt, der Dreherei und der Schweißerei vorzustellen. Dazu gehören Arbeitsschuhe, Overall, Arbeitshandschuhe, Schutzbrillen, Haarnetz und Schweißerhandschirm. Erklären Sie auf Englisch die Funktion der Schutz- und Sicherheitsausrüstungen.**

→ **PHRASES:** Presentations

WORD BANK

bar – (Metall-)Stange
grind (v) – schleifen
hand shield – Schutzschild
machinist – Maschinist(in); Maschinenarbeiter(in)
metal bar – Metallstab
metal plate – Metallplatte
milling shop – Fräserei
weld (v) – schweißen, verschweißen, zusammenschweißen

WORD BANK ◎

skilled worker – Facharbeiter(in)

A

NACH DIESEM MODUL:

- ✓ weiß ich, wie man sich auf Englisch begrüßt,
- ✓ weiß ich, wie ich mich selbst und andere einander auf Englisch vorstelle.

1

2

3

4

Meeting people

In the world of work you will often meet new people and it will be necessary to introduce yourself. In all industries developing relationships with colleagues and customers is the key to success. Not only is it important that you are polite, confident and friendly, but also that you know what to say, what information to include, and what the differences between formal and informal situations are.

1 Match the parts of the dialogues to form short conversations. Start with Speaker A.

Speaker A	Speaker B
1. Morning, Tom. That was a great game last night, wasn't it? 2. Hi guys, my name's Natalie. 3. Goodbye, Mr Bauer. See you next week. 4. It's nice to meet you, Simon.	a. Nice to meet you, too, Hannah. b. Goodbye, Mr Horvath. It was nice meeting you. c. Morning Chris. Yeah, it was amazing! d. Hi Natalie, I'm Mark. Welcome to the team.

2 Now match the conversations above with the appropriate picture (1–4) and decide which are formal and which are informal.

P **3** Which other phrases do you know for greeting somebody and saying goodbye? Make a list.

A | Saying "hello" and "goodbye" and giving your name

A trainee from Denmark has just arrived at Neureuther und Söhne in Kiel for a three-month internship.

R **1** **Listen to the two dialogues and write down the names of the people and their positions in the company.**
⊙ A 1.1

R **2** **Listen again and write down the phrases the people use for greeting and introducing one another.**
⊙ A 1.1

R **3** **Match the replies to the greetings and goodbyes in the two boxes.**

Formal greetings / goodbyes	Formal replies
1. Good morning. How are you today?	a. Good morning. I'm fine, thanks. And you?
2. Good night. Have a nice evening, Mr Dachs.	b. Goodbye, Mr Schäfer, and thanks for everything.
3. Goodbye, Mr Horvath. Have a nice journey home.	c. Good night, Ms Kistner, you too.
4. Good night, Silke.	d. Good night, Ms Hornbach.

Informal greetings / goodbyes	Informal replies
1. Hello, Mike. Haven't seen you for a long time.	a. Bye, Thomas. Give me a call, will you?
2. Lena, how are you this morning?	b. You, too, Florian. Thank you.
3. Morning. How was your weekend?	c. Fine, thanks. How about yours?
4. Bye-bye, Sevda.	d. I'm good, thanks. Yourself?
5. Have a nice weekend, Joe.	e. Yes, I was away on a trip last week.

P **4** **Make dialogues from the following prompts and present them to the class. Look at your lists of phrases from exercise 2 and check the info box on the next page.**

Example:
A: Hello, my name is Marina Kohler. I represent Toolcell in Leipzig.
B: Hello, Ms Kohler. I'm Amy Strong from Easytools in Bern. Nice to meet you.
A: Nice to meet you, too, Ms Strong.

Names: Denise Hofmann • Marina Kohler • Alice Campbell • Abel Kazich • Tanja Neuhäuser • Rudolfo Orvieto • Ursula Braun • Stefan Helm • Gerard Mathieu • your name

Job descriptions: I'm a trainee / intern • I work for ... • I come from ... • I represent ... • I'm training to be a ... • your job

Companies: Toolcell GmbH in Leipzig, Germany • Easytools in Bern, Switzerland • Tools Expert Pontypridd, Wales • DWT Electronics, Stuttgart • Smart EDV, Kiel • Xiang Piong Ltd, Hong Kong • Naturholz GmbH • your company

Situations: a first meeting with a new customer • a meeting with an existing customer / a colleague • a party • a company open day • a trade fair • a job fair for trainees • the first day in a new company

WORD BANK ⊙

intern – Praktikant(in)

I **5** **Introduce the people to each other according to the following structure. Use the prompts on the previous page.**

→ **PHRASES:** Meeting people

A: Fragen Sie **B** und **C**, ob sie sich schon kennen. B und C antworten mit Nein.
A: Stellen Sie **B** und **C** einander vor.

B: Begrüßen Sie **C** freundlich.

C: Sie grüßen **B** zurück und stellen eine Frage zu **Bs** Firma

B: Sie geben eine Auskunft über Ihre Firma. Sie fragen **C** nach seiner Tätigkeit.

C: Sie beantworten **Bs** Frage.

INFO BOX: Meeting people

First meeting / Formal introduction

A: Hello, my name is Ines Sacher.
B: Nice to meet you, Ms Sacher. My name is Joshua Hamsung.
A: Nice to meet you, too, Mr Hamsung.
Women – married or not – are addressed as Ms, not Miss.

A: Mr Jacobs, this is Mr Sykes.
B: How do you do?
C: How do you do?
"How do you do?" is rarely used for first introductions.

A: I'm Frank Warren of Wood Tools in Manchester.
Please call me Frank.
B: Pleased to meet you, Frank. My name is Joanne McNeill.
Do call me Joanne.
In English-speaking countries first names are often used from the start of a business realtionship. In South America or Asia, however, you don't usually use first names right away.

I hope you had a good trip. /
I hope you had no trouble finding us. /
Welcome to our stand.
Phrases like these are used to break the ice after an introduction.

Second meeting

A: Good morning, Ms Sacher. Do you remember me?
I'm Joshua Hamsung from Bell & Co in Chicago.
B: Good morning, Mr Hamsung. Nice to see you again.

Informal meetings

A: Hello Ines. Great to see you again. How are you?
B: Hi Joshua. Lovely to see you, too. I'm fine. And you?

B | Intercultural awareness

M **1** KMK II

Ihr Betrieb wird in Zukunft für einen amerikanischen Auftraggeber arbeiten. Ihre Vorgesetzte interessiert sich daher für folgenden Artikel aus einer englischen Fachzeitschrift. Sie bittet Sie, die wesentlichen Aussagen des Artikels stichpunktartig in übersichtlicher Form für sie auf Deutsch herauszuarbeiten.

Intercultural awareness

Politeness, pleasantries and profitability

Americans are known to be direct, but they do like to take a few minutes to chat before getting down to work. They may ask after your health, or if your trip was pleasant, or about where you are from. This gives both parties a chance to form an impression of the other and establishes a basis on which to do business.

Americans, including the president, like to be called by their given name. This is not an invitation to be personal, as you would expect in Germany if someone suggested using the familiar "Du". It is a way to set a framework for working together. While it is usual in business, it would not be expected in dealing with a doctor, a teacher or a professor, and in any case, you should wait until it is offered: "Hello, I'm James Smith, vice-president in charge of sales. Call me Jim." "Pleased to meet you! I'm Walter König; please call me Walter." (Note that in the United States you state your *given* name and then your *family* name, and not the other way around, except perhaps on a form that you have to fill out.)

Americans don't like to waste time. They get to the point, in conversations as well as in conferences. Although Milton Berle, a comedian from the 1950s and 1960s, is quoted as saying: "A committee is a group of people that keeps minutes and wastes hours."

Americans are generally very polite, and they tend to smile much more than we are used to. An American tourist was quite upset that perfect strangers didn't smile back at her when she walked through the streets of a small town in Germany. On the other hand, a German woman in New York became quite tired of being asked, again by perfect strangers, the person at the cash register, the bus driver: "How are you doing?" and commanded to "Have a nice day!" These pleasantries are intended to show that you are noticed and respected. More than "Thanks!" is not expected.

P **2**

Check the Internet to see what advice people from other countries get to prepare for meetings in Germany. Make a list of ten useful tips.

02

NACH DIESEM MODUL:

- ✓ kenne ich die englischen Begriffe gängiger Hand- und Elektrowerkzeuge,
- ✓ kann ich auf Englisch einfache Arbeitsprozesse in der Metallwerkstatt beschreiben.

Hand and power tools

Hand tools still play a big role in mechanical engineering. They are used not only in professional workshops but also in homes. A hammer, screwdrivers and pliers are typical hand tools in the DIY-enthusiast's toolbox.

1 Match the tools with their German meanings.

1. vernier calliper	a. Stahlbürste
2. spanner	b. Nietenzange
3. screwdriver bits	c. Winkel
4. hacksaw	d. Beißzange
5. riveting tongs	e. Feile
6. file	f. Schraubenschlüssel
7. steel brush	g. Schraubstock
8. round nose pliers	h. Schraubendrehereinsätze
9. vice	i. Messschieber / Schieblehre
10. set of Allen keys	j. Verstellbarer Schraubenschlüssel / Engländer
11. adjustable wrench	k. Bügelsäge
12. square	l. Satz Inbusschlüssel

R **2** Identify the tools in the photo. Say which tools in exercise 1 are not shown.

3 Look at the photo again and say which tools are not in your own toolbox.

A | Discussing hand tools

In mechanical engineering hand tools are used to do manual work on metal materials. For example, you can bend wire with pliers or you can clamp metal in a vice to cut it with a hacksaw. You can also debur sharp metal edges with a file. Handtools are also often used to join metals or to bore holes in metal.

1 Complete the sentences using the words in the box.

cut · screw · tighten/loosen · clamp · drill/bore · drive · join · tighten/loosen · counter

1. You can ? holes with a diameter of up to 6 mm using a hand drill.
2. You use a bench vice to ? a workpiece that you want to debur.
3. Allen keys are used in mechanical engineering to ? hexagonal head bolts.
4. For certain jobs a spanner is used to ? nuts.
5 You use a hacksaw to ? metal bars.
6. I use a hammer to ? nails into a wooden board.
7. An adjustable wrench is useful if you want to clamp a nut to ? a bolt.
8. Riveting tongs are used to ? tin sheet.
9. A screwdriver is necessary to ? bolts into metal.

2 SAFETY FIRST ⚠

1. Say how you can prevent these mistakes from happening in the workshop. Use the phrases in the bubbles for your answers.

Always use…

Never use … to …

Make sure that…

Example:
The screws will be damaged when you drive them into a wall with a hammer.
Never use a hammer to drive screws into a wall.

a. The workpiece falls on Jonathan's foot when he starts deburring its edges.
b. Jackie ruins the spanner when she uses it to drive nails into the board.
c. David uses a screwdriver to make a hole in the wooden board and ruins it.
d. Jennifer bends some wire with her bare hands and cuts herself.
e. Robert turns the bolt with an adjustable wrench and ruins the bolt head.
f. Tommy tightens a screw with a pair of pliers and damages the head of the screw.
g. After the sports lesson Brian doesn't change his trainers when he goes to the general workshop.
h. Sally cuts her hand on the tin sheet when she carries it to the general workshop.

2. ▲ Think of other mistakes that can happen when using hand tools in the workshop. Present your ideas to your class. → **PHRASES:** Presentations

WORD BANK

bench vice – Schraubstock
bend (v) – biegen
bolt – Bolzen; Schraubenbolzen
bore (v) – bohren
clamp (v) – einspannen
debur (v) – entgraten
DIY enthusiast – Heimwerker(in)
hexagonal head bolt – Innensechskant-Schraubenbolzen
manual – Hand-
pliers – Zange
power tool – Elektrowerkzeug
screwdriver – Schraubendreher
tin sheet – Metallblech
toolbox – Werkzeugkasten
wire – Draht

B | Power tools

Unlike hand tools, power tools usually have a motor which is driven by electric power. The power comes either via a cord connection from a wall socket, or from batteries as it is the case with cordless power tools. DIY stores offer a wide range of power tools: light-duty drills, impact drills, angle grinders, jigsaws and sanders.

1 **Give the English words for the power tools in the photos.**

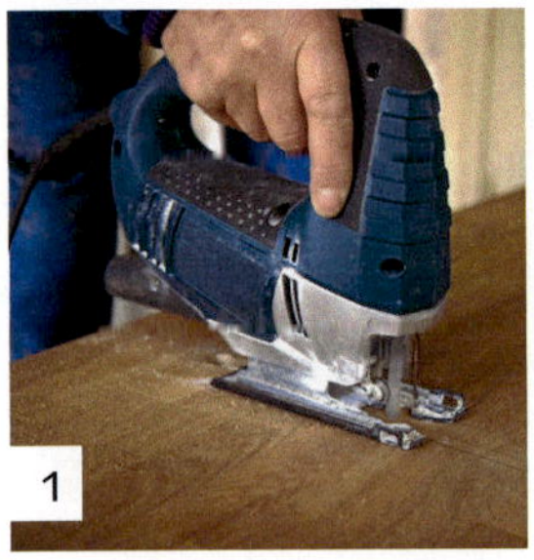
1

2

3

4

2 **Say which of the power tools you would use:**

1. to drill holes in a concrete wall
2. to debur the sharp edges on metal stock
3. to do light woodwork around the house
4. to drill a number of holes in wooden boards and to join the boards with screws.

P **3** **Search the Internet for information about different aspects of power tools using the key words below. Present your findings in class.**

→ **PHRASES:** Presentations

cordless power tools • power tool accessories • outdoor power equipment • power tool safety

4 **UNDERSTANDING TECHNICAL ENGLISH**

1. **Find the general and technical meanings of the words in the box in an English-German dictionary or in an online dictionary.**

   concrete • mount • nut • operate

2. **Complete the sentences using the correct form of the words in exercise 4.1.**
   a. All of the students enjoyed eating ? and crackers.
   b. The doctors ? on the patient behind the ? walls of the hospital.
   c. The mechanic ? the shelf on the wall before he ? the stairs to the assembly hall.
   d. The apprentices work with ? and bolts in the workshop.
   e. The manager has ? ideas on how to improve the company's position in the market.
   f. The instructor ? the machine tool very professionally.

C | Sales talk

1 **Find the English meanings of the German terms in the product description.**

Akku • Umlenkgetriebe • Werkzeugaufnahme • Durchmesser • vollisoliert • Metallschaltgetriebe • Gehäusedesign • Spannungsanzeiger • Schlagmechanismus

- 18 V-LI battery
- pneumatic hammer mechanism
- compact angle gear
- SDS-plus toolfitter
- compact ergonomic design
- fully insulated metal gearbox
- battery cartridge with battery life meter
- optimal for drilling diameters up to 12 mm

R **2** **Listen to the dialogue. The customer is interested in an impact drill.**
⊙ A 2.13 **What does the shop assistant recommend?**

R/M **3** **List the features of the drill in the dialogue. Then give their German meanings.**
⊙ A 2.13

M/I **4** **Sie arbeiten ein paar Stunden in der Woche in einem Elektrogeschäft.**
KMK II **Ein englischsprachiger Kunde interessiert sich für eine Schlagbohrmaschine. Geben Sie das folgende Verkaufsgespräch auf Englisch wieder.**

Begrüßen Sie den Kunden und fragen Sie, ob Sie ihm weiterhelfen können. →

Sagen Sie, dass Sie eine Bohrmaschine suchen.

Fragen Sie wozu der Kunde die Maschine braucht. *(What … for?)* →

Sagen Sie, dass Sie einige Arbeiten in Ihrer neuen Wohnung machen möchten.

Empfehlen Sie einen Akku-Schlagbohrer. Zeigen Sie Ihr neuestes Modell. →

Fragen Sie nach den Besonderheiten des Gerätes.

Nennen Sie den kraftvollen Motor mit einem 18 V-LI Akku und einem kompakten Umlenkgetriebe. →

Fragen Sie, ob das Modell auch einen Rechts-Links-Lauf hat.

Bestätigen Sie diese Eigenschaft. Fügen Sie hinzu, dass das Gerät über einen pneumatischen Schlagmechanismus verfügt. →

Erkundigen Sie sich nach dem Werkzeugwechsel, z. B. ob er schnell erfolgt. *(What about …?)*

Antworten Sie, dass das neue Modell über eine SDS-plus Werkzugaufnahme verfügt. →

Fragen Sie, ob Sie auch Löcher mit einem Durchmesser von 10 mm bohren können.

Bestätigen Sie, dass die Maschine Löcher mit einem Durchmesser bis zu 12 mm bohrt bei optimaler Lastdrehzahl. →

Ergänzen Sie, dass Sie das schon von dem Vorgängermodell kennen *(previous model)*. Fragen Sie nach weiteren Modellen.

WORD BANK

instructor – Ausbilder(in)
light-duty drill – Leichtbohrer
socket – Steckdose
sander – Schleifer; Schleifmaschine

WORD BANK ⊙

auto shut-off – automatischer Abschalter
charge (v) – (auf-)laden
charger – Ladegerät
chuck – Spannfutter
cordless – schnurlos
driver drill – Bohrschrauber
lock out (v) – abschalten
reversible – mit Rechts-Linkslauf
torque – Drehmoment

B

NACH DIESEM MODUL:

- ✓ kann ich verschiedene Firmenabteilungen auf Englisch erklären,
- ✓ kann ich Arbeitsplätze und Tätigkeiten auf Englisch beschreiben,
- ✓ kann ich eine Firmenstruktur auf Englisch beschreiben.

Your company

Regardless of whether your company builds houses, repairs cars, or makes furniture, there is likely to come a time where you will be required to talk about yourself, your job and your company in English. Whether you are greeting an English-speaking visitor, giving a tour of the factory, or talking to suppliers from another country, it is important you have the skills and vocabulary to express yourself clearly.

1 **Work on your own. Look at the photos and brainstorm words that describe what is shown in each of them.**

I/P **2** **Compare your list of words with your partner and work together to describe the pictures. Use these words to help you:**

building site • cable • construction worker • grease • hard hat • car mechanic • overalls • ratchet • server • timber • tools • wires • work gloves

WATCH OUT!

She ~~wears~~ a hard hat. She <u>is wearing</u> a hard hat.

P **3** **With your partner, think of three questions you would like to ask each of the four young workers shown in the photos.**

A | The company and its departments

P **1** **Use the words and phrases in the table to explain what the departments of Krone Elektronik GmbH do.**

Example: Sales and Marketing advertises and sells the products.

Department		
Sales and Marketing	distribute	the products are not damaged.
Production Planning	*advertise and sell*	new employees.
Accounts	check	raw materials.
HR (Human Resources)	buy	*the products.*
Production	deal with	the computer network.
Logistics	recruit and train	the finished products.
Purchasing	maintain	customer problems.
Customer Service	handle	the company's finances.
R&D (Research and Development)	make	new products.
IT (Information Technology)	organize	production schedules.
Quality Control	develop	the products to the customers.

P **2** **Use the information in the table to form sentences using *responsible for / in charge of*.**

Example:
The Production department is responsible for making the products.
The Production Planning department is in charge of …

P **3** **Look at the departments again and write down three questions. Then close your book and ask your partner.**

Example:
A: What is the Quality Control department responsible for?
B: It is responsible for …
A: Which department is in charge of …?
B: The … department is in charge of …

R **4** KMK I ⊙ A 1.2 **Der Ausbildungsleiter von Krone Elektronik, Herr Kirchner, zeigt Sean, einem Elektrotechnikstudenten aus Belfast, das Firmengelände und die einzelnen Abteilungen. Hören Sie sich das Gespräch an und beantworten Sie die folgenden Fragen auf Deutsch.**

1. Wann wurde Krone Elektronik GmbH gegründet, und von wem?
2. Wo hat die Firma ihren Hauptsitz?
3. Wie viele Produktionsanlagen hat Krone Elektronik insgesamt?
4. Wo wird nächstes Jahr eine neue Produktionsanlage eröffnet?
5. Wie viele Leute beschäftigt die Firma?
6. Woran arbeitet die Forschungs- und Entwicklungsabteilung gerade?
7. Welche drei Abteilungen befinden sich in dem Hauptgebäude?
8. Wo wird Sean zuerst arbeiten?
9. Wie viele Zylinderköpfe werden jährlich bei Krone Elektronik hergestellt?
10. Was passiert momentan in der IT-Abteilung?

WORD BANK

grease – Fett, Schmierfett
ratchet – Knarre
raw materials – Rohmaterialien
recruit (v) – anwerben
tool – Werkzeug

B | Tasks and responsibilities

Industrial companies are made up of many different people, who all have a variety of tasks and responsibilities. DWG Tech GmbH in Stuttgart manufactures machine parts for the automotive and aviation industry. Below, Tim Schieber, a DWG Tech GmbH employee, talks about his job and daily activities on DWG Tech GmbH's English website.

R **1** **Read the text and answer the following questions in your own words.**

1. What do CNC machines do?
2. What problems can occur with CNC machines?

Hi, my name is Tim Schieber and I work as a CNC machine operator here at the DWG Tech headquarters in Stuttgart. I've been with the company since completing my apprenticeship three years ago and next summer I am going to work at the DWG Tech branch in Detroit.

In my opinion, what we do here is very important. CNC is all about precision, and it is therefore essential that I concentrate at all times. These machines drill, shape, cut and polish the parts for automobiles and aeroplanes. As a CNC machine operator I am responsible for one machine. As I said, this job is all about precision, and the machines are programmed specifically for each job. I do not do the programming myself, but I learnt programming during my apprenticeship and I sometimes have to intervene when something goes wrong – such as a vibrating workpiece or broken cutting tools.

The CNC process is almost entirely automatic. It is my job to set up the machine for the production process, which means loading the machine with the correct tools and workpieces. Once the programming for an operation is done, I enter the commands into the machine. To do this we use a computer network. The next step is to let the machine work its magic.

The main part of my job is to monitor the machine and spot problems. This means checking that the machine is running smoothly, measuring finished workpieces to check that the dimensions are correct, and sometimes replacing tools. It is also important that the machine is kept cool and lubricated with a special lubricating oil – but this is also done automatically. Of course, another of my tasks is to make sure the machine is kept clean, and that the working area is safe.

My working day depends on what shift I am on. We generally work either early shift or late shift. Early shift is from 6am until 2pm, and the guys on late shift begin at 2pm and clock out at 10pm. Sometimes, if we have a lot of work to do, there is also a night shift – but that doesn't happen too often. I actually prefer early shift. Even though I don't enjoy waking up at 4:45am, it is great to have the afternoon to do whatever I like – especially in the summer.

I really enjoy my job and I am proud to be working for an international company like DWG. My colleagues and I are always very busy and it can be fairly stressful. But I love working with the machines and it is interesting to see the many technological developments in the industry.

2 **Find the synonyms in the text for the following words:**

1. to finish	4. accuracy	7. to like
2. very important	5. to observe	8. workmates
3. cars	6. usually	9. quite

R **3** **Decide whether the statements are true or false. Give reasons for your decisions in German.**

1. Tim is currently doing an apprenticeship as a CNC machine operator.
2. Once the machine starts running, Tim's work is over.
3. One of Tim's tasks is making sure that the cutting tools are not broken.
4. Tim rarely works in shifts.
5. Accuracy is very important for CNC work.
6. The technology used in CNC machining has hardly changed over the years.

P **4** **Your boss has asked you to write a short text for your company's English website. Make sure you include some basic facts about your company and details about your daily tasks and responsibilities. Use some of the phrases in Tim's text, e.g. *I work as, I've been with the company since*, etc.**

→ **PHRASES:** Your company

P/I **5** **Check the Internet for a job in your industry that interests you. Make notes on the daily tasks and responsibilities.**

I **6** **Explain the job you researched to your partner, but don't mention the job title. Your partner must guess what the job is from the description you give. Then swap roles.**

C | Organisational structure

P/M KMK II **Sie sind Auszubildende(r) in der DWG Tech GmbH. Ihr Vorgesetzter benötigt eine Übersicht über die Ingenieursabteilung der DWG Tech GmbH Niederlassung in Detroit. Auf deren Firmen-Homepage finden Sie die folgenden Informationen zu den Mitarbeitern. Zeichnen Sie ein Organigramm nach der vorliegenden Beschreibung.**

Who's who in DWG Tech GmbH Detroit's engineering department?

DWG Tech GmbH Inc. employs around 60 people in its engineering department. The department is led by Chief Engineer Dr. Adam Foster, who is supported by his Personal Assistant Helen Green and DWG Tech's Assistant Chief Engineer Dr. Tim Bayliss. The engineering department is split into two core areas: automotive and aviation. Shift leaders Chris Falsone and Sandra Borowski report to Michael Kellermann, the foreman. They all belong to automotive which is run by experienced Chief Automotive Engineer, Dr. Torben Brinkema. DWG Tech's aviation department is in the capable hands of Dr. Judith Sommer, Chief Aviation Engineer, who has been with the company for over 15 years. Dr. Sommer is supported by foreman Frank Kapowski. Barry Richardson and Jens Schmelzer are the two shift leaders and work closely with Mr Kapowski.

WORD BANK

aviation – Luftfahrt
CNC (computerized numerical control) – CNC (computerisierte numerische Steuerung)
dimensions – Maße
drill (v) – bohren
lubricated – geölt
lubricating oil – Schmieröl
measure (v) – messen
polish (v) – schleifen, polieren
precision – Genauigkeit
shape (v) – fräsen, formen
vibrate (v) – vibrieren
workpiece – Werkstück

WORD BANK ◎

braking system – Bremsanlage
cylinder head – Zylinderkopf
interface – Schnittstelle
manufacturing plant – Produktionsbetrieb
operating system – Betriebssystem

03

NACH DIESEM MODUL:

- ✓ kann ich auf Englisch den Gebrauch von Hand- und Elektrowerkzeugen erklären,
- ✓ kann ich auf Englisch spanabhebende Verfahren anhand von Hand- und Elektrowerkzeugen beschreiben.

1

2

3

4

Cutting processes with hand and power tools

The cutting processes in mechanical engineering all involve removing metal from material in the form of chips or swarfs. It depends on the type of job whether the cutting process is done with hand tools, power tools or machine tools. Cutting metal with hand tools, such as files, does not require as much precision as a machining job with a lathe, for example. If you want to cut metal to roughly the correct dimensions, you can use a hacksaw, or power tools such as angle grinders or power cutters. These are also cutting or chipping processes because chips or swarfs are produced.

R **1** Name the cutting tools shown above. Describe the jobs that are done with them.

2 Match the tools with the material that is removed in the cutting process.

R **3** Explain when a process is called a 'cutting process'.

R **4** Make a table of the hand tools and power tools used in metal cutting processes.

Hand tools	Power tools

5 Add the German words for the tools to your table. Use an English-German dictionary or an online dictionary.

A | Cutting metal with hand tools

Apprentices learn how to carry out easy cutting operations with hand and power tools. For example, the apprentices cut metal bars to a certain length with a hacksaw. Then they use different types of files to shorten the bars to a specific length.

1 **Read the text and match Alexander's questions with Sally's answers.**

Alexander Schröder and a Welsh apprentice, Sally Wade from Cardiff, are doing their training at Werkzeuge Maschinen Technik (WMT) in Karlsruhe. Their instructor, Stefan Hinz, has asked them to make a square base plate. First they cut a metal plate with a hacksaw to a length of 350 mm and a width of 150 mm. After that they use some files to work the metal plate to a length of 320 mm. The plate has a precision of a tenth of a millimetre and four right angles. The edges of the plate are deburred with a file. These jobs are started with a roughing file and continued with a finishing file. Alexander and Sally check the right angles of the four corners with a square. Then they use a scriber to mark four holes with a diameter of 5 mm in each corner of the metal plate. After centre punching the marks with a centre punch and a hammer, they are ready to bore the holes with a twist drill.

Alexander	Sally
1. Which file should you use first? 2. How are we going to work the edges of the plate? 3. How do we cut the metal plate to the correct length and width? 4. What tool can we use to get the precise length we want? 5. What can we use to bore the holes?	a. I guess we can use an electric drill with a twist drill. b. That's easy. We can debur them with a file. c. You can use a roughing file first. d. We should use a finishing file. e. The best thing to use is a hacksaw.

2 **Put the parts of the dialogue in exercise 1 into the correct order.**

3 **List the tools that are needed for the job in the technical drawing. Then describe the steps of the job from the raw material to the finishing process.**

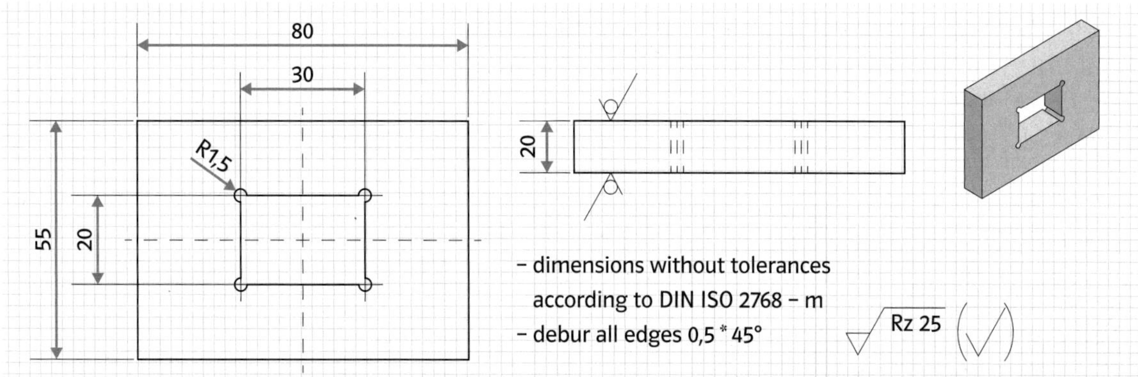

WORD BANK

base plate – Grundplatte
centre-punch – Körner
centre-punch (v) – körnen
chip – Span
chipping process – Zerspanungsprozess
cutting process – Zerspanungsprozess, spanabhebendes Verfahren
debur (v) – entgraten
diameter – Durchmesser
file – Feile
finishing file – Schlichtfeile
metal bar – Metallstab, -stange
metal plate – Flachmaterial
roughing file – Schruppfeile
scriber – Anreißnadel
square – Winkel (rechtwinkliges Messgerät)
swarf – Span
twist drill – Spiralbohrer

B | Cutting metal with power tools

Hand power tools are often used in workshops or garages to saw thick materials such as flat or round metal bars. An example of a hand power tool, which is often used in a metal workshop, is a circular saw. However, an angle grinder or power cutter is used more often in garages or on building sites to cut metal material to the approximate size or length. No matter which cutting job is processed, precision is not so important. The idea is to shorten the material before doing the next step in the finishing process.

R **1** **Give examples of the jobs for which hand power tools are often used. Where are they used?**

R **2** ⓞ A 2.14 **Alexander and Sally have to prepare some metal for a simple bench vice. Listen to the dialogue. Which tool does Alexander suggest using to cut the metal bar, and why?**

R **3** ⓞ A 2.14 **Listen to the dialogue again and say whether the statements are true or false. Correct the false statements.**

1. Alexander and Sally want to join the two metal bars.
2. Alexander cut the steel bars in the storeroom with a hacksaw.
3. The first bar is 218 mm long and 18 mm wide.
4. The second bar is 160 mm wide and 240 mm long.
5. Sally decides not to use the hacksaw because it is slower than the grinder.
6. They wear goggles so that they can see the metal bar properly.

M **4** KMK I **Alexander und Sally haben den Auftrag von ihrem Ausbilder bekommen, ein Abstract auf Deutsch über den Arbeitsprozess zu schreiben. Hören Sie den Dialog nochmals an und schreiben Sie das Abstract.**

P **5** **Check Internet catalogues for the hand tools and power cutter accessories below. Make notes about the products you find, including their prices. Present your findings in class.**

→ **PHRASES:** Presentations

1. roughing files
2. finishing files
3. a set of grinding discs for fine cutting-off jobs

P **6** **Decide which hand tools and power tools are suitable for the cutting jobs. Answer in complete sentences. Use a dictionary if necessary.**

Example:

cut off metal bars in the storeroom	*I would use a hacksaw to cut off metal bars.*

1. cut a metal bar to approximate dimensions on a building site
2. finish the base plate of a simple vice to precise dimensions
3. drill holes in a metal base plate
4. shorten the bars of a metal shelf
5. finish the surface of a car door that has been repaired
6. debur the edges of sawed bars

C | An advertisement for hand tools and power tools

M **1** Write down the main aspects of the article in German.

PTM (= PRECISION TOOL MAKER)

In addition to a variety of machine tools, our company offers a wide range of high-quality hand tools and power tools for use in production and in workshops, garages and training centres.

Just have a look at our online catalogue and you will find an attractive selection of hand tools.

For example, you will find sets of hand files, flat, round or half round and second-cut files with which you can finish a workpiece with a precision of a tenth of a millimetre. These files are suitable for use by professionals as well as trainees.

2 **UNDERSTANDING TECHNICAL ENGLISH**

1. **Find the general and technical meanings of the words. Use an English-German dictionary or an online dictionary.**

a. square	b. chip	c. (metal) plate
d. file	e. garage	f. training

2. **Complete the sentences using the correct forms of the words in exercise 1.**
   1. The finishing work is done on a ? with a file called the second-cut file.
   2. You use a ? to check that the corners of the metal are right angles.
   3. The trainees had steak and ? for lunch.
   4. After doing two hours of ? on the football field, the players were tired.
   5. If you want the metal to have a ? shape, you must make sure the sides are the same length.
   6. Sally takes her car to the ? to be checked.
   7. The precision finishing of the metal plate is done with a second-cut ?.
   8. The trainees put away the dirty ? and glasses after lunch.
   9. The technical drawing of the vice is stored in a ? on the instructor's computer.
   10. When the trainees work with cutting tools, they wear goggles to protect their eyes from ?.
   11. When Peter comes home from work, he puts his car in the ?.
   12. When the apprentices are in the second year of their ?, they start doing easy jobs on the centre lathe.

WORD BANK

circular saw – (Metall-)Kreissäge
cutting-off – Trennschleifen
grinding disc – Schleifscheibe
second-cut (file) – Doppelschlicht-feile
vice – Schraubstock
workpiece – Werkstück

WORD BANK ◎

clamp (v) – einspannen
drive (v) – antreiben
steel bar – Stahleisen, Stabstahl
stock – Material, Rohmaterial
storeroom – Materiallager

C

NACH DIESEM MODUL:

- ✓ kenne ich die wichtigsten Redewendungen um ein Telefongespräch zu führen,
- ✓ kann ich Maße, Namen und Adressen am Telefon auf Englisch weitergeben.

Telephoning

When you are on the job, chances are you will have your mobile phone with you – it does not matter what line of work you are in. Whether you are repairing a server, fixing a leak, or installing a telephone line, your phone can ring at any time. It could be a customer with a complaint, you may have to ring a supplier or check the status of an order. And if you have to talk in English, you need to have the necessary skills to understand and be understood, no matter what the situation.

P **1** **Look at the photos. What might the people be talking about on the telephone? Compare your answers with a partner. Use these words to help you:**

materials • problem • delay • support • help • breakdown • repair • solution • angry • confused • crash • computer network room

2 **Match the German words below with the English equivalents.**

1. Handy	a. message
2. Anrufbeantworter	b. hands-free device
3. Festnetz	c. extension number
4. Nachricht	d. mobile/cell phone
5. Durchwahl	e. answering machine
6. Freisprechanlage	f. area code
7. Vorwahl	g. country code
8. Ländervorwahl	h. landline

A | Making and receiving a phone call

R **1** **Which of the following phrases are used for making calls and which ones for receiving calls? Make a list.**

1. Could you put me through to Mr Warren, please?
2. I'm sorry, but Mr/Ms … is in a meeting at the moment.
3. How can I help you?
4. Thank you. I'll ring back later.
5. Can I ask what your call is about?
6. Would you like to leave a message?
7. Thank you very much for your help.
8. My name is Barry Potter and I'm calling from …
9. May I take your name, please?
10. I'd like to speak to somebody in the production department, please.
11. Hold the line, please. I'll put you through.
12. Could you tell him/her that …?

M **2** **Read the telephone conversation below and find the English equivalents for the following German expressions.**

→ **PHRASES:** Telephoning

1. Haben Sie etwas zum Schreiben?
2. Soll ich Ihnen seine Handynummer geben?
3. Er ist leider zurzeit nicht im Büro.
4. Ich hätte gerne mit … gesprochen.
5. Einen Moment, bitte.
6. Wie kann ich Ihnen helfen?

Christoph:	Smart EDV, Christoph Fink.
Caller:	Er, yes, hello. Do you speak English?
Christoph:	Certainly. How can I help you?
Caller:	This is the Smart IT company in Kiel, isn't it?
Christoph:	Yes, that's correct.
Caller:	Great. My name is Erik Pedersen and I'm calling from Danske Onlinebank Copenhagen. I'd like to speak to Mr Gebhardt, please.
Christoph:	Sorry, but Mr Gebhardt is not in the office at the moment. Can I take a message, or would you like his mobile number?
Caller:	Can you give me his mobile number, please?
Christoph:	Ok, do you have a pen?
Caller:	Just a second, please … ok, go ahead.
Christoph:	The number is 0049-170 557624.
Caller:	Sorry, I didn't catch that. Could you speak up a bit?
Christoph:	Yes, of course. The number is 0049-170 557624.
Caller:	Thank you very much.
Christoph:	You're welcome. Maybe you can give me your phone number.
Caller:	Certainly. It's 0045, that's the country code for Denmark, 32, the area code for Copenhagen, and then 54 58 11. Oh, and my extension number is 944.
Christoph:	0045-32 54 58 11, extension 944. Thank you very much. Goodbye.
Caller:	Goodbye.

WORD BANK

breakdown – Störung, Ausfall
crash – Absturz
leak – Leck

INTERCULTURAL BOX

Intercultural awareness – Telephoning in English-speaking countries

When talking on the phone in English it is important that you use suitable and polite phrases. For example, if you know the person you are calling, it is common to make a little small talk before getting down to business. One thing to remember: Although it is common for English people to quickly switch to first names, it is still important to remain polite and remember that you are talking to a customer or a colleague, and not your best friend.

Example: *How are you? I haven't spoken to you for a while.*

If you have to give bad news or talk about a problem, then you should begin with *I'm afraid …* or *Unfortunately … .*

Example: *I'm afraid we cannot install your wireless internet connection this week.*

A request often begins with *Could you possibly …* or *I would be grateful if you would / could … .*

Example: *I would be grateful if you would call me back later.*

When someone thanks you for your help, or for a job well done, you can simply say *You're welcome.* And be careful! Whereas in German, just saying *yes* or *no* may be fine, this is considered to be quite impolite in England. Instead, just say *Yes, I think so,* or *No, I'm afraid not.* If you call somebody, you should give your name, where you are calling from, and say who you would like to speak to.

Example: *Hello, my name is Felix Hirschbach, calling from Crown Electronics. Could I speak to Ms Cameron, please?*

P **3** **How would you say the following things more politely?**

→ **PHRASES:** Telephoning

1. Eh? Say it again!
2. Give me your number!
3. What do you want?
4. What's your name?
5. I can't hear you!
6. What?
7. He's not here!
8. Give me Ms Bauer!

I **4** KMK I **Sie arbeiten im International Calls Service Center von Smart EDV in Kiel und erhalten einen Anruf. Führen Sie das folgende Telefongespräch mit einem Partner auf Englisch.**

Smart EDV GmbH, Kiel.	Stefanie Berg, dänische Kundin
Nehmen Sie den Anruf entgegen. →	Nennen Sie Ihren Namen. Sie möchten mit Herrn Gebhardt sprechen.
Sagen Sie, dass Sie die Anruferin schlecht verstehen und bitten Sie sie, etwas lauter zu sprechen. →	Sprechen Sie etwas lauter und fragen Sie, ob Sie jetzt besser zu verstehen sind.
Bejahen Sie und fragen Sie, worum es geht. →	Erklären Sie, dass die Firma Smart EDV gestern in Ihrer Firma neue Hardware und Software installiert hat, und dass heute Morgen der Server abgestürzt ist. Es ist dringend!
Sagen Sie höflich, dass Herr Gebhardt in einer Sitzung ist und sich später melden wird. Fragen Sie, ob Herr Gebhardt die Nummer der Anruferin hat. →	Bejahen Sie. Bedanken Sie sich und beenden Sie das Gespräch.
Bedanken Sie sich auch und verabschieden Sie sich.	

B | Giving information over the phone

Making a quick call is often the fastest and easiest way of passing on valuable information, such as measurements or figures. However, misunderstandings can happen very quickly, so it is important to make sure any information is delivered clearly and correctly.

1 Match the English word to the German translation.

1. height	a. Breite
2. length	b. Gewicht
3. width	c. Höhe
4. weight	d. Tiefe
5. depth	e. Länge

INFO BOX: Saying weights and measurements

nine **point** five milimetres (9.5 mm)
thirty one **square** metres (31 m²)
one **point** two five litre engine (1.25 l)
170 kilometers **per** hour (170 kph)
100 **by** 30 **by** 15 (100 x 30 x 15)
twenty **cubic** metres (20 m³)
6000 revolutions **per** minute (6000 rpm)
two hundred **and** twenty volts (220 V)

2 What are the adjectives for the nouns in exercise 1?

I **3** Sit back to back with a partner. Take turns in giving each other different information over the phone. Partner A uses role card A, Partner B uses role card B (see Appendix).

I **4** Sit back to back and spell your name, the name and address of your company, and your email address. Use the table below to help you.

Symbol	Name	Example
@	at	info@
B / b	capital letter / lower case	NYC / asap
-	hyphen / dash	t-online
ö	o-umlaut / oe / o with two dots	Schönberg
:	colon	http:
/	slash / stroke / forward slash	org/news
\	backslash	\docs
.	dot	.de
_	underscore	customer_info

R **5** KMK I ◎ A 1.3 Alex Bauder works for Fertighaus Henke in Magdeburg and is called by Mr. Reid, an English customer who lives in Germany and who is currently building a house near Magdeburg. Listen to the conversation and answer the following questions in German.

1. Who is Mr Deschler?
2. Why can't Mr Reid speak to him personally?
3. Why does Mr Reid want to speak to Mr Deschler?
4. When will Fertighaus Henke begin building Mr Reid's cellar?
5. Why does the extractor fan need to be moved to the left?
6. Which changes is Mr Deschler not responsible for?
7. What should Mr Deschler do next?

R **6** ◎ A 1.3 Now listen to the conversation again and make notes of the changes Mr Reid wants, where he wants them, and details about the measurements, where given.

WORD BANK

cubic metre – Kubikmeter
revolutions per minute – Drehzahl
socket – Steckdose
square metre – Quadratmeter

WORD BANK ◎

construction manager – Bauleiter
diameter – Durchmesser
extractor fan – Dunstabzugshaube
foundation pit – Baugrube
hob – Kochfeld

04

NACH DIESEM MODUL:

- ✓ kenne ich die englischen Begriffe für die wichtigsten Werkzeugmaschinen und deren Bauteile,
- ✓ kann ich die Funktionen der wichtigsten Werkzeugmaschinenbauteile auf Englisch beschreiben.

Machine tools

The most important machine tools that are used in industry for production and for training are the lathe, the milling machine and the grinding machine. These machine tools have some basic machine elements in common: the main switch starts and stops the machine; the emergency stop rapidly halts all machine operations, if necessary. Another machine part is the machine frame, which carries various slides. In a lathe, for example, the turner moves the slides on the frame and feeds the lathe cutter to the workpiece which is held firmly in the chuck.

R **1** **Look at the photo and answer the questions.**

1. Which machine tool is the turner operating in the photo?
2. Which machine components are shown?

R **2** **Name the most important machine tools for cutting processes.**

3 **Complete the text using the correct machine parts from the box.**

main switch • cutter • chuck • emergency stop • machine frame

All metal-cutting machines have a **1** to power machine operations. An **2** immediately interrupts all machine processes. All machine tools have a **3**, a machine bed or base, and clamping elements such as the **4**. The lathe has different slides which feed the **5** to the metal that you want to cut.

WORD BANK

clamping element – Spannelement
feed – (Vor-)Schub; Zustellung
feed (v) – zustellen
gear and control unit – Steuerungseinheit
grinding machine – Schleifmaschine
lathe – Drehmaschine, Drehbank
lathe cutter – Drehmeißel
milling machine – Fräsmaschine
revolution speed – Drehgeschwindigkeit
turner – Dreher(in)

A | Machine tools and their parts

Lathes, milling machines and grinding machines all remove metal from workpieces in different ways. For this reason, they all have chucks to hold either the cutting tool or the workpiece. The main spindle rotates the chuck during the cutting process. The gear and control units determine the feed of the workpiece, the cutting tool and the revolution speed of the spindle.

R/M **Match the German terms in the box with the English labels.**

Anlass- und Ausschalter • Ständer/Säule • Sockel • Winkeltisch • Führungsarm • Schlitten mit Querschlitten/Support • Spindelkasten mit Getriebeblock • Hauptspindel mit Spannfutter • Hauptschalter • Werkzeughalter • Reitstock • Maschinentisch • beweglicher Schleiftisch • Schleifscheibe • Senkrechtschlitten • Steuerstange • Werkzeugschnellwechsler • Radsteuerung • Bedienungspult/Steuerpult • Spindel • Handvorschub für Schleiftisch • Notaus(-schalter)

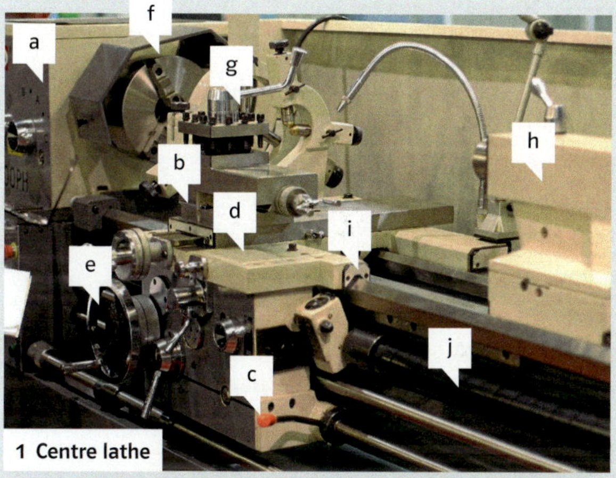

1 Centre lathe

a. headstock with gearbox
b. toolpost
c. main switch
d. saddle and cross slide
e. handwheel control
f. main spindle with chuck
g. tool quick exchange
h. tailstock
i. machine bed with slide
j. control rod

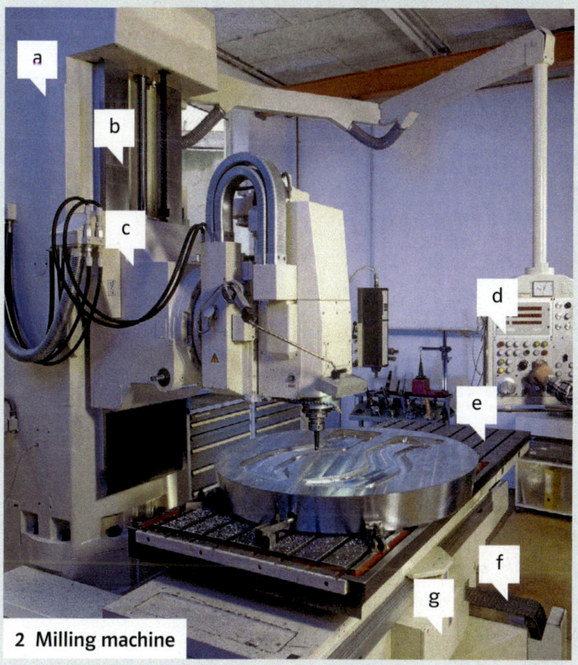

2 Milling machine

a. column
b. vertical slide
c. overarm
d. control panel
e. machine table
f. base
g. knee

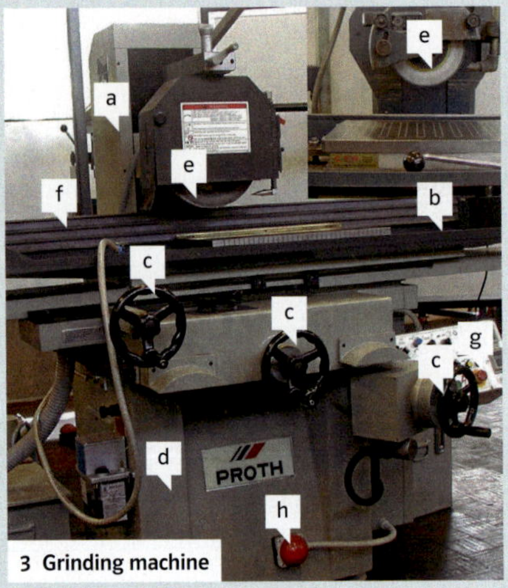

3 Grinding machine

a. column
b. machine table
c. table hand feed
d. base
e. grinding disc
f. table traverse
g. start and stop switch
h. emergency stop

B | The function of machine tool components

The machine tools differ in some basic functions. Round material is processed at the lathe by the rotating main spindle and the chuck which holds the workpiece. Flat material is operated in the milling process. The workpiece is clamped in the machine vice mounted on the machine table. The workpiece moves horizontally as it is milled. In grinding, the workpiece is fixed magnetically to the machine table. The table itself is fixed to the table traverse, which moves horizontally, too.

R **1** ⊙ A 2.15 **Sven Schäfer, a German apprentice, is at a trade show with Brian, an exchange student from York. Listen to the dialogue and say which parts have these functions:**

1. It houses the gears of a lathe.
2. It feeds the cutting tool during the turning operation.
3. It holds the workpiece during the milling process.
4. It feeds the workpiece to the grinding wheel.
5. It holds the workpiece during the lathe cutting process.
6. They drive the main spindle of all machine tools.
7. It rotates the workpiece in a turning operation.
8. It holds the lathe cutting tool.

R **2** ⊙ A 2.15 **Write down the list of parts 1–12 on a separate sheet. Listen to the dialogue again and note down which machine – lathe (L), milling machine (M) or grinding machine (G) – has which parts.**

1. base	5. three-jaw chuck	9. column
2. toolpost	6. vertical slide	10. overarm
3. motor-reversing switch	7. base table	11. machine table
4. saddle and cross-slide	8. table traverse	12. grinding wheel

I/P **3** **△ Use the role cards for Speakers A, B and C in the Appendix to discuss the function of the lathe machine elements on page 33.**

4 Match the parts of a milling machine with their functions.

1. knee 2. table handwheel 3. column 4. overarm 5. spindle	a. moves the table towards or away from the cutter b. houses the drive motor c. carries the machine table; houses various machine controls d. rotates the milling cutter during the operation e. houses the headstock and the main spindle

5 Complete the sentences about a grinding machine using the terms in the box.

grinding wheel • column • table traverse handwheel • table traverse • main switch • cross-feed handwheel

1. … provides the table cross-travel.
2. … carries the workpiece to the grinding wheel.
3. … controls the electricity supply to the machine (on/off).
4. … removes the material from the workpiece.
5. … provides the longitudinal table movement.
6. … carries the overarm with the spindle.

M **6** **UNDERSTANDING TECHNICAL ENGLISH**

Find the general meanings of the words in an English-German dictionary or an online dictionary.

a. column b. frame c. saddle d. knee e. feed

P/I **7** More sophisticated machine tools used for large-scale manufacturing are CNC machine tools. Check the Internet to find a CNC machine tool with lathe and milling functions. Find out the functions of the machine and present your results in class.

→ **PHRASES:** Presentations

P **8** KMK I Sie bekommen die Aufgabe, auf Englisch eine kurze Handreichung der Arbeitsprozesse zu erstellen, die erforderlich sind, um den Maschinenschraubstock in der Zeichnung herzustellen. Berücksichtigen Sie dabei auch detailliert die einzelnen Bauteile des Schraubstocks. Arbeiten Sie mit einem Partner.

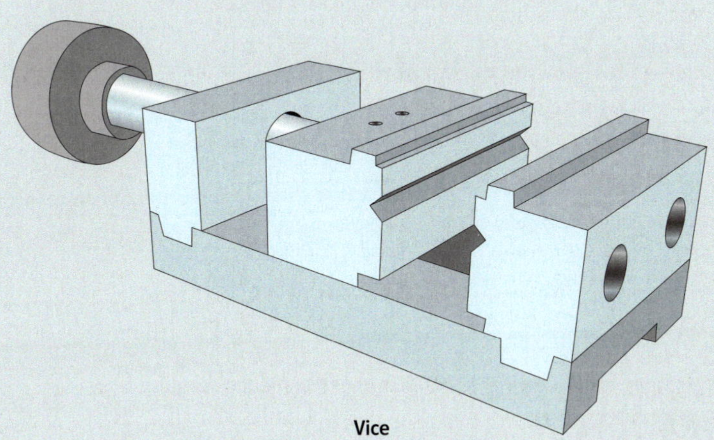

Vice

WORD BANK

component – Maschinenbauteil
drive (v) – antreiben
large-scale manufacturing – Massenfertigung
mount (v) – montieren
smooth (v) – glätten

WORD BANK ◎

cutting tool – Zerspanungswerkzeuge, Schneid-
gears – Getriebe
grinding wheel – Schleifscheibe
three-jaw chuck – Dreibackenfutter

cy8yn5

D

NACH DIESEM MODUL:

- ✓ kann ich auf Englisch kurze Anfragen, Angebote und Bestellungen als Brief, E-Mail oder Fax erstellen,
- ✓ kann ich englische Briefe, E-Mails und Faxe beantworten.

1

2

3

4

Written communication

Written communication such as emails, faxes and business letters play an essential role in business, both in the office and the workshop. For any company to run efficiently, it is necessary to have an effective communication system – making sure that enquiries are answered promptly, offers are made on time, and orders are placed and processed correctly. The standard business letter has been replaced in recent years by the faster email, and to a lesser extent, the fax. In all areas of business today it is common to have dealings with countries across the globe, meaning you need to be able to understand written communication in English.

P **1** **Look at the pictures above and describe them in your own words.**

P **2** **What are the advantages and disadvantages of the forms of written communication shown in the pictures? Create a list. Use these words to help you:**

confidential • instant • easy • time-consuming • reliable • signal • misunderstanding • slow • personal • formal • informal

3 **Compare your lists with a partner and come up with a final list for each form of communication. Share your final list with the class.**

A | Enquiries

Business transactions generally begin with an enquiry. In the example below, a car garage is looking for a new supplier of tools.

M **1** **Stephen Bains from City Garage in Wolverhampton, England is interested in buying some tools from Hauch Werkzeuge KG in Gelsenkirchen, a toolmaking company specializing in tools for car mechanics. Read Stephen's enquiry and sum up the main information in German.**

Dear Sir/Madam,	a. appropriate salutation
Automotive mechanic tool supplier	b. subject line
We saw your advertisement in this month's edition of *Under the Bonnet* magazine regarding your selection of tools for car mechanics.	c. source of address
We are a family-run car mechanic company in Wolverhampton, England, with over 20 employees.	d. introduction of your firm
We have recently expanded and are looking for a new supplier of quality tools for our new workshops. Therefore we would ask you to send us a copy of your latest catalogue and price list.	e. reason for enquiry f. request to send catalogue and price list
Please also inform us about your export prices and possible discounts as well as terms of payment and delivery and delivery times.	g. request for information on prices and discounts and terms of payment and delivery
As we would like to test your tools, we would appreciate it if you could send us some samples.	h. further requests
Thank you for your attention to this enquiry and we look forward to hearing from you.	i. closing phrase
Yours sincerely,	j. complimentary close

R **2** **Match these parts of an enquiry with the descriptions (a.–j.) above.**

1. Best wishes.
2. Your company was recommended to me by a colleague.
3. We are a large production company, specialising in machine components.
4. Please let us have a detailed cost estimate for configuring our IT network.
5. We hope to hear from you soon.
6. What are your terms of payment for regular customers?
7. As we are convinced that your products will sell well on the American market …
8. A visit by your representative would be greatly appreciated.
9. Please let us know whether you can supply from stock.
10. Machine component supplier

WORD BANK

bonnet – Motorhaube
car mechanic – KFZ-Mechaniker(in)
toolmaking company – Werkzeugmacher
workshop – Werkstatt

B | Offers

P **1** **Read the offer email below and complete it using the words from the box.**

bank transfer • discount • interest • business • working days • sample • attachment • delivery period • stock • orders

From: mailto:t.wolf@hauch...de **Sent:** 201_-05-30 14:52
To: mailto:info@citygarage.co...uk
Cc: mailto:k.mueller@hauch...de
Subject: Your enquiry

Attachments Hauptkatalog_2012.pdf

Dear Mr Bains

Thank you for your enquiry and your 1 in our products.

We are sending you our latest brochure and price list as an 2 .
For 3 of 200 units or more we are able to grant a quantity 4 of five per cent.
For large orders (over 250 units) we require a 5 of 10–14 6 .
Smaller orders can be delivered from 7 and within 3–5 working days.

Our usual terms of payment are by 8 to our account with the GDB Bank in Gelsenkirchen.

One 9 case of ratchets, sockets, wrenches and screwdrivers has been dispatched to you this morning and should reach you in the next few days.

Thank you again for your enquiry. We look forward to establishing regular 10 with you.

Yours sincerely

Tim Wolf

P **2** **Use the following notes to write an enquiry and an offer in English.**

→ **PHRASES:** Written communication

Enquiry
(You work at Construct World.)

- large DIY store in Poland (Construct World), looking to buy quality German-made tools
- saw your company (Hauch Werkzeuge KG) at a trade show in Hannover
- would like information about delivery times, discounts, copy of catalogue
- would like some samples to inspect
- polite ending

Angebot
(Sie arbeiten bei Hauch Werkzeuge.)

- Bedanken Sie sich für die Anfrage.
- Gerne schicken Sie Ihren aktuellen Prospekt inklusive Preisliste zu.
- Lieferzeit (nach Polen):
  große Bestellungen (über 500 Stück): 5–10 Werktage,
  kleine Bestellungen: 2–4 Werktage
- Preisnachlass ab Bestellwert von 2.500 € möglich (5 %)
- Sie würden sich freuen, mit Construct World zusammenarbeiten zu dürfen.
- höflicher Schluss

C | Orders

1 Read the order fax below and complete it using the prepositions in the box below.

for (2x) • by • of • to (3x) • with

TELEFAX Message

City Garage
17 Gorsebrook Rd.
Wolverhampton WV6 5PI
Tel.: 0044 (0)1902 554997… • Fax: 0044 (0)1902 554998…

To: Hauch Werkzeuge KG
Schmiedstrasse 44
45879 Gelsenkirchen
Germany

Attention: Mr Tim Wolf

Fax: 0049 209 721965…

From: Stephen Bains

Subject: Order

Dear Mr Wolf

Thank you very much **1** your email **2** 30 May.

Thank you also for sending us your catalogue and price list.
We were very impressed **3** your range of tools for car mechanics and would like to place a trial order **4** 16 socket sets, 16 screwdriver sets, 30 adjustable wrenches and 16 torque wrenches.

Please confirm this order indicating the bank account **5** which you wish to have the sum in question transferred.

Please deliver the tools **6** our workshop at 17 Gorsebrook Rd., Wolverhampton, WV6 5PI.

We look forward **7** receiving the consignment soon and to placing further orders **8** you.

Best regards

S.Bains

Stephen Bains

M **2** KMK II

Sie arbeiten bei Hauch Werkzeuge KG in Gelsenkirchen. Ihr Chef bittet Sie, das obige Fax für ihn auf Deutsch zusammenzufassen, damit er über den Auftrag informiert ist.

WORD BANK

ratchet – Knarre
screwdriver – Schraubenzieher / -dreher
socket – Steckdose, Stecknuss
torque wrench – Drehmomentschlüssel
(adjustable) wrench – (verstellbarer) Schraubenschlüssel

05

NACH DIESEM MODUL:

- √ kann ich die Hauptmerkmale von Zerspanungsprozessen auf Englisch benennen,
- √ kann ich die wesentlichen Dreh-, Fräs- und Schleifarbeiten auf Englisch beschreiben.

Cutting processes with machine tools

Conventional machines tools such as the centre lathe, the milling machine and the grinding machine are used for cutting processes in training centres. CNC (computerized numerical control) machines are used in industry for highly accurate, large-scale production. Each machine tool has a different function. The main difference between a centre lathe and a milling machine is the shape of the workpiece. Round material is machined or turned on a centre lathe and flat material is milled on a milling machine. A grinding machine is used to sharpen tools and to smoothen surfaces accurately.

R **1** **Which machine operation is illustrated in the photo?**

R **2** **Point out the main differences between the components that are machined on the different types of machine tools.**

P **3** **Decide which machining processes are suitable for the jobs below. Give reasons.**

1. The machinist wants to produce a stud bolt with a threaded shaft.
2. The apprentices have to manufacture steel plates with specified grooves.
3. The customer wants the surface of the steel plates and shafts to be processed accurately.
4. The machine tool company has received an order to produce 10,000 stud bolts within two weeks.

A | Working with machine tools

Compared with large-scale production in industry, small and medium-sized companies often produce limited quantities of parts. These parts are either turned on a lathe or milled on a milling machine.

R **1** ⊙ A 2.16 **Volker Feuerbach is an apprentice at a machine tool company in Berlin. He is discussing machining processes on a centre lathe with Philip, an English exchange student. Before you listen, look at the photo of a centre lathe on page 33. Listen to the dialogue and say which of the machine parts below they talk about. Two parts are not mentioned.**

page 33

> three-jaw chuck • headstock • gear and control units • main spindle • motor • motor-reversing switch • slideways • speed selection lever

R **2** ⊙ A 2.16 **Listen to the dialogue again and complete the sentences.**

1. The headstock is started by switching on the ? .
2. The power is transmitted to the different ? .
3. The ? rotates the workpiece.
4. The workpiece can be rotated clockwise or ? .
5. The ? speed is set with the speed selection lever.
6. The feed of the cutting tool is controlled via the ? .
7. The ? and cross-slide feeds the cutting tool.
8. The workpiece is clamped in the ? .

WORD BANK

cutting process – Zerspanungsprozess, spanabhebendes Verfahren
machine tool – Werkzeugmaschine
mill (v) – fräsen
process (v) – maschinell bearbeiten
process plan – Arbeitsplan
set up (v) – (eine Maschine) aufrüsten
shaft – Schaft
stud bolt – Gewindebolzen
technical drawing – technische Zeichnung
threaded – mit einem Gewinde versehen
turn (v) – drehen (auf der Drehbank)
working axis (Pl.) axes – Arbeitsachse; Messachse
workpiece – Werkstück

WORD BANK ⊙

clamp (v) – einspannen, aufspannen
three-jaw chuck – Dreibackenfutter

B | Setting up a milling machine

Before starting a milling operation, you have to plan the working steps. A process plan and a technical drawing are necessary to guarantee a safe and accurate milling job.

R **1** **Read the text and find the English terms for the words in the box.**

> Frästisch • Maschinenschraubstock • Arbeitsspindel • Steuerungspult • Nut • Fräser • Spannfutter

Preparing a milling job

The milling job starts by carefully reading the technical drawing and the process plan. The drawing shows a metal plate in the shape of a rectangle. Its dimensions are given on the process plan. The plan also specifies that the rectangle has two parallel grooves, which have to be 3 mm wide and 1.5 mm deep.

The job begins by setting the milling machine. The machine vice on the machine table is adjusted accurately to provide the working steps in the various working axes. These axes are the vertical Y-axis, the horizontal Z-axis and the X-axis, which runs at a right angle to the Z-axis or parallel to the working spindle.

Then the material is clamped into the machine vice and the milling cutter is clamped into the chuck. The required revolution speed of the spindle is set depending on the material to be worked. Finally, the feed values for the various axes are programmed into the electronic control panel.

I/M **2** **Discuss how you prepare a milling job in English using the prompts below. Present your dialogue in class.**

Example:

Speaker A: *I want to work a metal plate …*

Speaker A	Speaker B
1. Sagen Sie, dass Sie eine Metallplatte an einer Fräsmaschine bearbeiten möchten.	2. Antworten Sie, dass Sie als erstes die technische Zeichnung und den Arbeitsplan anschauen müssen.
3. Fragen Sie, was auf dem Arbeitsplan steht.	4. Antworten Sie, dass der Maschinenschraubstock exakt auf dem Frästisch auszurichten ist.
5. Fragen Sie, ob Sie jetzt das Werkstück in den Maschinenschraubstock einspannen können.	6. Antworten Sie mit ja. Dies ist der nächste Schritt auf dem Arbeitsplan.
7. Fragen Sie, welcher Arbeitsschritt nun folgt.	8. Sagen Sie, dass nun der Fräser in das Spannfutter eingespannt wird und die Vorschubwerte einprogrammiert werden können.
9. Sagen Sie, dass Sie die Vorschubwerte der drei Arbeitsachsen im elektronischen Steuerpult einprogrammiert haben.	10. Sagen Sie, dass nun die erforderliche Drehgeschwindigkeit der Spindel eingestellt wird.
11. Sagen Sie, dass die Drehgeschwindigkeit eingestellt ist.	12. Sagen Sie, dass die Fräsmaschine gestartet werden kann.

P **3** **Use the Internet to find tool suppliers of the latest end-mill cutters and cutting arbors, which could be used for your next training period. Make a note of the cheapest and most expensive items, their features and the suppliers. Decide which cutters and arbors are the best choice for the milling jobs in your workshop and present your findings in class.**

→ **PHRASES:** Presentations

M **4** **UNDERSTANDING TECHNICAL ENGLISH**

1. **Find the general and technical meanings of the words in an English-German dictionary or in an online dictionary.**

   a. adjust
   b. revolution
   c. value
   d. dimension

2. **Complete the sentences using the words in exercise 1. Then translate the sentences into German.**

   a. The students must ? the lines in their technical drawings to correspond to the ? in the process plan.
   b. After the ? thousands of people fled the country.
   c. When the machinist was setting the milling machine, he had to set the ? speed of the main spindle.
   d. The feed of the various milling axes was not correct because the apprentice had entered the wrong ?.
   e. The ? of the euro fell because of the worldwide economic crisis.

C | Working safely with machine tools

When operating machine tools, it is important that machinists are careful not to damage the machines by incorrect handling or ruin the workpiece or even the cutting tool. Machine operators have to wear suitable protective clothing such as goggles and gloves. They also have to check that the machinery is functioning properly.

P **1** **SAFETY FIRST ⚠**

1. **Decide whether the instructions refer to the worker's safety or to the correct use of machine tools. Some instructions refer to both.**

a. Always set the machine vice to an accurate working position on the machine table.
b. Always wear goggles during a grinding job.
c. Feed the cutting tool carefully to the workpiece to avoid damage to the cutter.
d. Check that the cutter is sharp before starting the machine operation.
e. Don't forget to set the required revolution speed of the main spindle before you start the machining process.
f. Tie back long hair and wear a hairnet during turning operations.
g. Make sure you can always reach the emergency stop.
h. Never leave the guard open during turning operations on the centre lathe.
i. When grinding a workpiece, it is safer to wear gloves as protection against sparks.
j. In case of an emergency, call an ambulance on the emergency phone.

2. **Give more safety instructions based on your experiences in the workshop.**

P/M **2** KMK I

Sie sollen die Fräsarbeit eines Rechtecks aus Aluminium mit verschiedenen Nuten ausführen. Bringen Sie die Arbeitsschritte für die Fräsarbeit in die richtige Reihenfolge. Dann übertragen Sie den Ablaufplan ins Deutsche.

1. Switch on the machine.
2. Put the workpiece on the milling table.
3. Adjust the cutter.
4. Read the order and the drawing.
5. Return the milling table.
6. Set the machine.
7. Clamp the end mill cutter.
8. Clamp the workpiece.
9. Remove the end mill cutter and the holding tool.
10. Have the end mill cutter and holding tool ready.
11. Unclamp and remove the workpiece.
12. Mill the workpiece.
13. Unclamp the end mill cutter.

WORD BANK

cutting arbor – Fräsdorn
emergency stop – Notaus; Notschalter
end-mill cutter – Walzenstirnfräser, Schaftfräser
guard – Schutzvorrichtung
machine operator – Maschinenbediener(in)
spark – Funke

E

NACH DIESEM MODUL:

- ✓ kann ich eine Stellenanzeige auf Englisch verstehen,
- ✓ kann ich meine Fähigkeiten und Qualifikationen auf Englisch beschreiben,
- ✓ kann ich eine Bewerbung auf Englisch schreiben.

1

2

3

4

Applications

The world today is full of opportunities. You might decide to work in your hometown, a big city, or even another country. Maybe you want to work for a small family-run company or a major corporation with branches across the globe. Whatever you decide, the opportunities are out there, but it is up to you to take them.

1 Look at the pictures above and describe them using the words below.

to apply • job advertisement • letter of application • CV • to search • job interview • employment contract • to invite • newspaper • to write

2 Put the steps of the application process shown in the pictures above into the correct order.

P **3** Work on your own. What skills and qualifications do you need for a job in your industry? Make a list. Use these words to help you:

hard-working • motivated • logical • good with numbers • good with your hands • communicative • good team player • technical skills • able to understand plans and diagrams • attention to detail • computer skills

4 Work with a partner and decide upon a final list. Share it with the class.

A | Job advertisements

M/R **1** **Read the three online job advertisements below and find the English translations for the following German words and expressions.**

1. verantwortungsbewusst
2. aktiv, praktisch
3. Bewerber
4. Störungssuche
5. pünktlich
6. lernbereit
7. begeistert
8. gültige Fahrerlaubnis
9. Erfahrung
10. abgeschlossene Ausbildung
11. gute Bezahlung
12. fließendes Englisch
13. teamfähig
14. Montage
15. Grundkenntnisse in CAD
16. freie Stelle

http://www.totaljobs...com

1	City Garage – Car mechanic (full-time)	City Garage in Wolverhampton is looking for a recently-qualified car mechanic to join our busy team. Are you enthusiastic, willing to learn, responsible and punctual? If so, then contact us. We offer good rates of pay and a pleasant working atmosphere. Applicants must have a clean and valid driver's license. Please send a written application and a CV to Michael McCarthy at the following address: City Garage 17 Gorsebrook Rd. Wolverhampton WV6 5PI Tel.: 0044 (0)1902 554997...
2	Harper Shipping Client Support Technician	We are looking for a client support technician for our IT team to provide support and troubleshooting for hardware and software installation. You will also be responsible for new system configuration and maintaining the desktop client software. You should have two years experience, good English skills and be able to work as part of a team. Salary: negotiable Email application to: careers@HS...com
3	Trafford Tools Mechatronic Technician	Trafford Tools is a leading supplier of high-quality tools. We have a vacancy for a hands-on person to work as a mechatronic technician. Tasks: fault finding, maintenance, assembly, assist with installation. Skills: completed apprenticeship, basic CAD skills, good knowledge of tools, fluent English. Contact: James Truman J.truman@TT...co.uk Tel: 0044 (0)161 929496...

I/M **2** **One of your colleagues does not speak English and asks you to tell him about one of the job ads. Choose one of the ads and give him a brief summary in German. Swap roles.**

WORD BANK

branch – Filiale
family-run company – Familien-unternehmen
job application – Bewerbung
maintain (v) – warten
opportunities – Möglichkeiten
qualifications – Qualifikationen
skills – Fähigkeiten
troubleshooting – Fehlerbehebung

B | Letter of application

R **1** **Read the letter of application and decide whether the following statements are true or false. Give reasons for your decisions.**

1. Erkan is in the final year of his apprenticeship as a car mechanic.
2. He has always wanted to be a car mechanic.
3. Erkan had a holiday job at *Werkstatt Kuhn.*
4. He is looking forward to working abroad.
5. Erkan has included his CV in the application.

Erkan Celik • Waldstrasse 48 • 50679 Köln • Germany

Michael McCarthy
City Garage
17 Gorsebrook Rd.
Wolverhampton
WV6 5PI
England

12 June 20_

Dear Mr McCarthy,

Application for job as car mechanic

I am writing to apply for the advertised position of a car mechanic at City Garage. I completed my apprenticeship as a car mechanic at a technical college here in Germany six months ago. I have been interested in cars since I was a child and being a car mechanic is my dream job.
As you will see from my CV, I recently completed a six-month internship at Werskstatt Kuhn. This not only gave me the opportunity to put my theoretical skills into practice, but I also had the chance to gain more experience with customers.
I am a very enthusiastic person. I am also reliable, responsible and willing to learn. Furthermore, I have good English skills and I would welcome the opportunity to gain some experience working in another country.
Thank you in advance for considering my application. If you require any further information, please contact me.

Yours sincerely,
Erkan Celik

Encl.: CV

WATCH OUT!
I am interested ~~for~~ cars. I am interested <u>in</u> cars.

M **2** KMK I **Fassen Sie mit Hilfe der unten stehenden Stichworte die wichtigsten Inhalte des Bewerbungsschreibens auf Deutsch zusammen.**

1. Beruf, für den sich Erkan bewirbt **2.** Berufserfahrung **3.** Motivation
4. Persönliche Qualifikationen/Fähigkeiten **5.** Kontaktperson

C | The CV

R **1** KMK II ⓞ A 1.4

Andrea Wagner ist Auszubildende bei einer IT-Firma in Nürnberg. Sie möchte sich für eine Praktikumsstelle in der englischen Niederlassung ihrer Firma bewerben und fragt David, einen Praktikanten aus England, ob er ihr ein paar Tipps geben kann. Hören Sie das Gespräch an und vervollständigen Sie die folgenden Sätze auf Deutsch.

1. Andrea möchte sich für eine Praktikumsstelle in ? bewerben.
2. Sie bringt am Montag ? mit ins Büro.
3. Der Lebenslauf sollte nicht länger sein als ?.
4. Man sollte niemals einen Lebenslauf ohne ? senden.
5. Man sollte den Lebenslauf dazu benutzen, seine ? und ? hervorzuheben.
6. Wenn man seine Arbeitserfahrung auflistet, sollte man mit ? anfangen.
7. In England muss ein Lebenslauf kein ? enthalten.
8. Man sollte sicherstellen, dass man zwei ? nennt.
9. Man sollte niemals ?.
10. Wenn der Lebenslauf fertig ist, sollte man ihn auf ? und ? überprüfen.
11. Es ist eine gute Idee, den Lebenslauf ? zu geben.
12. Wenn man den Lebenslauf abschickt, sollte man ? behalten.

P **2** KMK II

Verfassen Sie ein Anschreiben für eine der in Modulteil A ausgeschriebenen Stellen auf Englisch. Arbeiten Sie dabei die unten aufgeführten Inhalte ein.

→ **PHRASES:** Applications

- Wählen Sie einen geeigneten Betreff.
- Nehmen Sie Bezug auf die Stellenanzeige und bekunden Sie Ihr Interesse an der ausgeschriebenen Stelle.
- Sie werden bald Ihre Ausbildung als … abschließen.
- Bringen Sie zum Ausdruck, dass Sie ein geeigneter Bewerber sind: organisiert, erfahren, hoch motiviert, teamfähig, flexibel, lernbereit, zuverlässig. Sie haben gute Englischkenntnisse.
- Beenden Sie den Brief angemessen und unterschreiben Sie.
- Weisen Sie auf Ihren Lebenslauf hin.

WORD BANK

consider (v) – betrachten
gain (v) – sammeln
internship – Praktikum
letter of application – Bewerbungsschreiben
reliable – zuverlässig
require (v) – benötigen

INFO BOX: Translating German school types and qualifications

It is not always possible to find the equivalent of your school type or qualification in English. However, the following table gives some useful translations.

Schools			
Grundschule	Elementary school / Primary school	Berufsschule (Duales System)	Part-time vocational school (dual system)
Hauptschule	General secondary school	Berufsfachschule	Full-time vocational school
Realschule	Intermediate secondary school	Fachschule für technische Berufe	Technical college
Gymnasium	Upper secondary school	Fachoberschule	Upper secondary vocational school
Gesamtschule	Comprehensive school	Fachgymnasium	Specialized upper secondary school

Qualifications			
Hauptschulabschluss	secondary modern school qualification	Fachabitur	advanced vocational certificate of education
Mittlere Reife	secondary school leaving certificate	Zusatzqualifikation	additional qualification
Abitur	A level/high school diploma		

06

NACH DIESEM MODUL:

✓ kann ich die Eigenschaften und die Verwendung der wichtigsten Materialien in der Metallbearbeitung auf Englisch beschreiben.

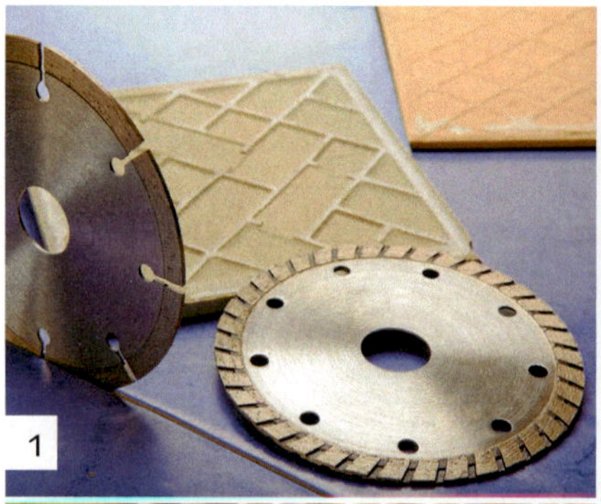
1

2

3

4

Engineering materials

In engineering it is important to find the most suitable material(s) for each job. The suitability of a material depends on its mechanical properties. For some jobs, a material has to be hard or dense, for others it must be malleable as is the case with sheet steel, which can be pressed or rolled. Cutting tools, such as lathe cutters, are often made of metal carbide steel so that they are hard enough to cut metal. Sawing discs must also be hard enough to cut stone, glass or ceramics. This is the reason why they are often coated with industrial diamonds. Steel is used in mechanical engineering as it is hard enough to be processed with machine tools.

R **1** Name the materials and cutting tools in the photos.

2 Describe the cutters in the photos in your own words.

3 Make a table like the one below. Add the properties of each material and the jobs it is used for in mechanical engineering.

Materials	Property	Job
sheet steel	?	?
steel	?	?
metal carbide steel	?	?
diamond-tipped sawing discs	?	?

A | Materials – an overview

In general, materials are divided into two groups, metals and non-metals. These two groups are divided into four sub-groups: ferrous and non-ferrous metals, natural and artificial materials.

1 Say which material in the chart each definition 1–4 refers to.

Metals			
ferrous metals		non-ferrous metals	
steels e.g. mild steel	iron ore cast iron	heavy metals e.g. lead	light metals e.g. aluminium
Non-metals			
natural materials		artificial materials	
stone paper		ceramic material e.g. glass	plastics

1. This material is made from iron ore which is heated until it becomes liquid. The material is usually brittle and breaks easily.
2. It is hard and can be cut with diamond- or carbide-tipped saw discs.
3. This material is a non-ferrous metal. It is heavy, rather soft and malleable. It is toxic if you touch it for too long.
4. A light non-ferrous metal which is corrosion resistant as an alloy.

P **2** Decide which sub-group to put the materials into.

1. copper   2. magnesium   3. wood   4. porcelain

R **3** Read the text about alloys and answer the questions.

1. Give a definition of an alloy.
2. Outline the advantages of stainless steel.

Alloys

The pure forms of metals are usually weak and corrode easily. However, when mixed with other metals or non-metals to form alloys, the properties of pure metals can be improved. Almost all metals can be used in alloys. Steel is an alloy of iron and carbon. It is harder than pure iron and more resistant to corrosion. In industry, alloys are much more widely used than pure metals. Pure aluminium corrodes easily but when alloyed it is suitable for the construction of aeroplanes, cars, and bicycles. Another alloy is stainless steel. It contains chromium which provides a long life and shiny appearance. Cast iron alone is brittle. When it is alloyed, its properties include excellent machinability, hardness and wear resistance. The applications of alloyed cast iron range from machine tools to cylinder blocks for the automotive industry.

M **4** Summarize the main points about cast iron in German.

5 Find alloys which are used for these things. Give reasons for your answer.

1. bridges   2. bikes   3. camper's cooking equipment

WORD BANK

automotive – Automobil-
carbon – Kohlenstoff
cast iron – Gusseisen
ceramics – Keramik
chromium – Chrom
corrode (v) – korrodieren, rosten
cutting tool – Schneidwerkzeug, Zerspanungswerkzeug
cylinder block – Zylinderblock
ferrous – Eisen-
hardness – Härte, Festigkeit
industrial diamond – Industriediamant
iron ore – Eisenerz
lathe cutter – Drehmeißel
malleable – verformbar, schmiedbar
mild steel – (Maschinen-)Baustahl
non-ferrous – Nichteisen-
press (v) – pressen, stanzen
property – (Material-)Eigenschaft
resistant – resistent, beständig
roll (v) – walzen
sawing disc – Sägeblatt
sheet steel – Stahlblech

B | Steel

The alloys of steel all have different properties. Mild steel, for example, is widely used in mechanical engineering because it is malleable. When it is machined, it must be strong enough to withstand a certain load. It must also be durable and last a long time. Another alloy of steel is tungsten carbide steel, which is very hard. It is often used for cutting tools such as reversible carbide tips, which are easy to exchange when they become blunt.

R **1** **Outline the applications of mild steel and tungsten carbide in industry. Refer to their properties in your answer.**

→ **PHRASES:** Presentations

2 **Complete the statements using the correct information in the brackets.**

1. Steel is an ? of iron and contains up to 1.7% carbon. (alloy / property / product)
2. Low-carbon steel is made from ? and contains about 0.2% carbon. (cast iron / iron / steel)
3. High-carbon steels include ?. (1% or more of carbon / less than 1% of carbon / no carbon)
4. Apart from carbon, steel sometimes contains elements such as manganese, phosphorous or silicon. This kind of steel is called ?. (high alloy steel / combination steel / alloyed steel)
5. Steels with ? amounts of other metals are called carbon steels. (small / large / very large)
6. ? steel with up to 20% tungsten is used for cutting tools. (The most malleable / The most expensive / The hardest)
7. You can work steel by hammering it while it is still hot or press it between rollers to produce ?. (steel bars / sheet steel / steel alloy)

R **3** ◎A 2.17 **Darren Wilson is an apprentice machinist from Bradford. He is doing an exchange with a college in Stuttgart. He is telling the German trainer, Sebastian Zimmermann, about an e-mail which he has just received. Listen to the dialogue and write down the materials and properties which they talk about.**

R **4** ◎A 2.17 **Listen to the dialogue again. Decide whether the statements are true or false. Correct the false statements.**

1. Sebastian and Darren made an aluminium box in college last month.
2. The components have to clamp the jaws of the vice securely.
3. The vice has to be rigid or it will not be able to hold the component properly.
4. The thread will be machined in the handle of the spindle.
5. The spindle is harder than the threading tool.

P/I **5** **Use the Internet to find information about aluminium alloys and steel alloys. Point out their advantages and disadvantages for the automotive industry. Present your results in class.**

→ **PHRASES:** Presentations

C | The mechanical properties of metals

The choice of materials that are used in a manufacturing process depends on the mechanical properties and also on the application of the material. As steel is malleable, it can be machined easily. In the case of cutting tools, however, the required property of the material that is used is hardness.

1 Match the properties of metal with the correct definition.

1. durability 2. ductility 3. elasticity 4. malleability 5. hardness	a. It returns to its original shape and size after being deformed. b. It can be worked into a new shape by hammering, rolling or pressing. c. It is resistant to abrasion, cutting, etc. d. It is stretched without losing its strength and it keeps the new shape. e. It is resistant to corrosion.

M **2** Give the German words for the properties. Summarise the definitions in German.

3 Say which properties the statements refer to. Give reasons for your answer.

1. This is an important property for the moving parts of machines or cutting edges of tools in a lathe or a milling machine.
2. Two metals with this property are gold and platinum.
3. Sheet steel needs two properties to be used in industrial production.
4. This property is required for steels that are used in spring steel.

M **4** **UNDERSTANDING TECHNICAL ENGLISH**

1. Find the general and technical meanings of the words in an English-German dictionary or an online dictionary.
   a. material b. thread c. property

2. Translate the sentences into English.
   a. Die wichtigste Materialeigenschaft von Baustahl ist seine Verformbarkeit.
   b. Für den Bau des Wohnblocks wird ein Grundstück am Stadtrand gesucht.
   c. Um die Hose zu nähen, braucht man guten Zwirn.
   d. Das Gewinde von Schrauben kann geschnitten oder gerollt werden.

P **5** KMK II Ein Schüler Ihrer Partnerschule in Cardiff bittet Sie um Hilfe. Er soll die Materialeigenschaften verschiedener Schneidwerkzeuge beschreiben und den entsprechenden Zerspanungsarbeiten zuordnen. Schreiben Sie auf Englisch in ganzen Sätzen.

Schneidwerkzeuge	Zerspanungsarbeiten
drill universal drill lathe tool reversible carbide tip sawing discs	sawing drilling turning as is the case in wood work, metal work and masonry

WORD BANK

durable – haltbar, strapazierfähig
high-carbon steel – (unlegierter) Hartstahl
load – Last
low-carbon steel – weicher Stahl, kohlenstoffarmer Stahl
manganese – Mangan
phosphorous – Phosphor
reversible carbide tip – Wendeplatte aus Hartmetall
roller – Walze
silicon – Silizium
spring steel – Federstahl
tungsten carbide steel – Hartmetall, Werkzeugstahl

WORD BANK ◎

clamp (v) – einspannen
clamping jaw – Spannbacke
control spindle – Steuerspindel
machine vice – Maschinenschraubstock
thread – Gewinde
threading tool – Gewindeschneidwerkzeug

F

NACH DIESEM MODUL:

- ✓ kann ich *Small Talk* auf Englisch machen,
- ✓ kenne ich die Regeln des *Small Talk*,
- ✓ kann ich auf Englisch Essen erklären und bestellen.

1

2

3

4

Socialising

Socialising is very important. It can strengthen relationships with your colleagues and improve the working atmosphere in a company. It can also be a good way of getting to know your customers or potential customers a little better. And in today's global world, English has become the world's language. So although the people you meet and work with are likely to come from a wide range of cultural backgrounds, you will often be required to communicate in English. That means that it is important to not only have the necessary language skills, but also the intercultural knowledge so that you can make a good first impression and develop professional and personal relationships.

I **1** Look at the pictures above. What relationship do you think these people might have to each other? Discuss with your partner.

2 Brainstorm a list of topics these people might be talking about.

P **3** Choose one of the pictures and create a small dialogue.

4 Look at photo 1. Brainstorm what cultural misunderstandings could take place when a German employee meets a person from another country.

P **5** Make a list of situations when a German technician might have contact with foreign colleagues – for example, customers, suppliers, manufacturers, etc.

A | Small talk

Your company has visitors from a subsidiary in Poland. Fabian, a German trainee, has been asked to show Jan, a Polish trainee, around the company.

R **1** ⦾ A 1.5 **Listen to the dialogue between Jan and Fabian. Take notes of the topics the two are talking about. Then listen again and make a list of the phrases they use.**

2 **Name other topics that Jan and Fabian could also talk about.**

3 **Which of the following topics would / wouldn't you talk about? Why? Discuss in class.**

free-time activities • films you have recently seen • sex • your job or school course • politics • money • personal problems • fashion • sports • food • the boss's wife • the weather • your favourite music • religion

P **4** **Small talk is not that difficult. All that is needed is an 'ice breaker' to get things going. Look at the following examples and come up with appropriate answers.**

→ **PHRASES:** Socialising

In the workshop:
a. Did you see the game last night?
b. How was your weekend?
c. It's warm today, isn't it?

In the car:
a. How was your trip / flight?
b. Is this your first time in Germany?
c. How's the weather in Sao Paolo?

At a trade fair:
a. Did you have any problems finding our stand?
b. Would you like a brochure?
c. If you like, I could give you a demonstration.

In the canteen:
a. Have you tried the tiramisu? It's amazing!
b. Is anybody sitting here?
c. Ah! I see you like spicy food.

P **5** **Now it's your turn to break the ice! Think of at least three ice breakers for each of the following situations:**

→ **PHRASES:** Socialising

1. You are at a bar with colleagues on Friday evening.
2. You work with a new colleague one afternoon.
3. You are at the "Green Technology" conference. It's time for a coffee break.
4. You've just arrived at work and you're in the lift. A person you don't know enters.

I **6** **Choose one of the four situations above. Start a conversation and try to keep it going for as long as possible. Then end the conversation politely and act it out in front of the class.**

→ **PHRASES:** Socialising

P **7** **Check the Internet and create your own 'Dos & Don'ts' guide to making small talk and present it to your class. Also include some intercultural aspects.**

Dos	Don'ts
Make eye contact.	Ask personal questions.

WORD BANK

subsidiary – Tochtergesellchaft
trainee – Auszubildende(r)

B | Small talk in business

R **1** KMK II

Ihr Arbeitgeber hat im Internet folgenden Artikel gefunden. Da er nur wenig Englisch kann, bittet er Sie, die folgenden Fragen auf Deutsch zu beantworten.

1. Was wird oft in abwertender Weise über Small Talk gesagt?
2. Was passiert, wenn man sich nicht am Small Talk beteiligt?
3. Was sind die positiven Auswirkungen von Small Talk?

Small talk in business

Small talk is often dismissed as a waste of time, or as the art of saying nothing with a lot of words. Some people say it has no place in the business world, since the subjects discussed are often 'unimportant' – i.e. the weather, sports, fashion or other trivial matters. However, if you don't take part in small talk, your business partners might feel that you are being unfriendly or antisocial. When people just stand next to one another, without any signs of communication between them, it can lead to a feeling of uneasiness, and even tension. And this is certainly not good for future business or private relations. Small talk is in fact a very important and effective tool for avoiding an awkward silence between people who don't know each other, especially business partners who may want to form a relationship. Making small talk with strangers helps to break the ice; you discover what they like or dislike, so you can find a common ground of some sort. It helps, for example, if you support the same football team, like the same kind of car, or read the same kinds of books. However, it is also important to know who you are making small talk with. The rules of small talk are not international and different cultures have their own dos and don'ts. For example, you may have been told to always make eye contact when talking to your counterpart – but this may offend a material supplier in China. If you are going to have contact with someone from a different cultural background, it is a good idea to do a little research to avoid any embarassing mistakes.

M **2** KMK II

Ihr Arbeitgeber bittet Sie, für die Mitarbeiter stichwortartig ein kurzes Merkblatt anhand dieses Textes auf Deutsch zu erstellen.

R **3**

Sind Sie ein guter Smalltalker? Bewerten Sie die Aussagen zum Small Talk in einem Online-Test mit „Yes“ oder „No“. Notieren Sie die entsprechenden Buchstaben.

Statements	Yes	No
1. Small talk deals with rather unimportant topics. Another word for it is chitchat.	a	c
2. Religion always makes a good topic, because it is controversial.	d	e
3. Answering questions with 'yes' or 'no' during small talk is appropriate.	i	e
4. A good answer when asked if you'd like something to drink is: "I'd love a cup of coffee, thank you."	g	h
5. "That's great" is an acceptable answer to the statement: "I got the job!"	b	i
6. The noun "talk" can also mean speech.	a	c
7. Small talk is an icebreaker.	b	f

Addieren Sie die Buchstabenwerte a = 3, b = 3, c = 1, d = 0, e = 3, f = 1, g = 3, h = 1, i = 1.
Wer hat die höchste Zahl? (Maximum 21)

C | Eating out

1 Look at the German words (1.–16.) below and match them with the English equivalent (a.–p.).

1. Speisekarte	a. well-done
2. Rechnung	b. pork
3. Rind	c. side order
4. Vorspeise	d. bill
5. Schweinefleisch	e. game
6. Wild	f. dessert
7. durchgebraten	g. savoury
8. Hauptgericht	h. fork
9. Geflügel	i. menu
10. Kellner(in)	j. main dish
11. Nachtisch	k. beef
12. Trinkgeld	l. poultry
13. Beilage	m. starter
14. vegetarisch	n. waiter / waitress
15. herzhaft	o. vegetarian
16. Gabel	p. tip

I/M **2** Partner 1: You are taking a foreign colleague out to dinner in a traditional German restaurant. Study the menu below and explain the dishes to him / her.
Partner 2: Take the role of the foreign colleague and ask questions about the menu.

Gasthaus Sonne

Tagesmenu (10,95 €)

Vorspeisen
Lauchcremesuppe **oder** *kleiner gemischter Salat*

***

Hauptgerichte
Rinderrouladen mit Kartoffelklößen & Sauerkraut
oder
Putenschnitzel mit Pommes Frites
oder
Forelle Müllerin mit Salzkartoffeln

***

Nachtisch
Rote Grütze mit Sahne **oder** *Gemischtes Eis (Vanille / Erdbeere / Schoko)*

Inklusive ein alkoholfreies Getränk (0,3 l)

WORD BANK

avoid (v) – vermeiden
awkward – unangenehm
common ground – gemeinsame Basis
dismiss (v) sth. as – etwas abtun als
tension – Spannung
trivial – unbedeutend
uneasiness – Unbehagen

I **3** Now the two of you are ready to order. The young German waitress / waiter doesn't mind taking the order in English. Study the eating out phrases at the end of the book and create a role play. Practise, and perform it in front of the class.

→ **PHRASES:** Socialising

07

NACH DIESEM MODUL:

- ✓ kann ich auf Englisch die Bedeutung der Materialprüfung für die industrielle Fertigung erklären,
- ✓ kann ich auf Englisch die wichtigsten Materialprüfgeräte und deren Anwendung für die Prüfverfahren beschreiben.

Material testing

Before processing a metal, tests are carried out to determine its properties and whether it is suitable for mechanical processing. For example, is the metal hard and malleable enough for cutting processes? Is it brittle and will it break easily? A tensile test demonstrates what happens when a material is loaded in tension, an impact test shows how it reacts when it is hammered.
The mechanical properties which are tested in industry include tensility, ductility and toughness. Tensility or tensile strength describes the ability of a material to withstand a limited stretching force or stress. Ductility means that a metal can be stretched and deformed without breaking. Toughness or hardness refer to the resistance of a material to a sudden impact.

R **1** Say which test can be carried out on the machine in the photo.

R **2** Outline the testing processes used in industry and the properties which are tested with them.

3 Give the German words for the properties you found in exercise 2.

4 Decide which material properties correspond to the definitions below.

1. When you change the shape of the material, it does not break.
2. Materials do not break when a load is applied quickly.
3. Materials can be stretched to a certain point before they break.

A | The tensile test

Metals such as steel are elastic. The tensile test is a way of finding out how far metals can be stretched before their elastic limit is reached. In other words, it measures the stress required for a metal to fail. The tensile test is done before a metal is processed and afterwards as a quality control test. The test specimen is usually wider at both ends, these are the shoulders. The middle of the specimen is narrower and this is where it necks or breaks during the test.

1 Match the terms with the parts of the diagram.

shoulders • tensile gauge length • necking/fracture point • original gauge length

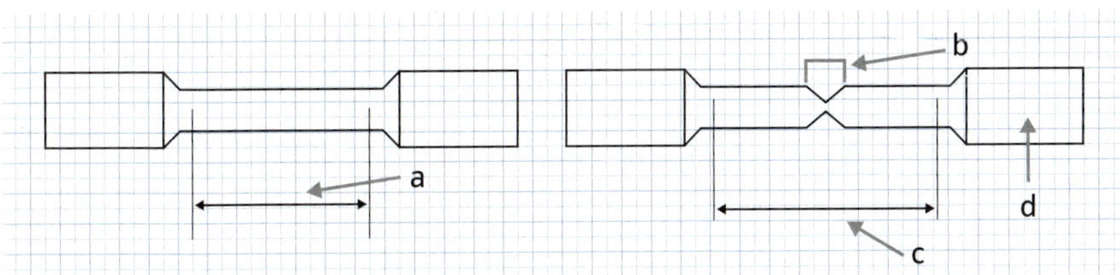

Standard tensile test specimen

2 Give the German terms for the parts of the diagram.

R **3** ⓞ A 2.18 Nina and Carsten are doing an internship with a company in Frankfurt that manufactures test equipment. Listen to the dialogue with Luke, an intern from a subsidiary near London, and note down the properties of metals that they mention.

R **4** ⓞ A 2.18 Listen again and put the steps of the tensile test into the correct order.

1. The shoulders of the specimen are fixed in the tensile tester.
2. The distance between the gauge marks is measured again.
3. The tensile strength is measured by a computerized system.
4. One end of the specimen is pulled away from the other fixed end.
5. The specimen necks at the fracture point.
6. The distance between the gauge marks is measured to get the original gauge length.
7. The maximum stress is achieved.
8. Gauge marks are made on both sides of the point where the fracture point will occur.

5 **UNDERSTANDING TECHNICAL ENGLISH**

1. Give the general and technical German meanings of the word 'apply'.

2. Translate the sentences using the correct meaning of 'apply'.
   a. The tensile test is applied to test the quality of a processed material.
   b. After Carsten passed his exams, he applied for a job in Australia.
   c. The tensile gauge length applies to the length of a specimen after the tensile test.

WORD BANK

deform (v) – verbiegen
elastic limit – Elastizitätsgrenze
fail (v) – ausfallen, versagen
hammer (v) – hämmern
impact – Schlag, Stoß
load – Last
load (v) – belasten
stress – Belastung, Spannung
stretching – Dehn-
tension – Zugspannung
test equipment – Prüfgerät(e)
test specimen – Prüfstück

WORD BANK ⓞ

elongation – Längung, Dehnung
gauge mark – Messpunkt
sheet steel – Stahlblech

B | The impact test

When metal is processed on a machine tool, it is important that it does not break suddenly or fracture. An impact test is carried out beforehand to determine the toughness of the metal. Toughness describes the ability of a material to resist a sudden impact. The impact test measures the energy required to break a material.

R **1** Explain the importance of the impact test.

R **2** Complete the description of an impact test using the words in the diagram. You will not need all of the words.

The impact test

In the illustration a weighted pendulum hammer is fixed and centred at a point above the **1** with the metal specimen. First the **2** is swung upwards and held stationary. The height and speed of the hammer at impact must be constant. When the hammer is released from the **3**, it swings to the opposite side. The hammer impacts the **4**, which breaks and absorbs energy. The height attained by the hammer after impact is shown in joules by a pointer on a fixed **5**. A material that is tough absorbs a large amount of energy and therefore the upward swing of the pendulum is small.

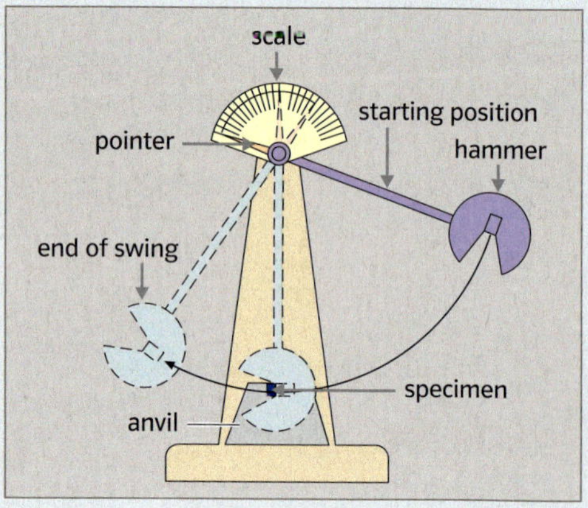

I **3** Explain some of the parts of the impact test in the illustration to your partner. He or she must guess which parts you mean.

Example:

Speaker A: It is the part of the tester which breaks the specimen.
Speaker B: You mean the hammer.

M **4** Describe the sequence of steps in the impact test in German.

C | Testing and measuring hardness

The mechanical property of 'hardness' can be defined as the resistance to scratching, abrasion and cutting, or as the resistance to being deformed, bent or broken when a load is applied. Three types of hardness test are mainly used: the Brinell, the Rockwell and the Vickers hardness tests. All three tests measure hardness by determining the resistance of a material to penetration under a given load within a certain time. Depending on the hardness of the metal, the indentation can be shallow or deep.

1 Answer the questions in your own words.

1. Define the mechanical property 'hardness'.
2. Name the most common hardness tests.
3. Explain how hardness is measured by these tests.

R **2** **Read the text and say whether the statements are true or false. Correct the false statements.**

1. The zero or reference position is determined by a minor load test force.
2. A major load is added to allow the metal to recover elastically.
3. The final position is compared with the zero position.
4. The resulting measurement is converted to a Brinell rate.

The Rockwell hardness test

The Rockwell hardness test is the most frequently applied test in industry. Metals with a wide range of hardness can be tested with the tester. The Rockwell hardness tester measures the permanent depth of an indentation made in a specimen. In the test, a penetrator, such as a hardened steel ball, is applied under a certain load. First, a test force called a preload or minor load is applied to a specimen using the indenter. This is the zero or reference position that breaks through the surface to reduce the effect on the surface finish. Then, a major load force is added to reach the total test force required. This force is held for a certain amount of time to allow the metal to recover elastically. Then the additional test force is released. The final position is measured against the zero position and converted to a Rockwell hardness number.

3 **Find the English terms for the words and phrases in the text.**

1. Härtegrad
2. eine gehärtete Stahlkugel
3. Hauptlast
4. Tiefe
5. Prüfspitze

P/I **4** **Use the Internet to find out about tests done with the Brinell or Vickers testers. Present your results in class.**

→ **PHRASES:** Presentations

I/M **5** **Use the role cards for Speakers A, B and C in the Appendix to discuss the application of test procedures for certain materials in English.**

M **6** KMK I **In Ihrem Praktikumsbericht sollen Sie die Hauptmerkmale eines Rockwell Prüfgerätes zusammenfassen. Schreiben Sie diese Zusammenfassung auf Deutsch in ganzen Sätzen.**

The Rockwell hardness tester

Like the Brinell tester, the Rockwell hardness tester measures the resistance of a metal to penetration. Unlike the Brinell tester, which measures the diameter of an indentation, the Rockwell tester measures its depth. The hardness of the material is indicated directly on a scale on the tester. The rule is the shallower the penetration, the higher the hardness number. Two types of penetrators are used with the Rockwell tester, a diamond cone and a hardened steel ball. The load that forces the penetrator into the metal is the major load, and this is measured in kilograms. The results of each penetrator and load combination are given by letters on separate scales. The penetrator, the major load, and the scale vary with the kind of metal being tested.

WORD BANK

abrasion – Abrieb, Verschleiß
fracture (v) – brechen
indenter – Eindringkörper
joule – Joule
machine tool – Werkzeugmaschine
minor load – Anfangsbelastung, Anfangslast
preload – Vorlast(-spannung)
recover (v) – sich wiederherstellen
reference position – Bezugspunkt, Referenzpunkt
resist (v) – widerstehen, standhalten
surface finish – Oberflächenbeschaffenheit, -güte
weighted – gewichtet; beschwert

WORD BANK ◎

elongation – Längung, Dehnung
gauge mark – Messpunkt
sheet steel – Stahlblech

G

NACH DIESEM MODUL:

- ✓ kann ich eine englische Präsentation vorbereiten,
- ✓ kann ich auf Englisch präsentieren.

1

2

3

4

Presentations

At some point in your career you may be required to present your company, or their products or services, either informally or on a more formal level. This could mean presenting a new product to a potential customer, or presenting the company as a whole, or something more specific, such as assembly instructions or a positional sketch. Whatever you may be presenting, the ability to give an oral presentation is a key skill. It is also a skill that can be developed and improved.

P **1** **Look at the pictures above and describe them using the words below.**

to present • meeting • flipchart • graph • chart • laptop • preparation • to explain • sales pitch • audience • projector

P **2** **For what reasons might you have to give a presentation? Write a list.**

3 **With a partner, decide upon a final list and share it with the class.**

4 **With the same partner brainstorm what you think is important to remember when giving a presentation. Write your answers in a word web like the one below.**

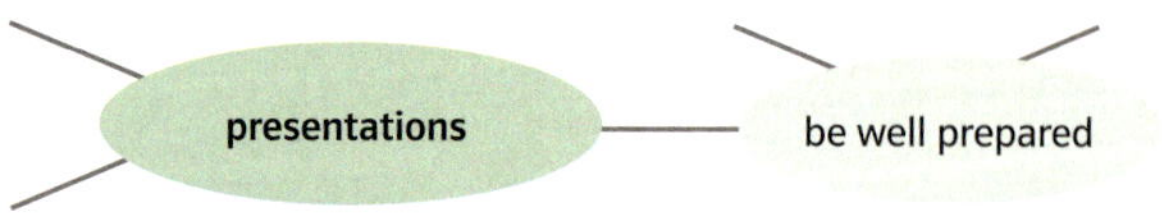

A | Preparing a presentation

1 **In the following table are words which are linked to presentations. Match the English words (1.–10.) with the appropriate German words (a.–j.).**

1. audience	a. Augenkontakt
2. prompt cards	b. beschreiben
3. body language	c. Zusammenfassung
4. eye contact	d. visuelle Hilfsmittel
5. handout	e. Publikum
6. to prepare	f. Schaubild
7. graph	g. Stichwortkarten
8. visual aids	h. Körpersprache
9. to describe	i. vorbereiten
10. summary	j. Informationsblatt

M **2** KMK II **Fassen Sie den folgenden Text über die Vorbereitung einer Präsentation unter Beantwortung folgender Fragen auf Deutsch zusammen.**

1. Warum soll eine Präsentation nicht schriftlich ausformuliert werden?
2. Wie soll eine Präsentation gegliedert sein?
3. Was ist „signposting“?
4. Welche Vorteile bieten visuelle Hilfsmittel?
5. Wie müssen Präsentationsfolien aussehen, damit sie wirken?

How to make a presentation

You have been asked by your boss to give a presentation? Here are a few tips:

- → Do not write out your presentation in full. Instead, use numbered prompt cards with key words – they are the best way to remember important points.
- → Remember: your presentation needs to have an introduction, a main part, and a conclusion.
- → Begin by giving a brief overview of the points to be covered.
- → Use "signposting" phrases to lead through your presentation, e.g.:

  I would like to begin by ... • Let me start by showing you ... • Next, I would like to say something about ... • Another important point is ... • Finally, I will talk about ... • In conclusion, ...

- → Always finish with a conclusion.

Visual aids

You can use visual aids, such as Powerpoint, to help reinforce what you say. Visual aids help you explain complicated ideas or technical details more easily and hold the interest of your audience. They also make your presentation look more professional.

If necessary, you can print them out and use them as a handout for the audience. Visual aids could include graphs, pictures, plans, diagrams, or short texts. However, if you do use your visual aids to show text, then follow these guidelines:

- → Limit the text to six lines.
- → Try to use no more than six words per line.
- → Print the text in large letters, using upper and lower case letters.
- → Use dark colours, such as black, red, blue, or green. Light colours are difficult to read.

WORD BANK

assembly – Montage
positional sketch – Technologieschema

3 Match the visual aids (1.–6) with the pictures below (a.–e.).

1. plan 2. pie chart 3. line graph 4. bar chart 5. diagram 6. table

a.

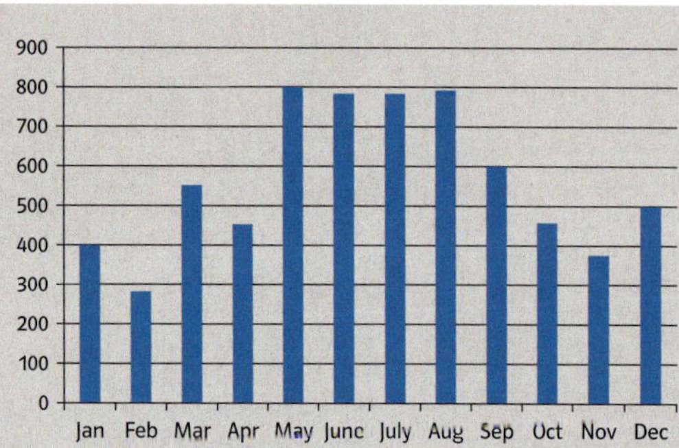

b.

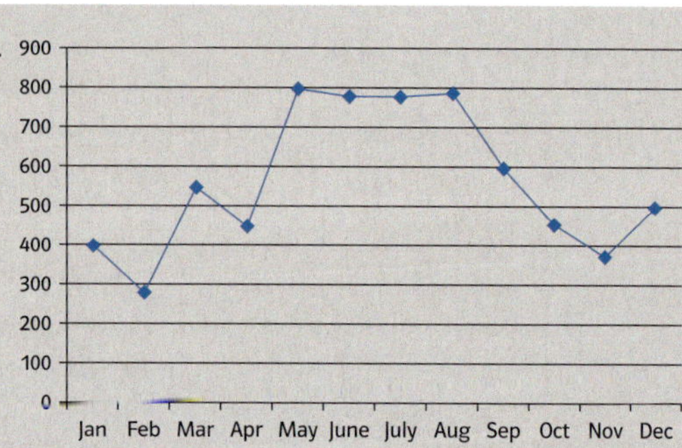

c.

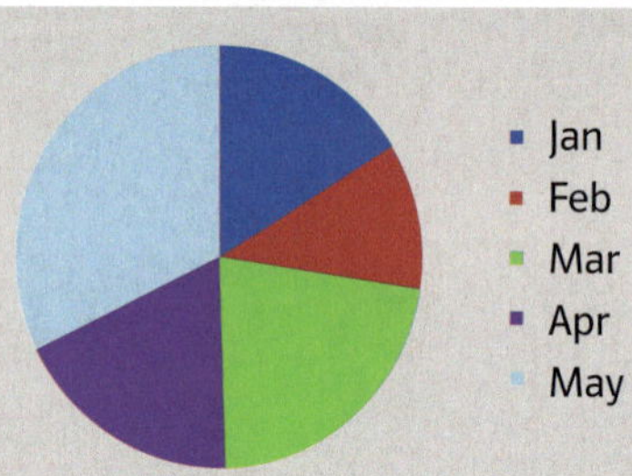

d.

2012		
Jan	$1,256	-6%
Feb	$1,477	+4%
Mar	$1,288	-5%
Apr	$1,543	+9%

e.

f.

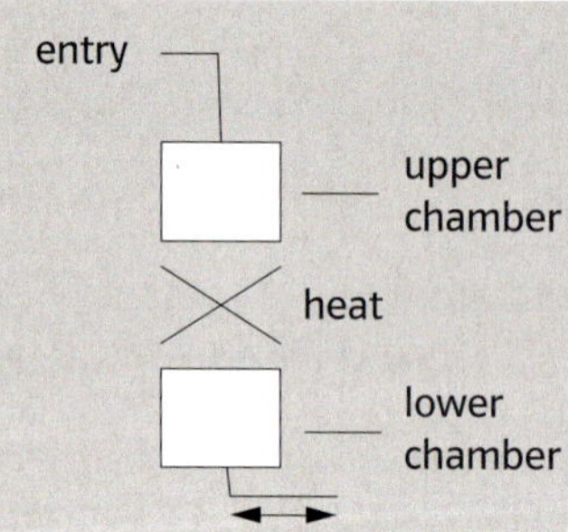

B | Describing materials and products

P **1** Think of something that you often use and describe it by using the terms in the box to help you. Don't name the item you are describing. Try and write 3 to 5 sentences.

I **2** Take it in turns to read your sentences to each other and see if you can guess what your partner is describing.

INFO BOX: Useful phrases for describing materials and products

It is a | strong · sturdy · rigid · flexible · lightweight · shiny · robust · matt | material.
The design is | modern · state-of-the-art · classic · elegant · old-fashioned.
It is | user-friendly · difficult to operate · reliable · innovative · hand-crafted.

C | Delivering a presentation

R **1** ◎ A 1.6 **Max Wiesinger, a trained carpenter who works for a furniture design company, is presenting a new line of furniture at a trade show. Listen to the presentation and complete the following text.**

Good morning ladies and gentleman. Today **1** our new range of **2**, *Simply Wood*. The range, which is shown here on the first slide, includes chairs, a large table, a lounger, and benches. I would like to start by talking about the **3** used in the furniture. All of the *Simply Wood* range is made from single softwood timber and has been **4** by our highly-skilled carpenters and joiners. If you look at this picture, you can see that the benches and the seats are designed with a low back, deep seats and long arms to offer a great deal of comfort and convenience. Thanks to a special varnish, the furniture is 100% **5** and will not suffer from discolouring. **6** from this final slide, the furniture is also available in white, to give it a classic, timeless look. And do not worry, we have used a durable white polyurethane coating that is suitable for every environment. On your handout you will see more details about each piece, including the measurements. **7** this morning. Are there any questions? Yes …

P **2** **Now it's your turn. Work in small groups and design a chair, a pocket torch, or any other object of your choice. Present your ideas in class. Use the following words and phrases to help you:**

→ **PHRASES:** Presentations

We have designed a … • Our idea was to … • Our design is made of … • The advantage of the material we used is … • Its measurements are … • length • diameter • weight • width • height • rectangular • circle • circular • square • smooth edges • glued/screwed together • made out of one piece

M **3** KMK I **Ihre Kollegin muss nächste Woche eine wichtige Präsentation halten und bittet Sie um Ihre Hilfe. Sie hat den folgenden Text gefunden, versteht aber leider nur wenig Englisch. Übertragen Sie den Text für sie sinngemäß ins Deutsche.**

7 Ways to Do it Right: Presentations

1. Keep it short and simple (KISS).
2. Do not use too many visual aids.
3. If you are presenting in a group, decide beforehand who will say what.
4. Practice at least once in front of an audience.
5. Do not read from your notes. Look at your audience.
6. Structure your presentation with phrases so your audience can follow more easily.
7. Tell the audience when they can ask questions – either during the presentation, or at the end.

WORD BANK

carpenter – Tischler(in) / Schreiner(in)
circle – Kreis
circular – kreisförmig
diameter – Dicke
furniture – Möbel
height – Höhe
length – Länge
rectangular – rechteckig
smooth – glatt
square – quadratisch
trade show – Messe
weight – Gewicht
width – Breite

WORD BANK ◎

durable – haltbar
joiner – Tischler(in) / Schreiner(in)
polyurethane coating – Polyurethanbeschichtung
softwood – Weichholz
timber – Holz
varnish – Lack

08

NACH DIESEM MODUL:

- √ kann ich die gängigsten Messinstrumente in der Metalltechnik auf Englisch beschreiben,
- √ kann ich die Funktionen dieser Messinstrumente auf Englisch erklären.

1

2

3

4

Measuring and gauging

In mechanical engineering it is essential to work as accurately as possible. Sophisticated measuring instruments and gauges such as vernier callipers, micrometers and dial gauges ensure that machining processes are correct and precise. Less complex instruments can also be used. For example squares are used to measure right angles. Measuring instruments have different functions to fixed gauges or calibres. You use a measuring instrument to measure the length or diameter of a workpiece. You can check calibrated measurements with a fixed gauge such as a slip gauge or gauge block. In this way you can see whether the measurements of a workpiece you have machined are good / no good or go / no go.

R **1** Say which instruments are in the photos and describe what you can do with them.

2 Decide which measuring or gauging instrument to use for the tasks below.

1. Measure the right angles of a metal block.
2. Check the diameter of a turned metal bolt.
3. You have worked a workpiece on a lathe. Now check it accurately.
4. Check the precision of a cylindrical pocket hole turned on a lathe.
5. Measure a slot on a metal plate.

A | Measuring with a vernier calliper

The vernier calliper is one of the most versatile measuring instruments in mechanical engineering. It is used for external, internal and depth measurements.

R/M **1** **Match the German terms with the parts of the diagram.**

Tiefenmaß • Feststellschraube • Backen für Innenmaße • Hauptskala • Backen für Außenmaße • feststehender Backen • beweglicher Backen • Nonius

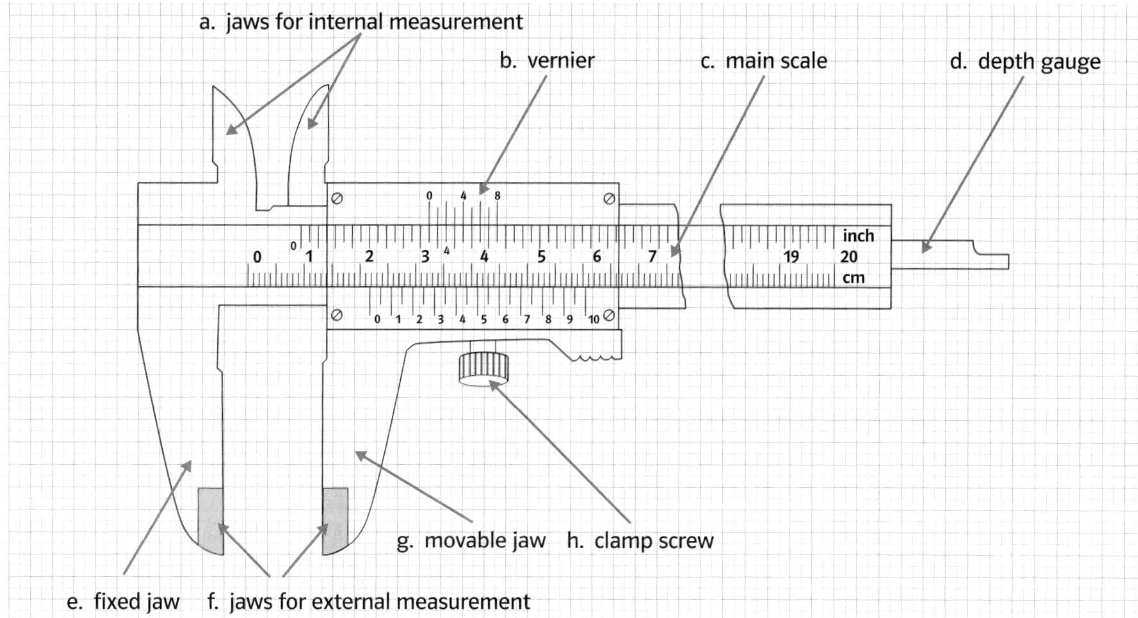

Vernier calliper

2 **Complete the text using some of the terms in the diagram in exercise 1.**

The vernier calliper consists of three main components, two sets of jaws and a [1] which is used to measure depth. In order to measure the length of a workpiece, you adjust the pair of [2] until they fit around the workpiece. If you want to measure the inside of a pipe, you adjust the [3] until they fit into the pipe. The movable jaws are fixed with the [4] to guarantee an exact reading of the measurements. While you are adjusting the jaws, you move two scales against each other. The [5] on the fixed jaw is calibrated into millimetres. The small auxiliary scale on the movable jaws is called [6] or nonius. This scale allows you to read measurements of up to a tenth of a millimetre, i.e. 10 parts on this scale represent 9 mm on the main scale.

R **3** ◎ A 2.19 **Claus Huck is an apprentice in a machine tool company in Bonn. He is talking to Sharon, an exchange student from York. Listen to the dialogue and list the parts of the vernier calliper they talk about.**

R **4** ◎ A 2.19 **Listen to the dialogue again and write down the measurements of the tube.**

WORD BANK

auxiliary scale – Hilfsskala
bolt – Bolzen, Schraubenbolzen
calibrated – kalibriert, geeicht
calibre – (Prüf-)Lehre
fixed gauge – (Prüf-)Lehre
gauge – Messgerät, Eichmaß, (Prüf-)Lehre
gauge (v) – nachprüfen
good / no good, go / no go – geeignet oder ungeeignet
grinding machine – Schleifmaschine
groove – Nut
lathe – Drehmaschine, Drehbank
slot – Nut
square – Winkel

WORD BANK ◎

thread – Gewinde

5 **Study the example scale and give the measurements in illustration 1.**

Example:
Read off the whole millimetres on the main scale (32 mm). Read off the 1/10 mm value on the vernier scale (0.3 mm) where the two scales are aligned. Add the two readings (result: 32.3 mm).

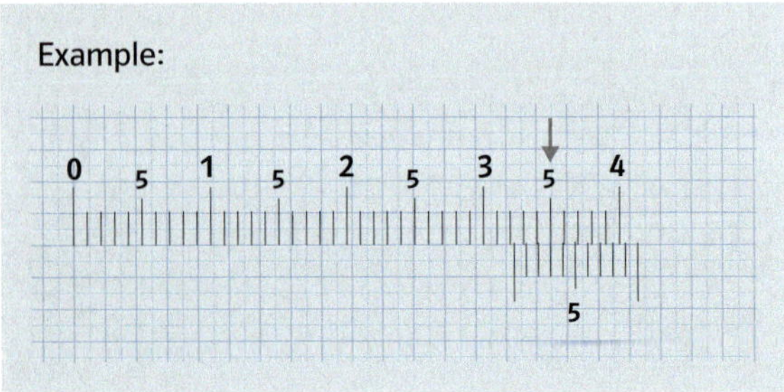

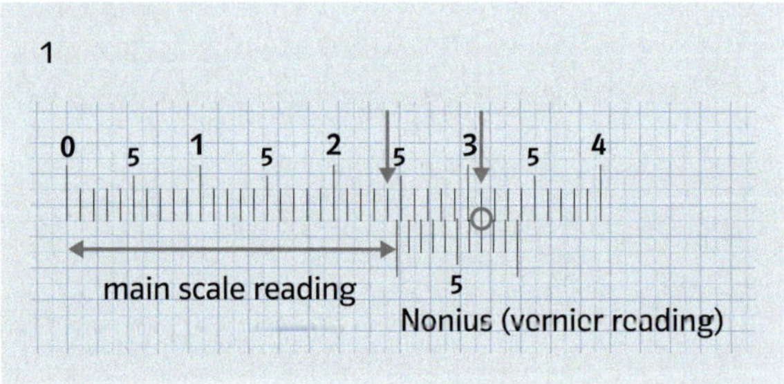

B | Gauges

Gauges are as important in industry as measuring instruments. Gauges are used to check the precision of engineering components according to the SI base units.

1 **Match the gauges in the photos with the tasks you can do with them.**

thread ring gauge

gauge block

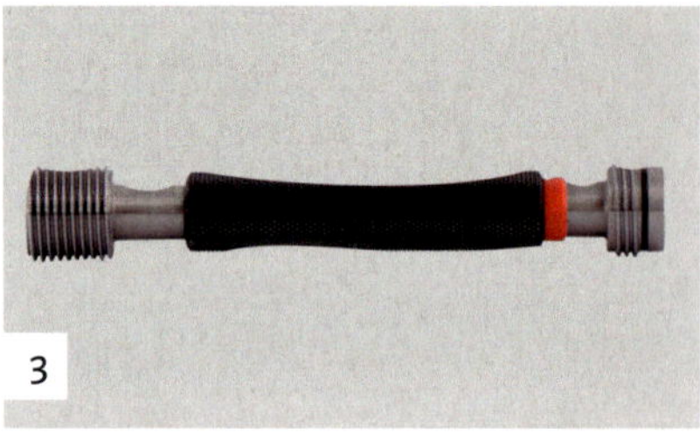

thread gauge

Tasks
a. A slot in a metal block is checked with this type of gauge.
b. It is used to check internal threads.
c. It can be used to check the external thread of a bolt.

M **2** **UNDERSTANDING TECHNICAL ENGLISH**
Give the German meanings of the word 'gauge'. Use a dictionary or the Internet.

1. By turning the thread ring gauge onto the bolt we checked its thread.
2. He used the micrometer to gauge the diameter of the turned steel bolt.
3. The dial gauge of the tester showed the hardness of the metal.
4. The mechanic uses a slip gauge to see if the slot in the metal is go/no go.
5. The apprentice checked the measurements of the component with a gauge.
6. The fuel gauge tells us when we have to refill the petrol tank.

C | The International System of Units

The International System of Units (SI) allows for seven base units which are defined in an absolute way, i.e. they do not refer to any other units. The units are the basis for measurement worldwide. The system guarantees an international standard for measurements. SI stands for *Système international d'Unités* and was introduced in Paris in 1960.

WORD BANK

amount of substance – Stoffmenge(-nanteil)
current – Stromstärke
mass – Masse
SI base unit – SI-Einheit
thread gauge – Gewindelehre
thread ring gauge – Gewindelehrring
value – (Mess-)Wert

P **1** **Find out the full names and abbreviations of the SI base units for the base quantities below.**

1. length
2. mass
3. time
4. current
5. temperature
6. light intensity
7. amount of substance

I **2** **Ask and answer questions about measuring with the base units using the phrases in the table and information in exercise 1.**

Example:
Speaker A: What unit is used to measure mass?
Speaker B: The … is used to measure mass.

Questions	Answers
What base unit is used to measure …? What quantity do you measure with a (name of unit)? What unit is used …?	You measure a … with … You use a … to measure … … is measured using (name of unit) … The (name of unit) is used to measure …

P **3** KMK I **Ein Austauschschüler aus Warschau an Ihrem Ausbildungszentrum bittet Sie um Hilfe. Er spricht wenig Deutsch, aber gut Englisch, und braucht Hilfe beim Messen und Prüfen der abgebildeten Schraubbolzen und Beschläge aus der Sanitärinstallation. Nennen Sie ihm auf Englisch die erforderlichen Mess- oder Prüfgeräte und die vorzunehmenden Messungen.**

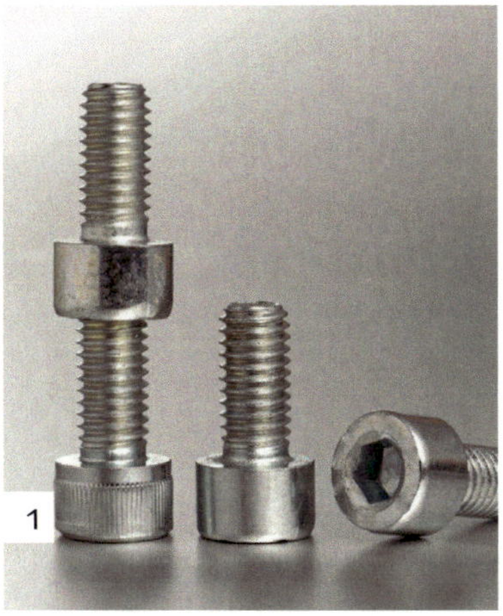

Thread bolts

Pipe with internal and external thread

Fittings used in plumbing

H

NACH DIESEM MODUL:

- ✓ kann ich auf Englisch auf Kundenbeschwerden reagieren,
- ✓ kann ich auf Englisch mit unzufriedenen Kunden umgehen.

Dealing with customers

The way a company deals with its customers is the key to its success. Whether you are arranging appointments, handling enquiries, or dealing with complaints, it is essential that you are able to express yourself clearly, confidently, and politely. And remember: the customer may not always be right, but they are very important.

1 Brainstorm words that describe what is shown in the photos above.

P **2** Compare your list of words with your partner and work together to describe the pictures. Use these words to help you:

complaint • hotline • builder • hard hat • building site • meeting • customer • plans • mechanic • explain • repairs • bonnet • overalls • engine

3 Which of the customers above do you think are happy, and which are unhappy? Explain your answer.

P **4** In what situations do you deal with customers in your job? Copy and complete the word web below to brainstorm reasons for talking to customers.

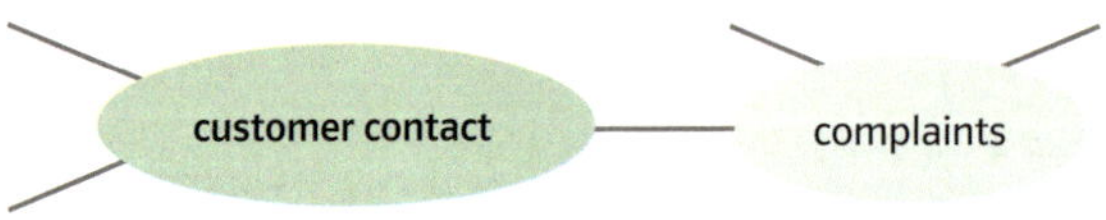

A | Complaints

1 **Match the common causes for complaint on the left with the suggested solutions on the right. Several options may be appropriate.**

1. delay in delivery	a. offer a price reduction
2. faulty goods	b. improve the service
3. damaged goods	c. repair the goods
4. unsatisfactory services	d. replace the goods
5. wrong goods	e. send the goods by air freight
6. too many/too few goods received	f. send the missing goods
7. too early delivery	g. take the goods back
	h. collect the surplus goods
	i. send a credit note

P **2** **What about your industry? Which are the most common reasons for complaints? Make a list and compare it with a partner. Be as specific as possible.**

R **3** **Which of the following phrases are used for making complaints and which ones for replying to complaints? Make a list.**

→ **PHRASES:**
Dealing with customers

1. This is very inconvenient for us because we need the goods urgently.
2. We are sorry for any inconvenience this has caused.
3. We will keep the damaged goods until we hear from you.
4. Please return the damaged goods at our expense.
5. We can assure you that this will not happen again.
6. Some items were badly damaged.
7. We regret to inform you that the order has not yet arrived.
8. We think the damage may have occurred in transit.
9. We are experiencing difficulties with our new logistics software.
10. Could you please look into this problem immediately?
11. Please accept our apologies.
12. The reason for the mistake is that we are extremely busy at this time of the year.
13. Please send us replacements as soon as possible.
14. We hope that this proposal will find your approval.
15. We believe the problem is down to human error.

R **4**
KMK II
A 1.7

You work for *Deutsches Netz*, an IT company in Hamburg. Your boss, Mr Bauder, receives a voicemail message on his mobile phone from Mr Jenkins, owner of *New Wave Marketing*, a subsidiary of an English marketing company based in Hamburg. Listen to the message and answer the following questions.

1. What did the technicians from Deutsches Netz do for New Wave Marketing?
2. What problems are the employees having (three things)?
3. What is the most serious problem?
4. Why is this a serious problem?
5. How should Mr Bauder contact Mr Jenkins?

WORD BANK

bonnet – Motorhaube
builder – Bauarbeiter
building site – Baustelle
hotline – Informationsdienst
repairs – Reparaturen
technician – Techniker(in)

P **5** Mr Bauder asks you to respond to Mr Jenkins' phone call. He sends you the following email and asks you to draft a short email to the customer.

→ **PHRASES:** Dealing with customers

Von: mailto:s.bauder@DNetz...de
An: mailto:info@DNetz...de
Betreff: Bitte an Herrn Jenkins schreiben (eilt!!)

... diese Firma ist ein sehr wichtiger Kunde von uns und wir wollen ihn **auf keinen Fall** verlieren!! Bitte sagen Sie ihm folgendes:

- Es tut uns sehr leid, dass es diese Probleme gegeben hat.
- Wir verstehen völlig, dass es jetzt sehr ungelegen und ärgerlich ist.
- Wir vermuten, dass das Problem durch menschliches Versagen verursacht wurde.
- Wir werden sofort jemanden schicken, um das Netzwerk zu reparieren. (selbstverständlich auf unsere Kosten!)
- Der Techniker wird spätestens um 17 Uhr dort sein.

Bringen Sie nochmals unser Bedauern für das Problem zum Ausdruck und versichern Sie ihm, dass sich dies nicht wiederholen wird.

Danke,
Bauder

M **6** You work for a plumbing and heating installation company in Leipzig. Your supervisor, Mr Hüber, receives an email about a recent job done for an American family living in the area. Your supervisor does not speak very good English and asks you to read the email and to sum it up in German.

Von: mailto:j.t.levine@kwq...net
An: mailto:info@sippelheizung_sanitaer...net
Betreff: Problems with the heating

Dear Mr Hüber,

I am writing in reference to the heating system installed by your company at my house last week. Unfortunately, my family and I have been having some problems. Firstly, the water in the bathroom takes a long time to warm up – sometimes over 5 minutes!

Secondly, the temperature in the house is too low, and I cannot make it warmer. Also, I cannot find the instruction manual – did your technician take it with him? My final problem is that the underfloor heating does not seem to be working in the bathroom. The tiles on the floor are still cold in the morning. Is something wrong?

As it is winter, and very cold, I would ask you to send someone to my house as soon as possible to find a solution to these problems. Please give me a call, or send me an email to confirm.

Thank you in advance,

John Levine

B | Customer service

P **1** What five tips would you give a colleague about dealing with unhappy customers?

2 Compare your list with a partner.

How to deal with unhappy customers

No company has happy customers 100 % of the time.
Things can always go wrong and customers can become unhappy – or worse, upset. Here are some tips on how to avoid making the situation worse.

Stay calm: The customer may be angry at somebody, but it does not help the situation if you get just as angry. The last thing you want to do is start an argument – that is very unprofessional and unhelpful. Try to calm the customer down.

Listen, listen, listen: You will only be able to understand what has upset the customer if you listen, and listen carefully. Before you start talking, listen actively to the customer until you fully understand why they are unhappy. If you don't know what's wrong, you will not be able to do anything about it.

The customer is king: Show the customer that they, and their problem, are important to you. Tell them quickly how sorry you are for their problem and reassure them that you will do everything you can to help them. And, always be patient and polite.

Stay positive: Do your best to stay positive at all times. Remember that your goal is to solve the problem and you can do this better if you have a positive frame of mind. Regardless of how negative and furious the customer gets, it is important that you do not let it affect your mood.

No excuses: No matter what the problem is, or who you think caused it, do not blame other people or try to make excuses. Instead, take the initiative and do whatever you can to solve the problem.

R **3** Find the synonyms in the text for the following words and expressions:

1. to stop sth. from happening
2. disagreement
3. to aim
4. to fix
5. attitude
6. very angry
7. reason
8. to take control

R **4** Sie lesen den oben stehenden Artikel im Internet. Beantworten Sie die folgenden
KMK II Fragen dazu in ganzen Sätzen auf Deutsch.

1. Warum ist es wichtig zu wissen, wie man mit unzufriedenen Kunden umgeht?
2. Was sollte man tun, wenn der Kunde sehr verärgert ist?
3. Warum ist es wichtig, dem Kunden ganz genau zuzuhören?
4. Wie kann man einem Kunden zeigen, dass man sein Problem ernst nimmt?
5. Wann ist es gerechtfertigt, jemand anderem die Schuld für das vorliegende Problem zu geben?

I **5** Choose one of the problems you listed in exercise A1 and create a short role play. One of you should play the unhappy / angry customer and the other the employee. Act out your role play in front of the class.

WORD BANK

instruction manual – Bedienungsanleitung
plumbing and heating – Heizung und Sanitär
underfloor heating – Fußbodenheizung

09

NACH DIESEM MODUL:

✓ kann ich auf Englisch die wichtigsten Montagewerkzeuge benennen sowie ihre Merkmale und Funktionen beschreiben.

1

2

3

4

Joining and assembly

Metal parts can be joined using different joining techniques. Screws, nuts, bolts, rivets and fitting parts are used for mechanical joints and assemblies. When parts are welded or soldered, heat is applied and we talk about non-mechanical joining. Laser technology is often used for specified joints and for dismantling processes. Bonding techniques that use adhesives are often applied in automotive engineering.

R **1** Divide the joining techniques in the photos into mechanical and non-mechanical techniques. Make a table like the one below.

Mechanical joining technique	Non-mechanical joining technique

R **2** Add the other joining techniques in the text above to your table.

3 Complete the sentences using the tools in the box.

riveting tongs • spanner • welding torch • screwdriver • rivet gun

1. Bolts are usually loosened with a ? .
2. Screws are tightened with a ? but you drive rivets with ? or a ? .
3. A pipe is welded with a ? .

A | Choosing joining and assembling techniques

Joining or assembling parts is an important task in mechanical engineering. Joining describes a process where parts of the same material, or of different materials, are fastened. Assembling describes a more detailed kind of joint, for example, when parts are mounted on top of each other. The parts can be dismantled again for repair work.

R **1** **Read the text and say what you should think of when joining materials.**

Before you apply any joining and assembling methods, it is important to know the property of the material to be joined. If you want to assemble metal plates or sheet metal, the riveting technique is applied. This technique produces a perfect, non-detachable joint, which is popular in shipbuilding and in the construction of bridges. Fasteners such as bolts and nuts are often used in mechanical engineering to assemble parts. However, if a joint has to be sealed so that liquid cannot pass through, bolts and nuts are unsuitable fasteners. This is why plumbers apply fitting techniques. For example, they use press fits, fitting grooves and fitting strips, or folded joints which are formed under a certain amount of pressure. When parts are not joined mechanically, they are usually welded or soldered. In modern industrial production, advanced adhesives are used more and more often to bond materials such as glass, polymers, ceramics and even metals.

R **2** **Decide whether the statements are true or false. Correct the false statements.**

1. Welding is a technique that is used to join metals with heat.
2. When you want to join two metal plates mechanically, you can solder them.
3. It is possible to join different materials by welding or soldering them.
4. A modern, non-mechanical joining technique is bonding with adhesives.

M **3** **Describe the joining techniques in exercise 1 in German.**

I/P **4** **Discuss the most suitable joining techniques for the tasks. Use the prompts given.**

A		
I want to I've got to	join tighten / loosen bond	two metal bars a glass plate and a plastic plate two broken ceramic parts nuts and bolts two sheets of metal two copper wires

B		
Why don't you You can You need to	weld solder rivet screw / unscrew use	adhesive riveting tongs soldering iron screwdriver spanner welding torch

WORD BANK

adhesive – Kleber, Klebstoff
assemble (v) – montieren, fügen
assembly – Fügen, Montage
bond (v) – kleben
dismantling process – Demontage
fitting groove – Passnut
fitting part – Passstück, Passteil
fitting strip – Passleiste
folded joint – Falzverbindung
join (v) – fügen, verbinden
joining technique – Fügetechnik
joint – Verbindung, Verbindungsstelle
plumber – Klempner(in), Installateur(in)
polymer – Kunststoff
press fit – Presspassung
sheet metal – Blech

B | Joints with fasteners

Fasteners such as screws, bolts, nuts, rivets and washers are used in mechanical joints. The form and application of the materials to be joined determine which fasteners are used. Thin materials are likely to be riveted, for example, and solid parts are mainly joined with screws and bolts.

R **1** **Match the terms with the numbered parts below. Then give the German word for each fastener.**

slotted screw • hexagonal headed bolt • cross-slot screw • washer • nut

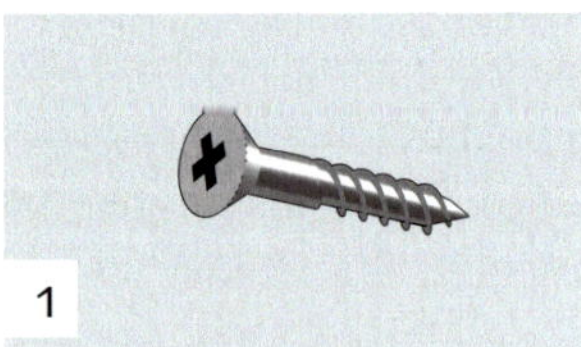
1

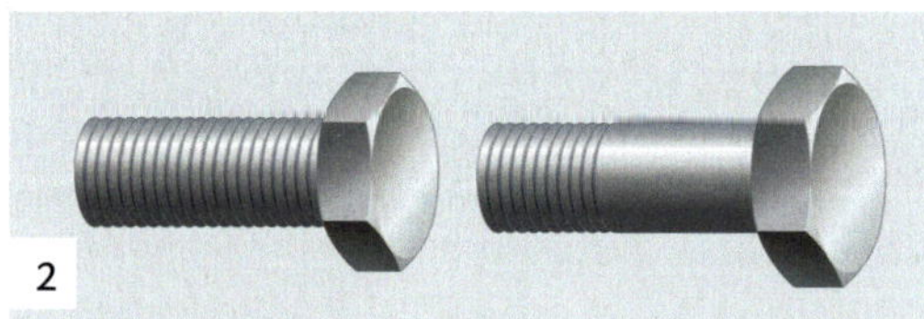
2

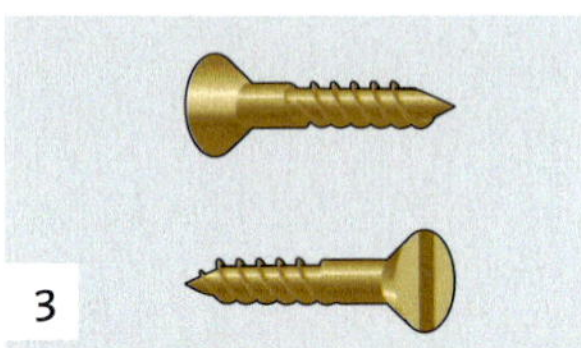
3

4

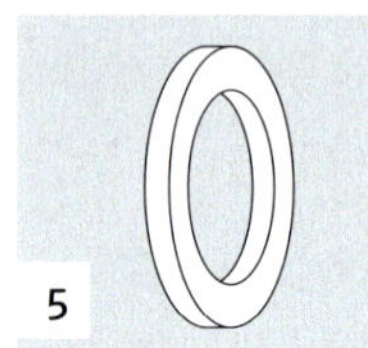
5

2 **Decide which fastener can be used or is described below.**

1. The joint between the bolt and nut has to be as tight as possible.
2. Two wooden boards have to be joined.
3. Some thin sheet steels have to be assembled.
4. This is the most widely used fastener in metalwork.
5. You need a fastener to counter a bolt.

M **3** **Match the German terms for the fasteners with the English ones.**

1. hexagon nut	a. flache Unterlegscheibe
2. Allen screw	b. Senkkopfniete
3. countersunk rivet	c. Sechskantmutter
4. flat washer	d. Senkkopfschraube geschlitzt
5. spring washer	e. Inbusschraube
6. slotted countersunk head screw	f. Federscheibe

4 **Complete the sentences below with suitable fasteners from exercise 3.**

1. Before countering the bolt with a ?, the apprentice inserted a washer to save the joint.
2. You use a screwdriver to loosen a ?.
3. Stefan could not find the riveting tongs in order to drive in the ?.
4. He held the ? with an Allen key and turned the nut with a spanner.

C | Assembly by fitting

Sheet metals or sheet steels can be joined by means of fitting parts, press fits or folded joints. For example, sheet steels are assembled using a locking seam. First the seam is folded. Then the edges are tapped down with a rubber mallet to avoid scratching or denting the surface. The seams are hooked together and tapped down until they are locked.

R **1** **Match the terms with the parts of the illustration.**

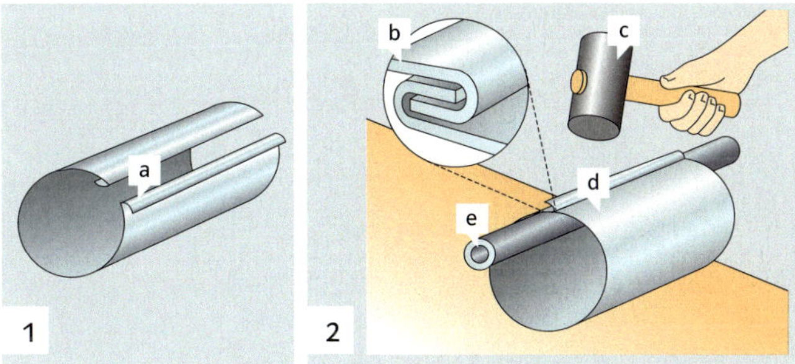

folded seam
rubber mallet
sheet edges
seam in detail
metal pipe

R **2** **The instructor Stefan Hinz shows the apprentices Harry and Timo how to fold a**
⦾ A 2.20 **locking seam. Listen to the dialogue and complete the sentences.**

1. The trainees have learnt different ? and assembling methods.
2. Today they want to ? a seam on two sheets of metal.
3. We ? the first sheet in the bench vice.
4. We carefully ? the edges by nearly 180 degrees.

R **3** **Listen again and write down the steps not listed in exercise 2.**
⦾ A 2.20

M **4** **Explain the steps of the joining process of two sheet metals in German. Use the steps in exercises 2 and 3.**

5 **UNDERSTANDING TECHNICAL ENGLISH**

1. **Give the general and technical meanings of the verbs and nouns in German.**
   a. bend, to bend   b. counter, to counter

2. **Translate the sentences into German.**
   1. The police car drove around the bend at high speed after the suspect.
   2. The machinist bent the wire to 90 degrees to shape it like a hook.
   3. In the pub the two friends went to the counter and ordered two pints.
   4. The mechanic countered the hexagon socket screw with an Allen key.

P **6** **Ihr Ausbilder bittet Sie, eine Präsentation auf Englisch über verschiedene Montage-**
KMK II **und Fügetechniken zu entwerfen. Stellen Sie die Unterschiede zwischen mechanischen und nicht mechanischen Fügetechniken anhand der Stichwörter heraus.**

Nietverbindungen • Schraubverbindungen • Presspassungen • Passnuten • Passleisten • Falzverbindungen • Klebverbindungen • Schweiß- und Lötverbindungen

WORD BANK

counter (v) – kontern
fastener – Verbindungselement; Fügeteil
washer – Unterlegscheibe
dent (v) – verbeulen
fit (v) – fügen durch Passungen
hook together (v) – festhaken
lock (v) – festklemmen
locking seam – Falzverbindung
seam – Falz
sheet steel – (dünnes) Stahlblech

WORD BANK ⦾

bench vice – Schraubstock
bend (v) – biegen
clamp – einspannen
marker line – Markierungslinie
pliers – Zange
scribe (v) – vorreißen

10

NACH DIESEM MODUL:

- ✓ kann ich auf Englisch Schweiß- und Lötapparate sowie deren Funktionen beschreiben,
- ✓ kann ich Schweiß- und Lötarbeiten sowie die dabei relevanten Sicherheitsaspekte auf Englisch beschreiben und erklären.

1

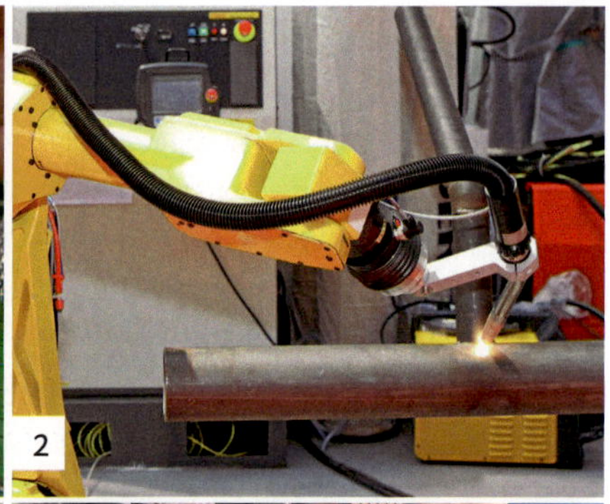
2

3

4

Welding and soldering

Welding and soldering are joining techniques which make a permanent joint without using mechanical fasteners. If you dismantle a welded joint for repair work, it is difficult to reassemble it again. In comparison, a joint made with mechanical fasteners such as screws or nuts is reversible.
The materials to be joined and the use of the end product determine whether you can weld or solder them. Welding is used where the joint has to bear a lot of weight or pressure. For example, steel is welded to build steel girders for bridges. In automotive engineering, car body parts are welded by robots to produce accurate weld joints. Soldering is primarily applied in electrical engineering, for example, to connect wires or to fix electric parts onto printed circuit boards (PCBs). In the plumbing trade, soldering is often used to join metal parts such as pipes.

R **1** Identify the joining techniques in the photos and then say how they are used.

R **2** Complete the tasks.

1. Give as many examples of the uses of welding and soldering as you can think of.
2. Outline the differences between welding and soldering techniques as compared to mechanical joining.
3. Explain why robots are preferred for welding jobs in the car industry.

A | Welding

Welding is divided into two categories: gas welding and electric welding. Gas welding is mainly oxyacetylene welding, in which oxygen and acetylene are mixed. The flame generated at the tip of the torch heats the metals to be joined. The welding wire then melts to make the joint. Valves and gauges on the gas cylinders regulate the pressure of the gas and the working pressure of the torch. Electric welding such as arc welding is operated with standard power. The power flows between the contact tip and the ground clamp, which is clamped to the material. This generates a high temperature and heats the material to be joined. The flux core melts and makes the joint.

R **1** ⓞ A 2.21 **Bernd and Oli, two German apprentices, and Amélie, an exchange student from France, are talking to the instructor about welding equipment. Listen to the dialogue and say which things they do not talk about.**

regulator • fire-resistant • acetylene • wire speed • torch • 300 °C

R **2** ⓞ A 2.21 **Listen to the dialogue again and identify the labelled parts.**

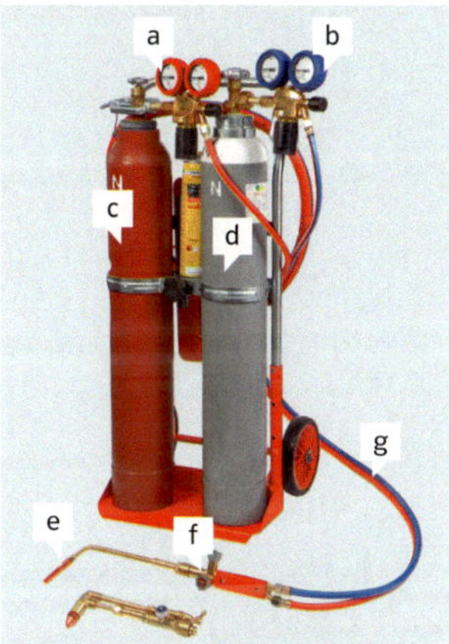

Gas welding gear

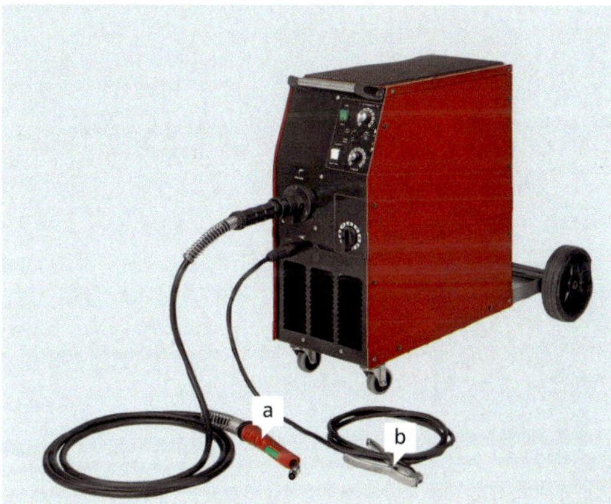

Arc welding gear

3 **Match the product features of an arc welding system with the German phrases.**

Product features	Produktmerkmale
1. Runs on standard power 2. External polarity plugs for quick changeover 3. Thermal overload protection (automatic shut-off) 4. Four position heat setting 5. Wire speed control 6. Perfect for welding thin sheets of stainless steel or aluminium 7. Includes flux core wire, contact tips, ground clamp 8. Portable	a. Tragbar b. Vierstufige Temperaturauswahl c. Ideal zum Schweißen dünner Bleche aus Edelstahl oder Aluminium d. Überhitzungsschutz (automatisches Abschalten) e. Beinhaltet: Fließdraht, Kontaktierungsklammern, Erdungsklemme f. Drahtgeschwindigkeitsregelung g. Funktioniert mit Standardspannung h. Externe Polaritätsstecker für schnelle Umstellung

WORD BANK

arc welding – Lichtbogenschweißen
automotive engineering – Automobilbau
car body – Karosserie
contact tip – Kontaktierungsklemme
electric welding – Elektroschweißen
electrical engineering – Elektrotechnik
fastener – Verbindungselement
flux core – Fließdraht
gas welding – Gasschweißen
gauge – Messgerät
ground clamp – Erdungsklemme
joint – Verbindungsstelle
oxyacetylene welding – Autogenesschweißen, Schutzgasschweißen
printed circuit board (PCB) – Leiterplatte
solder (v) – löten
steel girder – Stahlträger
torch – Schweißbrenner
valve – Ventil
weld (v) – schweißen
weld joint – Schweißverbindung
welding wire – Schweißdraht
working pressure – Betriebsdruck

WORD BANK ⓞ

flip-front helmet – Helm mit Klappvisier
welding process – Schweißverfahren
wire speed – Drahtzufuhr

B | Soldering and brazing

Soldering and brazing are joining techniques which are applied at high temperatures, although the temperatures used in welding are higher. Both soldering and brazing are primarily applied in electrical engineering and plumbing work. Electrical engineers solder electric wires and parts to radio and TV boards, and plumbers apply brazing to join pipes in houses and other buildings. In soldering the melting point of the solder is lower than in brazing.

M **1** **Give a summary of the text about soldering and brazing in German.**

Soldering and brazing

In soldering the parts to be joined are heated to temperatures of up to 450°C. The solder begins to melt when it is pressed against the parts and flows into the joint. When the material has cooled down, the joint is finished. In brazing, the solder works at higher temperatures, i.e. the melting point is between 450°C and 900°C. Brass, silver, copper and steel are all suitable for brazing. Soldering equipment consists of a soldering station with a soldering iron tip, or a soldering piston tip, and an iron holder, as well as solder paste, solder tin and solder wire. A brazing torch and mixer are used in brazing. Oxygen is taken from a blue cylinder and acetylene from a yellow one through hoses. The oxygen and acetylene regulators control the temperature of the flame.

R **2** **Identify the labelled parts of the soldering and brazing gear using words from the text in exercise 1.**

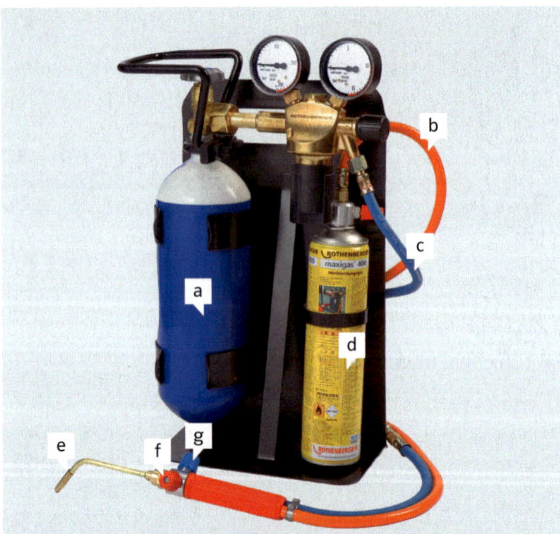

Brazing equipment

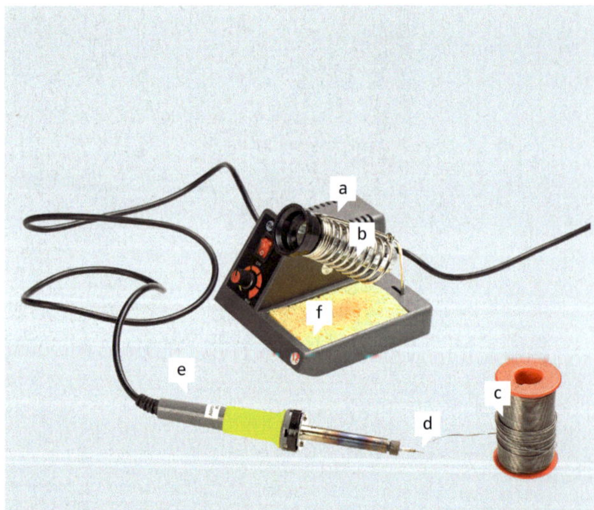

Soldering station

3 **Look at exercise 1 again and say if the following statements are true or false. Correct the false ones.**

1. When the solder flows into the joint, the joint is then finished.
2. The blue cylinder contains oxygen and acytelene comes from the yellow cylinder.
3. The temperature of the flame is varied by the regulators.
4. Gold and silver are suitable metals for brazing.

M **4** KMK II

Sie haben die Produktbeschreibung einer digitalen Lötstation in einem englischen Katalog gelesen und möchten Ihrem Ausbilder die Leistungsmerkmale auf Deutsch nennen. Fassen Sie die Merkmale auf Deutsch zusammen.

Digital processor-soldering station

The station turns automatically into 'sleep mode' when the soldering iron is left in the iron holder for longer than 15 minutes. In sleep mode, the temperature goes down to 200° C. This function prolongs the life of the soldering tip and saves electricity.
When the soldering job is taken up again or any key is pressed, the station automatically goes back to the operating mode and heats up to the preset temperature.

Features

- Integrated automatic "Sleep function"
- Temperature range 150°C – 500°C
- Short warm-up time
- LCD display
- Power 60W
- Precise, rapid temperature control
- 24V soldering iron with 1.0mm tip
- Weight: 2.450kg

R/I **5**

SAFETY FIRST ⚠

1. **Name the protective gear in the photo using the words in the box.**

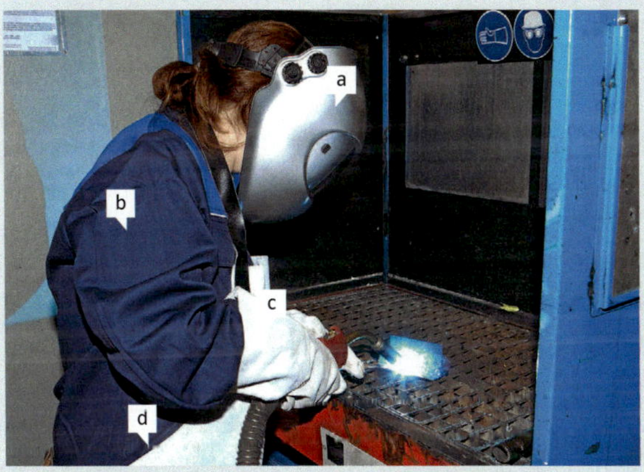

with button-up collar
welding helmet
filtered lens
fire-resistant jacket
leather apron
welding gloves

2. **Speaker A wants to weld two steel frames together. Speaker B tells him/her which protective gear to use to avoid injuries and mentions the risks involved. Use the role card below and the card for Speaker B in the Appendix.**

Speaker A
Which / eye protection
Why / hands / in danger
How / protect / arms / upper body
Best way / cover / working clothes

P **6**

Find out about the uses of laser welding and laser soldering in the automotive industry. Present your results in class.

→ **PHRASES:** Presentations

WORD BANK

acetylene – Azetylen
board – Platine, Leiterplatte
braze (v) – hartlöten
brazing torch – Lötlampe
electrical engineer – Elektroingenieur(in)
iron holder – Lötkolbenhalter
melting point – Schmelzpunkt
mixer – Mischregler
regulator – Regler
solder – Lot, Lötmetall
solder paste – Lötfett
solder tin – Lötzinn
solder wire – Lötdraht
soldering iron tip – Lötkolbenspitze
soldering piston tip – Lötkolbenspitze
soldering station – Lötstation

11

NACH DIESEM MODUL:

- √ kann ich auf Englisch die wesentlichen Merkmale der CAD- und CAM-Technik beschreiben,
- √ kann ich auf Englisch erklären, wie diese Technologie bei CNC gesteuerten Maschinenprozessen funktioniert.

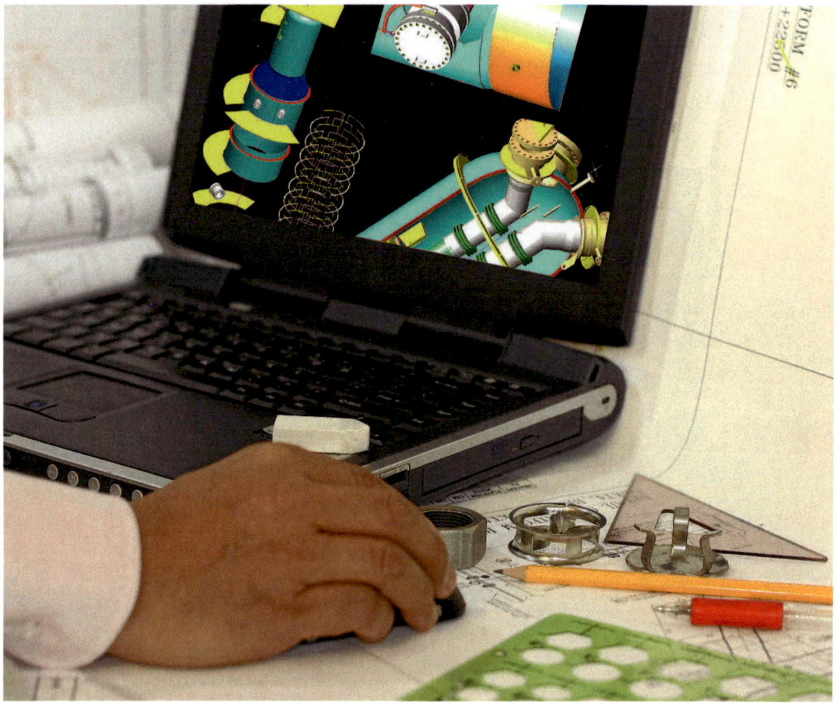

CAD-CAM and CNC

CAE (computer aided engineering) is an integrated system. It includes CAD (computer aided design) and CAM (computer aided manufacture), which communicate with each other under the control of the machine operator. Programmed data are stored in a central database or data warehouse where they are managed. Another technology in the integrated computerized system is CNC (computerized numerical control): it programmes machine-cutting processes in manufacturing and in training centres.

R **1** Which CAE integrated system is shown above? Give a reason for your answer.

R **2** Explain how CAE integrated systems are managed.

P **3** Describe your own experiences with CAD-CAM.

4 Ask and answer questions about CAD-CAM and CNC using the verbs and phrases. A asks questions and B gives recommendations.

Example:
Speaker A: Which system would you use to create a technical drawing?
Speaker B: I'd use CAD.

create • change • design • calculate • test • simulate … on screen • mill • carry out	2,000 workpieces • functions of a robot arm • *technical drawing* • details in a technical drawing • end product • quality control check

A | CAD-CAM technology

CAD technology is applied in areas such as automotive and mechanical engineering, electronics and architecture. Originally CAD systems were used as drafting tools and replaced bulky drawing boards to create technical drawings. Nowadays, it is possible to produce three-dimensional models and simulate their operation, or design digital mock-ups using CAD.

R ⊙ A 2.22 **1** **Listen to the interview with a CAD-CAM expert at a trade fair. Note down the advantages of CAD-CAM technology.**

R ⊙ A 2.22 **2** **Listen to the dialogue again and say whether the statements are true or false. Correct the false statements.**

1. CAD systems are used to build prototypes.
2. Using digital mock-ups saves manufacturers a lot of money.
3. You need several computers with CAM technology to control each machine.
4. Without CAM technology it is easy to quickly implement design changes.
5. Digital mock-ups allow designers to find the stress and load of a material.

3 **Complete the sentences about CAM technology using the words in the box.**

> tactile sensors • assembly lines • sensory devices • welding • CAM systems • operator

Many steps of production on **1** in the automotive industry could not be performed without robots. Especially potentially dangerous **2** processes are unimaginable without robots. Robot technology improved enormously after the implementation of **3**. An **4** can program robots to carry out tasks such as spray painting. A CAM progam can also tell a robot which component to mount where. Complex, multitasking robotic systems are equipped with **5** to collect information for particular jobs. For example, **6** allow the robot to pick and place objects correctly.

4 **Find headings for the photos in the completed text in exercise 3.**

1

2

3

M **5** **Give a summary of the main features of CAM systems in German.**

WORD BANK

automotive engineering – Automobilbau, -technik
CAD – computergestützte Konstruktion
CAE – computergestützte Bearbeitung
CAM – computergestützte Fertigung
CNC – CNC Steuerung
component – Bauteil
control – Steuerung
database – Datenbank
digital mock-up – virtueller CAD Prototyp
drafting tool – Konstruktions-, Zeichnungswerkzeug
drawing board – Zeichenbrett
machine operator – Maschinen-bediener(in)
mechanical engineering – Maschinenbau
mill (v) – fräsen
model – Modell
mount (v) – montieren, anbauen
multitasking system – Mehrprogrammbetrieb
quality control check – Qualitäts-kontrolle
sensor device – Sensorgerät
spray painting – Sprühlackierung
tactile sensor – Berührungssensor
three-dimensional – dreidimensional

WORD BANK ⊙

load – Last, Belastung
prototype – Prototyp
stress – Spannung, Belastung

B | CNC technology in industry

Machine tools that are used for machining processes in large-scale production are usually computerized numerical control or CNC machine tools. The working steps are programmed into a control panel as commands. A skilled machine operator monitors the machine tool during the milling or drilling or cutting operation.

R **1** **Read the text about the operation motions of a CNC machine. Name the operation motions and say how they are controlled.**

CNC machine tools

The working axes of a CNC machine tool operate automatically, precisely and consistently. There are two types of axes, the linear axis and the rotary axis. The linear axis is driven along the straight motion path, and the rotary axis is driven along the circular motion path. The motion control can be positioned along the length of travel. The linear or rotary motions are controlled by programmed commands. Rapid motions can be programmed in most CNC machine tools as can the feed rate of the material. Cutting processes are carried out by one of the cutting tools in the tool station of a CNC lathe or in the turret of a CNC milling machine. The material is clamped in the three-jaw chuck and countered by the tailstock in a turning operation. A CNC turning command causes the drive motor to rotate a number of times, which in turn rotates the ball screw and drives the linear axis. The ball screw has a feedback device to confirm that the programmed number of rotations has been performed. The machine operator has to be protected from flying chips while he or she observes the machine operation. This is why all CNC machines have a safety guard with transparent glass doors.

2 **Which machine tools are shown below? Give reasons for your answer.**

3 **Name the labelled parts of the CNC machines in the photos.**

1

2

4 Match the CNC processes with the corresponding machine components.

CNC processes	Machine components
1. It controls the position of the working axes.	a. feedback device
2. It operates in a straight line.	b turret
3. It is the control centre of CNC; it works with commands.	c. feed rate
4. Control commands programme this feature as well as the motions of the axes.	d. control panel
5. It stores the cutting tools that are required in turning operations.	e. ball screw
6. It holds the milling cutters which are programmed for CNC milling jobs.	f. motion control
7. It is rotated by the drive motor.	g. tool station
8. It shows that the performance of the turning operation has been programmed correctly.	h. linear and axis

P **5** KMK II

Ihr Ausbilder bittet Sie, bei einem englischen Hersteller von CNC Werkzeugmaschinen anzufragen. Er möchte wissen, ob die Firma eine CNC Fräsmaschine hat, die für Ausbildungszwecke geeignet sei. Schreiben Sie eine E-Mail, in der Sie folgende Leistungsmerkmale anfragen:

Leistungsmerkmale
- *Programmierbar für unterschiedliche Geschwindigkeiten der Hauptspindel*
- *Revolveraufnahme für mindestens 14 verschiedene Fräswerkzeuge*
- *ein Steuerpult mit ausreichend großem LCD Bildschirm für deutliches Ablesen der programmierten Werte der X-, Y- und Z-Achsen und der Zahlen für die Vorschubgeschwindigkeiten*
- *Gute Eignung für die Ausbildung durch umfassenden Schutz vor Späneflug, optimale Sicht in den Arbeitsraum sowie Schutzvorrichtung mit großen Türen aus Sicherheitsglas*

6 SAFETY FIRST ⚠

Make a table like the one below. Fill in the phrases about safety regulations and good work practices under the appropriate headings.

Before you start	While you are working	When you finish

1. Don't forget to wear gloves to protect your hands against sharp chips.
2. Clamp the workpiece securely.
3. Clean the safety guard.
4. Take care that the emergency shut-off is always accessible.
5. Clean the working area.
6. Make sure that visibility through the safety guard is good.
7. Check that the tools are clamped securely.
8. Close the guard doors completely.
9. Make sure that the working area is absolutely clean.

→ **PHRASES:** Written communication

WORD BANK

axis, (plural) axes – (Funktions-)Achse
ball screw – Kugelrollspindel
CNC machine tool – CNC Werkzeugmaschine
command – Befehl, Eingabe
control panel – Bedienungs-, Steuerpult
counter (v) – kontern
cutting operation – Zerspanungsarbeit
drilling operation – Bohrarbeit
drive motor – Antriebsmotor
emergency shut-off – Notaus(schalter/knopf)
feed rate – Vorschubgeschwindigkeit
feedback device – Messwertgeber
length of travel – (Arbeits-)Weglänge
linear axis – Linearachse
milling operation – Fräsarbeit
motion control – Strecken-, Bahnsteuerung
motion path – Funktions-, Arbeitsweg
operation motion – Betriebs-, Funktionsbewegung
rotary axis – Drehachse
safety guard – Schutzvorrichtung
tailstock – Reitstock
three-jaw chuck – Dreibackenfutter
tool station – Werkzeugwender
turret – (Werkzeug-)Revolverkopf
visibility – Sicht, Sichtbarkeit, Sichtweite

12

NACH DIESEM MODUL:

- √ kann ich Anwendungen zur Wartung und Instandsetzung von Werkzeugmaschinen auf Englisch beschreiben,
- √ kann ich auf Englisch Maßnahmen zur Feststellung von maschinellen Störungen und deren Beseitigung nennen und beschreiben.

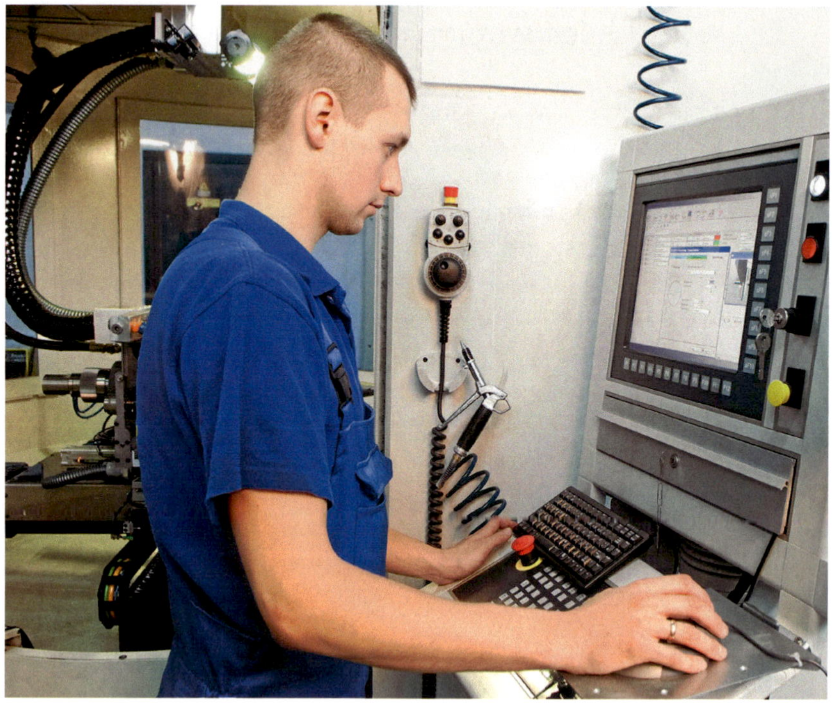

Maintenance and troubleshooting

Machinery that is not maintained by the machine operator is likely to break down or damage components and workpieces. In addition, warranties cannot be claimed if machinery has been neglected or treated carelessly. Machinery that lies idle after a breakdown costs a company thousands or millions in lost working hours.
Thus it is important that machinery is serviced regularly. Even if a machine is properly maintained, problems such as faults in the working programme of a CNC machine can arise. Then the operator has to follow a troubleshooting procedure to locate the fault.

R **1** **Choose the appropriate working step to describe the photo.**

1. The operator is maintaining and servicing the machine.
2. The operator is troubleshooting a fault in the CNC programme, which controls the machining process.
3. The operator is repairing the control panel of the machine.

2 **Say if the steps describe maintenance or troubleshooting procedures.**

1. Make sure that there is enough coolant in the centre lathe.
2. Check the set revolution speed and the sharpness of the drill.
3. Check if the electronic components of the control are functioning properly.
4. Check the cutting programme that has been entered.

A | Troubleshooting

Troubleshooting becomes necessary when a machine does not perform the required operation, e.g. when the centre lathe does not cut a workpiece properly. This may happen when the revolution speed of the main spindle is not set correctly or the feed of the lathe cutter needs to be adjusted. Another reason could be that the lathe cutter is blunt or some coolant needs to be applied.

1 Match the verbs with the parts and functions to describe troubleshooting procedures.

Verbs	Machine parts and functions
1. turn on 2. release 3. set 4. check 5. set anticlockwise 6. clamp	a. correct revolution speed of the cutter b. safety button c. cutter tightly in the toolpost d. table on the gear box for the correct revolution speed e. main switch f. rotation of the cutter

R **2** ⦾ A 2.23 Listen to the apprentices, Lukas Drechsler from Hamburg and Chris Neville from Manchester. Find out what mistakes Chris has made.

R **3** ⦾ A 2.23 Listen again. What does Lukas recommend Chris should do?

I **4** Make dialogues about the problems 1–7 using the phrases in the box.

Example:
Speaker A: The drilling machine won't start.
Speaker B: Check if the safety button is released.

Problems:
1. *The drilling machine won't start.*
2. There are scratches on the material after the grinding process.
3. The drilled hole is oval rather than round.
4. The cutter produces smoke during the turning operation.
5. The slot is not milled to the correct depth.
6. The grinding disc does not run properly during the grinding operation.
7. The twist drill broke after a few rotations of the column drill.

You should check *Check if* You should have checked … before you Why don't you …? It would be better if you (past tense) Make sure that	the set revolution speed and feed of the spindle. the abrasives of the grinding disks are worn out. the machine vice is properly adjusted. the grinding disc is balanced. the drill is clamped tight in the chuck. use some coolant. *the safety button is released.*

WORD BANK

abrasive – Schleifmittel, -korn
clamp (v) – einspannen
column drill – Ständerbohrmaschine
control panel – Steuerpult
coolant – Kühlmittel
feed – Vorschub
gear box – Getriebe
grinding – Schleif-
lathe cutter – Drehmeißel, -stahl
main spindle – Hauptspindel
main switch – Hauptschalter
maintain (v) – warten, instand halten
maintenance – Instandhaltung, Wartung
mill (v) – fräsen
operator – Bediener(-in)
revolution speed – Drehgeschwindigkeit, -zahl
safety button – Notaus, Sicherheits-, Notschalter
service (v) – warten, instand halten
toolpost – Werkzeughalter
troubleshoot (v) – Fehler suchen und beheben
troubleshooting – Fehler-/Problemsuche und -lösung
twist drill – Spiralbohrer

WORD BANK ⦾

lock in (v) – arretieren, sperren
longitudinal turning – Längsdrehen
mild steel – (Maschinen-)Baustahl
milling shop – Fräserei
revolution – Umdrehung
stress – Last, Belastung
three-jaw chuck – Dreibackenfutter

B | Maintenance

All DIY power tools for use in the home, such as drills, angle grinders and electric saws, are supplied with a manual or you can download one from the Internet. Before using a tool you are unfamiliar with, or when a problem arises with a tool, it is a good idea to read the operating instructions in the manual.

R **1** **Find the English equivalents for the German words in the text below.**

1. Durchmesser
2. Spiralbohrer
3. Hartmetallbohrer
4. Mehrzweckbohrer
5. Hochleistungsstahl-
6. Zentrierspitze
7. Bohrgeschwindigkeit
8. Eigenschaft

http://www.drillingapps...uk

Before using a drill certain aspects have to be considered, for example, the type of material you want to drill a hole in. The properties of wood, metal, and masonry such as stone or concrete vary greatly. They determine the kind of drill bit that should be used as well as the correct drilling speed. A twist drill bit with a brad point is suitable for drilling holes with small to medium diameters in wood. When drilling metal, a high-speed steel drill bit is normally used. When drilling stone or concrete, a tungsten-carbide drill bit is the best option.
Information about the correct drilling speed is given on the packaging or in the operating instructions. A basic rule says that the smaller the drill bit diameter, the higher the speed, and the larger the drill bit diameter, the lower the speed. Another rule states the softer the material, the higher the speed, and the harder the material, the lower the speed. DIY markets sell multi-purpose drills that can cope with most materials. However their multi-purpose carbide-tipped bits wear out easily.

M **2** **Give a summary in German of the application of drills in the text above.**

R **3** **Complete the operating instructions for a power drill.**

impact drilling • screwdriver bits • centre-punch • HSS • hard metal tips • pre-drill • deforming • vice

1. Use ? of the correct size and shape.
2. ? the hole when working with hardwoods or screws with a large diameter.
3. Switch to ? for concrete, stone, and marble.
4. Use drill bits with soldered ? to drill stone or concrete.
5. Before drilling a hole in sheet metal, mark and ? the position of the hole.
6. For safety reasons always clamp sheet metal firmly in a ?. Otherwise the sheet metal might rotate with the drill and injure the person operating it.
7. Place a block of wood under thin metal to avoid ? the metal.
8. Use ? drill bits.

R **4** Read the instructions about the maintenance of a power drill. What recommendation is made for all maintenance procedures?

http://www.toptool...com

TOP TOOL

- Keep ventilation slots clear at all times to avoid overheating.
- Remove dust regularly from the chuck when doing impact drilling: hold the machine vertically with the chuck facing down, open and close the chuck completely. Any dust that has collected in the chuck will fall out.
- We recommend the regular use of cleaning spray for the clamping jaws and the clamping jaw borings.
- Use only original TOPTOOL spare parts and accessories. If components which have not been described in the manual need to be replaced, contact TOPTOOL by email or call our hotline. (See list of guarantee/service addresses).
- Check out our permanently updated online catalogue to find all available accessories with their part numbers. We also recommend downloading the TOPTOOL DVD with more than 5,000 exploded views, 150,000 data sets and video-animated service operations.
- Do not hesitate to register for the TOPTOOL newsletter. You will always be up-to-date on our latest products.

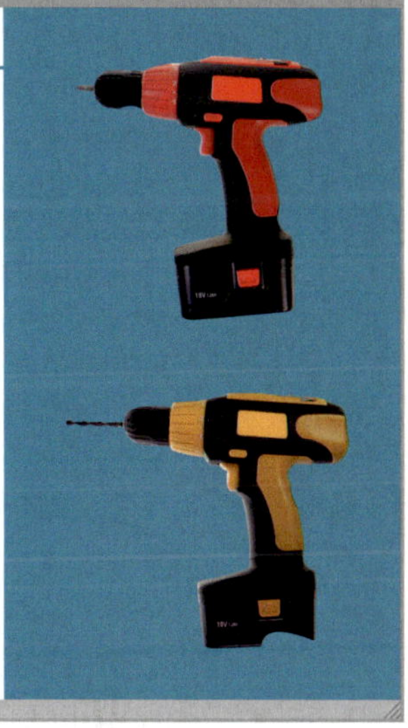

M **5** Write an e-mail in German to a friend in Stuttgart telling him or her about the most important maintenance procedures in the instructions above.

→ **PHRASES:** Written communication

P **6** Check the Internet for the different warranties and the service a customer can expect when an impact drill breaks down within the warranty period.

7 **SAFETY FIRST** ⚠

Match the two parts of the sentences to complete the safety instructions.

1. Only unplug the machine	a. while working on stonework. It could contain toxic substances.
2. Do not remove chips	b. by leading it behind you.
3. Always wear goggles	c. while the machine is still running.
4. Wear a mask when dust is produced	d. during all machine operations.
5. Keep the connection cable out of the working range of the machine	e. they must be connected with a residual current device (RCD).
6. Always switch off the machine	f. when it is switched off.
7. When appliances are used outdoors	g. before carrying out any maintenance work on it.

P **8** KMK I

Sie sind zuständig für die Materialbeschaffung Ihrer Firma. Eine relativ neue Anschaffung, ein Schlagbohrer Typ Power Turbo 1024, schaltet bei Bohrarbeiten in Beton automatisch ab. Schreiben Sie eine E-Mail auf Englisch an den Hersteller. Schildern Sie das Problem und bitten Sie um Mitteilung einer Servicestelle in der Nähe, da Sie die entsprechende Information im Internet nicht finden können. Bitten Sie auch um Informationen über eventuelle Garantieleistungen für die Reparatur der Maschine, die Sie vor 18 Monaten gekauft haben.

WORD BANK

angle grinder – Winkelschleifer
boring – Bohrung
centre punch (v) – zentrieren
chuck – Spannfutter
clamping jaws – Spannbacken
cleaning spray – Reinigungsspray
connection cable – Verbindungskabel
drill – Bohrer; Bohrmaschine
drill bit – Bohreinsatz
exploded view – Explosionszeichnung
residual current device (RCD) – Fehlstromschutzschalter
saw – Säge
solder (v) – löten
ventilation slot – Lüftungsschlitz
working range – Arbeits-, Wirkungsbereich

V1 Company tour

lingua tv
we watch languages!

Before watching
1. Describe the photo.
2. Who do you think the men in the picture are?

While watching
3. Watch the film and find out the following:
   a. the number of countries SAND Machinery delivers to.
   b. the names of three departments that the men have visited.
   c. the number of people who work for the company.
   d. whether SAND Machinery has other sites and if so, where they are.
4. Watch the film again and answer the questions.
   a. What will Mr Kramer's main tasks be during the internship?
   b. What is made at the company's production site?

After watching
5. Explain the sentences from the clip in your own words.
   a. "I'm eager to get in and get my feet wet."
   b. "… around the globe, around the clock."

V2 Telephoning

lingua tv
we watch languages!

Before watching
1. Describe the photo.

While watching
2. What problem does Ralf have at the beginning of the call?
3. Watch the film again and answer the questions.
   a. Who is calling?
   b. Who does he want to speak to?
   c. What is the purpose of his call?
   d. Why can Ralf's boss not contact the caller until the 15th of the month?
4. Find out the following technical information about the vehicle in question:
   a. the engine size
   b. the top speed
   c. the distance that can be travelled on a single charge.

After watching
5. Use the information in parts 3 and 4 to write a short memo for Ralf's boss explaining who called and what the call was about, and giving other key information.
6. How does Ralf handle the phone call? Discuss what he did well and what he could improve.

V 3 Job interview

lingua tv
we watch languages!

Before watching

1. Describe the photo.

While watching

2. Write down three of the questions that the interviewer asks.
3. Watch the film again and answer the questions.
   a. What is the applicant's name?
   b. What position is he applying for?
   c. What position did the applicant hold in his last job?
   d. According to the applicant, what is his greatest strength?
   e. What is the applicant's weakness?
   f. What questions does the applicant ask the interviewer?

After watching

4. Do you think the applicant will get the job? Give reasons for your answer.

V 4 Technical support

lingua tv
we watch languages!

While watching

1. What does 'rebooting the system' mean?
2. Watch the video again and decide whether the following statements are true or false.
   a. The caller cannot connect to the Internet.
   b. He has been having problems for two days now.
   c. He has tried rebooting the system.
   d. Turning the modem on and off did not help the problem.
   e. The scanner is not connected to the caller's computer.
   f. The technical support employee is unable to solve the problem with the scanner.

After watching

3. Make a list of problems that employees may have with their computers.
4. Record the call by copying the headings onto a sheet of paper and filling in the information.

Name of caller • Problem(s) • Solution(s) • Further action necessary: Yes/No

V5 Waste – the future's most valuable resource

ZDF.enterprises

Before watching

1. What things do you recycle every day, and how?
2. How many different waste bins does your city or community provide per household?

While watching

3. Watch the film and find out the following information:
   a. How many tons of rubbish does Germany produce each year?
   b. What nations are eager to pay for our rubbish?
   c. What metal is particularly desirable for recycling?

4. Watch the film again and answer the following questions:
   a. How many tons of copper were stolen in Germany?
   b. How much heat can one ton of residual waste produce?

After watching

5. Explain these phrases/sentences from the film in your own words.
   a. "modern urban warfare"
   b. "Our waste is getting a second lease on life."

V6 Pipe inspection

ZDF.enterprises

Before watching

1. What do pipelines transport?

While watching

2. Watch the film and find out the following information:
   a. What is the inspection device called?
   b. How long is it?
   c. How fast does the device travel?
   d. How many days does it take to inspect 300 km of pipeline?

3. Watch the film again and answer the following questions:
   a. Where are the data analyzed?
   b. How accurate is the data grid?
   c. What does the device use to identify defects?

After watching

4. What may cause defects in or damage to pipelines?

V7 High voltage work

ZDF.enterprises

Before watching

1. What do you think the men in the steel basket are preparing to do?

While watching

2. Watch the film and find out the following:
   a. what weather conditions are necessary for repairing overhead power lines.
   b. how many volts of electricity high-voltage lines carry.
   c. how the repairmen get to the damaged lines.
   d. what safety measures are taken.

3. Watch the film again and answer the following questions:
   a. How long does the job shown in the film take?
   b. Where is the electricity switched off and on?

After watching

4. Why is it important that the men work quickly?
5. Explain in your own words: "A power cut can quickly bring an entire city to its knees."

V8 Ras Laffan

ZDF.enterprises

While watching

1. Watch the film and find out the following:
   a. where Ras Laffan is located.
   b. what is processed there.
   c. how much is processed each year.
   d. how large the Ras Laffan industrial region is.

2. Watch the film again and answer the following:
   a. What problems do the construction workers face?
   b. How is the concrete cooled, and why?
   c. Why is the gas cooled?

After watching

3. Explain the phrase "liquid gold".

V9 Pipelines

2DF.enterprises

Before watching

1. Name some things which are transported in pipelines.

While watching

2. Watch the film and find out the following:
   a. what alloy is popular for making long-distance pipelines.
   b. how thick are the steel plates that are formed into round pipes.
   c. the welding technique used in the factory shown.
   d. what the expander is for.

3. Watch the film again and answer the following:
   a. What conditions do offshore pipelines have to cope with?
   b. Why do they have an additional outer casing of concrete?

After watching

4. Explain why quality-control checks are important in the production of pipelines.

V10 Robots in the hospital

2DF.enterprises

While watching

1. Watch the film and find out the following:
   a. What hospital is shown as an example? Which parts of the hospital do we see?
   b. How many robots do they have?
   c. What powers the robot couriers and how do they navigate?
   d. What is a 'lift-and-tunnel system'?

2. Watch the film again and answer these questions:
   a. What metal in the plates keeps the food warm?
   b. Do the robots distribute the food to the patients?
   c. How many containers are used to transport food?
   d. How does the hospital director feel about using robots to transport patients?

After watching

3. What else do you think the robots transport in the hospital?
4. Where else might transportation robots be used?

V11 Portable power stations

BBC Motion Gallery

Before watching

1. Think of situations in which a portable power station like the one in the photo could be useful.

While watching

2. Watch the film and list the uses of electrical power 'out in the open' that the reporter mentions.

3. Watch the film again and answer the following:
   a. What supplies the power for the 12-volt portable power station?
   b. Why are batteries not such a good choice?
   c. Where was the portable power station invented?

After watching

4. Do you think the inventor will be able to sell his power station in Germany? Where might the need for it be greater?

V12 Car speed control

BBC Motion Gallery

Before watching

1. What speed limit is acceptable
   a. on city streets?
   b. on the motorway?

While watching

2. Watch the film and find out the following:
   a. how many people die in road accidents in the UK every year.
   b. what the MIRA is working on.
   c. what the satellite positioning system does.

3. Watch the film again and answer the following:
   a. Is speed control popular with car manufacturers? Why or why not?
   b. Do speed cameras have any effect on driving habits?
   c. How is the speed-control system being tested?

After watching

4. Would you buy a car with a speed-control system? Give reasons for your answer.

KMK-Prüfungssätze

KMK Stufe I *(100 VP)*

1 Rezeption (Hörverstehen) **20 VP**

⊙ A 6.1 Sie interessieren sich für eine Stelle im englischsprachigen Ausland, z. B. ein Praktikum oder eine längerfristige Anstellung nach der Gesellen- oder Facharbeiterprüfung. Die Virtual Employment Agency (VEA) vermittelt solche Praktika. Sie laden einen Podcast mit vier Stellenangeboten herunter. Erstellen Sie hierzu eine Tabelle mit folgenden Stichwörtern und hören Sie den Podcast zweimal an. Füllen Sie Ihre Tabelle auf Englisch aus.

Information number	1 *(5 VP)*	2 *(5 VP)*	3 *(5 VP)*	4 *(5 VP)*
trade / position offered				
length of practical				
company and location of practical				
requirements				
extra information: email address, telephone number if given				

2 Rezeption (Leseverstehen) **20 VP**

Sie möchten Ihren Arbeitgeber überzeugen, Sie während Ihrer Ausbildung für ein Praktikum im Ausland freizustellen und haben dazu folgendes Informationsmaterial von der Internetseite der VEA heruntergeladen. Ihr Arbeitgeber bittet Sie, folgende Fragen zu diesem Text auf Deutsch zu beantworten.

1. Was erfahren wir über die Organisation der VEA? *(2 VP)*
2. Welche Vorteile eines Praktikums werden genannt? *(3 VP)*
3. Was konkret bietet die VEA an? *(3 VP)*
4. Was wird über eine Bezahlung / Kostenzuschuss für die Praktikanten gesagt? *(3 VP)*
5. Wie lange dauern die angebotenen Praktika? *(3 VP)*
6. Wer kann sich bei der VEA bewerben und welche Voraussetzungen sollten die Bewerber mitbringen? *(3 VP)*
7. Wie bewirbt man sich? Welche Unterlagen müssen geschickt werden? *(3 VP)*

London-based VEA offers job placements

Who we are

VEA is an organisation funded by the European Union and European companies. Our aim is to help to make European companies fit to operate more effectively in a global world by giving their trainees a chance to work abroad, improve their English language skills and become acquainted with a new culture. The trainees who take part in the programme have a chance to see different work techniques and learn to adapt to new working conditions.

▶

What we offer

VEA helps trainees to find work placements in England, Scotland and Wales. We have lists of companies in all kinds of trades who offer work placements. All placements take place in an authentic work environment. We can help you to establish contacts with companies and to plan your stay. We have a telephone hotline if problems should come up.

What payment is given

VEA does not pay trainees any money for the work placement, but we can pay a fixed amount towards your travelling expenses. However, most of the companies that we have under contract offer small salaries that will enable you to cover daily expenses such as food and board.

How long do work placements last?

The duration of work placements depends on the companies. Placements usually last between eight and ten weeks, but most companies are flexible if you want to arrange different periods. The shortest possible placement is three weeks.

Who can apply

All trainees can apply after their first or second year of training. The applicants should have a fair working knowledge of English. They should be communicative, interested in our culture and willing to participate in social activities if these are offered by the company.

How to apply

Send an email and a CV as an attachment in English telling us why you would like to take part in our work placement programme. You should also send written consent and a letter of recommendation from your company. And don't forget to mention the dates you would like to do the placement and the trade you would like to work in. Send your application by email to info@vea...biz subject matter "work placement."

(363 words)

3 Produktion — 30 VP

Sie wollen sich per E-Mail bei der VEA um ein Praktikum bewerben (Adresse: info@vea...biz). Schreiben Sie, dass Ihre Firma es lieber hätte, wenn Sie zunächst einmal nur 3 Wochen auf ein Auslandspraktikum gingen. Geben Sie an, welchen Beruf Sie lernen und in welchem Jahr Ihrer Ausbildung Sie sich befinden. Nennen Sie einen Zeitraum von drei Wochen (mit genauem Datum), in dem Sie ein Praktikum machen möchten.

4 Mediation — 30 VP

Auf der Internetseite befinden sich auch Erfahrungsberichte früherer Absolventen. Einer hat Ihnen besonders gefallen. Sie übertragen ihn ins Deutsche, um ihn ebenfalls Ihrem Arbeitgeber vorzulegen. Auf eine wörtliche Übersetzung legt er keinen Wert, lediglich auf eine inhaltlich korrekte Wiedergabe.

My name is Michael. I'm in my third year of training as a car mechanic. I've just come back from a three-month placement in South Wales. It was sponsored by the Leonardo Programme. My company in Germany ▶

encouraged me to apply for the placement. They even sponsored me by paying my wages even though I wasn't working for them for three months.
I worked in a company based near Cardiff that makes parts for the automobile industry. First I spent a few days in each department of the company, and then I was fully involved in the production process.
I worked with a Welsh colleague in the CNC centre. Of course I had some experience with CNC from my own company. I must say, I learned a lot, especially how to work more efficiently and independently.
In the beginning the language was a bit of a problem, but after a couple of weeks we managed to communicate quite well, and I learned many technical words and phrases.
This placement was a great opportunity for me, and my boss sees it as a real plus for our company and our business with British customers.

(193 words)

KMK Stufe II *(100 VP)*

1 Rezeption (Hörverstehen) — 8 VP

A 6.2 **Ihre Firma stellt Hydraulikaggregate her. Sie werden gebeten, eine Nachricht auf dem Anrufbeantworter Ihrer Firma abzuhören und eine kurze Telefonnotiz auf Deutsch zu erstellen.**
Bevor Sie die Nachricht abhören, bereiten Sie auf einem Blatt eine Telefonnotiz mit folgenden Überschriften vor.

1. Name des Anrufers und der Firma *(2 VP)*
2. Sitz der Firma *(1 VP)*
3. Nachricht für … *(1 VP)*
4. Grund des Anrufes *(2 VP)*
5. Auftragsnummer *(1 VP)*
6. Rückrufnummer *(1 VP)*

2 Rezeption (Hörverstehen) — 12 VP

A 6.3 **Für die Herstellung von Steuerungen und Motoren sind seltene Erden unverzichtbar. Ihr Ausbildungsleiter hat zu seltenen Erden einen englischen Podcast gefunden. Da der Ausbilder nicht so gut Englisch kann, bittet er Sie, sich den Podcast anzuhören und folgende Fragen auf Deutsch zu beantworten.**

1. Was wird über den Bedarf an seltenen Erden in der Einführung gesagt? *(1 VP)*
2. Welche Hinweise werden in der Einführung über die Rolle Chinas gegeben? *(2 VP)*
3. Ihr Ausbildungsleiter hat nicht genau verstanden, ob und wie seltene Erden wiederverwertet werden können. Notieren Sie die Aussage des Sprechers auf Deutsch. *(1 VP)*
4. Der Podcast nennt einige Bereiche, in denen seltene Erden unverzichtbar sind. Nennen Sie vier dieser Bereiche. *(2 VP)*
5. In welchem Bereich werden gleich mehrere Kilogramm an seltenen Erden pro Einheit gebraucht? *(1 VP)*

6. Wie selten sind seltene Erden nach Auskunft des Podcasts wirklich? *(1 VP)*
7. Es werden Produktionszahlen für China genannt: Wie hoch ist der Anteil der Chinesen an den geschätzten Reserven weltweit? *(1 VP)*
8. Welche anderen Länder werden genannt, in denen seltene Erden gefördert werden? *(2 VP)*
9. Welche Sorgen plagen das amerikanische Repräsentantenhaus? *(1 VP)*

3 Rezeption (Leseverstehen)

20 VP

Im Umgang mit Druckluft müssen bestimmte Sicherheitsregeln beherzigt werden. Bei einem Druckluftwerkzeug, das Ihre Firma geliefert bekam, war folgendes Faltblatt beigefügt. Ihr Ausbilder stellt Ihnen dazu ein paar Fragen, die Sie anhand dieses Textes auf Deutsch auf einem gesonderten Blatt beantworten sollen.

1. Der Text zählt eine Reihe von Druckluftwerkzeugen auf. Nennen Sie acht davon in der Reihenfolge, in der der Text sie aufführt. *(4 VP)*
2. Welche Sicherheitsausrüstung muss laut Text benutzt werden? *(2 VP)*
3. Was muss zum Schutz Ihrer Mitarbeiter getan werden? *(2 VP)*
4. Wie sind laut Text Druckluftwerkzeuge zu behandeln? *(3 VP)*
5. Was wird über die Zusatzgeräte ausgesagt? *(1 VP)*
6. Welche allgemeinen Eigenschaften sollen die Schläuche haben (bitte in der Reihenfolge aufführen wie im Text)? *(2 VP)*
7. Welche speziellen Eigenschaften hinsichtlich des Druckes sind bei den Schläuchen einzuhalten? *(2 VP)*
8. Was müssen Sie laut Text tun, bevor Sie Werkzeuge an den Druckluftschlauch anschließen? *(1 VP)*
9. Welchen Anforderungen müssen die Schlauchverbindungen entsprechen? *(2 VP)*
10. Druckluft wird gerne auch zur Reinigung verwendet. Was wird über die Reinigung mit Druckluft in diesem Text ausgesagt? *(1 VP)*

What are pneumatic tools?

- Pneumatic tools are powered by compressed air. Common types of these air-powered hand tools that are used in industry include buffers, nailing and stapling guns, grinders, drills, jack hammers, chipping hammers, riveting guns, sanders and wrenches.

How do you use pneumatic tools safely?

- Review the manufacturer's instruction before using a tool.
- Wear safety glasses or goggles, or a face shield and, where necessary, safety shoes or boots and hearing protection.
- Post warning signs where pneumatic tools are used. Set up screens or shields in areas where nearby workers may be exposed to flying fragments, chips, dust, and excessive noise.
- Ensure that the compressed air supplied to the tool is clean and dry. Dust, moisture, and corrosive fumes can damage a tool. An in-line regulator filter and lubricator increases tool life.
- Keep tools clean and lubricated, and maintain them according to the manufacturer's instructions.

▶

- Use only the attachments that the manufacturer recommends for the tools you are using.
- Be careful to prevent hands, feet, or body from injury in case the machine slips or the tool breaks.
- Reduce physical fatigue by supporting heavy tools with a counter-balance wherever possible.

How should you handle air hoses?

- Use the proper hose and fittings of the correct diameter.
- Use hoses specifically designed to resist abrasion, cutting, crushing and failure from continuous flexing.
- Choose air-supply hoses that have a minimum working pressure rating of 1035 kPa (150 psig) or 150 % of the maximum pressure produced in the system, whichever is higher.
- Check hoses regularly for cuts, bulges and abrasions. Tag and replace, if defective.
- Blow out the air line before connecting a tool. Hold hose firmly and blow away from yourself and others.
- Make sure that hose connections fit properly and are equipped with a mechanical means of securing the connection (e.g. chain, wire, or positive locking device).
- Install quick disconnects of a pressure-release type rather than a disengagement type. Attach the male end of the connector to the tool, NOT the hose.
- Do not operate the tool at a pressure above the manufacturer's rating.
- Turn off the air pressure to hose when not in use or when changing power tools.
- Do not carry a pneumatic tool by its hose.
- Avoid creating trip hazards caused by hoses laid across walkways or curled underfoot.
- Do not use compressed air to blow debris or to clean dirt from clothes.

What should you avoid with compressed air?

- Cleaning with compressed air is dangerous.
- Do not use compressed air for cleaning unless no alternate method of cleaning is available. The nozzle pressure MUST remain below 207 kPa (30 psi). Personal protective equipment and effective chip guarding techniques must be used. (…)

(489 words)

4 Mediation **30 VP**

Im Lernfeldunterricht Ihrer Berufsschule bekommen Sie folgenden (siehe nächste Seite) englischen Text vorgelegt. Lesen Sie ihn durch und übertragen Sie die wichtigsten Punkte in zusammenhängenden Sätzen ins Deutsche. Eine wörtliche Übersetzung ist nicht gewünscht.

Processes for joining metals

When metals are to be joined different processes can be applied such as welding, soldering and brazing. There are two kinds of welding: gas welding and electric-arc welding. By definition, welding is a fusion process that joins materials of the same kind, usually metals or thermoplastics. This is often done by melting the workpieces and adding a filler to form a pool of molten material that cools to become a strong joint; pressure is sometimes used together with high temperature, up to 3000°C, to produce the weld.
This is in contrast to soldering and brazing, which use a material with a lower melting point between the workpieces to form a bond between them without melting the workpieces.
The solder used in soldering has a melting point of up to 450°C. The parts which are to be joined are heated, and the solder is pressed against them. The solder melts and flows into the joint. After the material has cooled down, the joint is finished.
Higher temperatures are needed in brazing: the solder has a melting point of between 450°C and 900°C. Metals suitable for brazing are steel, copper, silver and brass.
Electrical engineers apply soldering to join electronic parts onto a PCB (printed circuit board), for example. Plumbers use this joining technique to fit water or gas pipes, to join drain pipes or gutters, or to generate roof sealings.

(233 words)

5 Produktion **30 VP**

Ihre Firma plant einen Messeauftritt auf der *Automotive Testing Expo* in Shanghai. Zur Vorbereitung hatte sie zwei Monate vor dem Messetermin den Besuch eines Mitarbeiters in Shanghai geplant, um mit chinesischen Zulieferern den Auftritt zu besprechen. Leider wurde der Termin von chinesischer Seite kurzfristig um zwei Wochen verschoben. Schreiben Sie eine E-Mail mit folgenden Punkten an das Royal Victoria Hotel in Shanghai info@royalvictoria...com .

- Bedanken Sie sich für die Reservierung eines Einzelzimmers mit Dusche, Satellitenfernseher, schnurlosem Telefon und Internetanschluss für Nichtraucher sowie für die Reservierung eines Sitzungsraumes für kurze Geschäftsbesprechungen für den Zeitraum 01.–08.08.20...
- Teilen Sie mit, dass Sie die Reservierungen leider stornieren müssen, weil Ihre Geschäftsreise um zwei Wochen verschoben werden musste.
- Fragen Sie an, ob Sie Ihre Buchungen ebenfalls um zwei Wochen verschieben können, und zwar auf den 15.–22.08... .
- Bitten Sie um eine schriftliche Bestätigung der neuen Buchungen.
- Bitten Sie um die Empfehlung eines anderen Hotels für den Fall, dass das Royal Victoria Hotel zu dem gewünschten Termin keine Zimmer mehr frei hat.
- Denken Sie beim Verfassen Ihrer E-Mail auch an die äußere Form der E-Mail wie Betreff, Anrede, Schluss und Grußformel.

Role cards

Module 4 Machine tools, B 3

Speaker A

1. Ask Speaker B about the function of the parts of the lathe on page 33.
You can use the following phrases:
What is … needed for? • What is a … used for? •
What's the function of …?

2. Answer Speaker C's questions.
You can use the following phrases:
It is needed to … • It is used for … • The function of … is to …

Module 7 Material testing, C 5

Speaker A

1. Fragen Sie Sprecher B, wie Sie einige geschmiedete Metallteile prüfen können.
2. Auf Anfrage von Sprecher C geben Sie die Auskunft, dass die Härte eines Metalls mit dem Rockwell Versuch geprüft wird.

Module 10 Welding and soldering, B 5

Speaker B

Use the phrases and the protective gear in the photo on page 79 to advise Speaker A.

- It is necessary to wear ? to stop your clothes catching fire.
- The ? will protect your upper body and arms from hot flying sparks.
- You should use ? to protect your eyes from the bright welding arc.
- Think of the hot sparks. Don't forget to protect your hands with ? .

Module 7 Material testing, C 5

Speaker B

1. Sagen Sie Sprecher A, dass geschmiedete Metalle mit dem Brinell Test geprüft werden.
2. Fragen Sie Sprecher C, wie Sie die Elastizität eines Metallstabes prüfen können.

Module 4 Machine tools, B 3

Speaker C

1. Answer Speaker B's questions on the lathe on page 33.
You can use the following phrases:
It is needed to … • It is used for … • The function of … is to …

2. Ask Speaker A about the function of the parts of the lathe on page 33.
You can use the following phrases:
What is … needed for? • What is a … used for? •
What's the function of …?

Module C Telephoning, B 3

→ **PHRASES:** Telephoning

Speaker A

Give your partner the following information:
1. The room is $54\,m^2$.
2. The wire needs to be 128.5 cm long.
3. The doors are 80 cm x 220 cm.
4. Each of the components weighs around 0.75 kg.

Module 7 Material testing, C 5

Speaker C

1. Sagen Sie Sprecher B, dass die Elastizität von Metallen durch den Zugversuch bestimmt wird.
2. Fragen Sie Sprecher A, wie Sie prüfen können, ob ein Metall für die Herstellung von Metallbolzen hart genug ist.

Module 4 Machine tools, B 3

Speaker B

1. Answer Speaker A's questions about the parts of the lathe on page 33.
You can use the following phrases:
It is needed to … • It is used for … • The function of … is to …

2. Ask Speaker C about the function of the parts of the lathe on page 33.
You can use the following phrases:
What is … needed for? • What is a … used for? •
What's the function of …?

Module C Telephoning, B 3

→ PHRASES: Telephoning

Speaker B

Give your partner the following information:
1. The table is 2 m x 3 m.
2. The engine runs at 7500 rpm.
3. 220 V sockets are standard in Germany.
4. The customer would like the work surface to be 24 mm thick.

Phrases

A | Meeting people

Formal greetings	Formelle Begrüßung
Good morning / afternoon / evening, Ms Robinson / Mr Jones.	Guten Morgen / Tag / Abend, Frau Robinson / Herr Jones.
Good morning / afternoon / evening, ladies and gentlemen.	Guten Morgen / Tag / Abend, meine Damen und Herren.
Informal greetings	**Informelle Begrüßung**
Good morning, Susan / James.	Guten Morgen, Susan / James.
Hi / Hello / Morning, Karl.	Tag / Morgen, Karl.
Hi everybody!	Tag zusammen!
Formal goodbyes	**Formelle Verabschiedung**
Goodbye! It's been nice / pleasant meeting you.	Auf Wiedersehen! Es war nett / angenehm, Sie kennen zu lernen!
Thank you for your help / your time. Let's keep in touch.	Danke für Ihre Hilfe / Ihre Zeit. Wir bleiben in Kontakt.
Informal goodbyes	**Informelle Verabschiedung**
Bye!	Tschüss / Ciao!
See you later!	Bis später!
See you around!	Wir sehen uns!
See you tomorrow / on Monday / next week!	Bis morgen / Montag / nächste Woche!
Formal introduction	**Formelle Vorstellung**
May I introduce myself?	Darf ich mich vorstellen?
Hello, my name is / I'm Lukas Hansen from ATW Shipping.	Hallo, mein Name ist / ich heiße Lukas Hansen von ATW Shipping.
Pleased to meet you. / Nice to meet you. / How do you do?	Angenehm. / Sehr erfreut.
It's a pleasure to finally meet you in person.	Es freut mich sehr, Sie endlich einmal persönlich kennen zu lernen.
Informal introduction	**Informelle Vorstellung**
Hi. I'm Peter, Peter James.	Hi. Ich bin Peter, Peter James.
Hello, my name is Sarah O'Neill.	Hallo, ich heiße Sarah O'Neill.
Hi Sarah. Nice to meet you.	Hi Sarah. Freut mich, dich kennen zu lernen.

Introducing others (formal)	Andere miteinander bekannt machen (formell)
Have you met our managing director?	Haben Sie schon unsere Geschäftsführerin / unseren Geschäftsführer kennen gelernt?
Ms Hall? May I introduce you to Christian Eriksen, our new intern? Christian, Georgina Hall from our sales department.	Frau Hall? Darf ich Sie Christian Eriksen, unserem neuen Praktikanten, vorstellen? Christian, das ist Georgina Hall von unserer Verkaufsabteilung.
Introducing others (informal)	**Andere miteinander bekannt machen (informell)**
Here's someone I'd like you to meet.	Ich möchte euch gerne jemanden vorstellen.
Christian, this is Joe. Joe, Christian.	Christian, das ist Joe. Joe, das ist Christian.
Let me introduce you to the team.	Darf ich dich dem Team vorstellen?
Use of first names	**Verwendung von Vornamen**
Please call me Martin.	Bitte nennen Sie mich ruhig Martin.
My name's Marianne.	Ich heiße Marianne.
My first name's Andrew, but everybody calls me Andy.	Mein Vorname ist Andrew, aber alle nennen mich Andy.
May I call you Anna?	Darf ich Anna zu Ihnen sagen?

B | Your company

Introducing the company	Die Firma vorstellen
Our company was founded in 1997.	Unsere Firma wurde 1997 gegründet.
In 2005 we were taken over by …	2005 wurden wir von … übernommen.
We are a leading manufacturer of engines.	Wir sind ein führender Hersteller von Motoren.
We are a medium-sized family firm.	Wir sind ein mittelständisches Familienunternehmen.
We are a manufacturer of industrial cleaning machines specializing in high-pressure cleaners.	Wir sind ein Hersteller von industriellen Reinigungsgeräten und sind auf Hochdruckreiniger spezialisiert.
I work for a major construction company.	Ich arbeite bei einem bedeutenden Bauunternehmen.
We are a subsidiary of …	Wir sind eine Tochtergesellschaft von …
We are a chain of electronics suppliers.	Wir sind eine Kette von Elektronik-Anbietern.
Describing the company's products / services	**Die Produkte / Dienstleistungen der Firma beschreiben**
We offer sustainable solutions.	Wir bieten nachhaltige Lösungen an.
Our products are environmentally friendly.	Unsere Produkte sind umweltfreundlich.
Our products are well-known in Europe.	Unsere Produkte sind europaweit bekannt.
Our components are both reliable and long-lasting.	Unsere Komponenten sind zuverlässig und haben eine lange Lebensdauer.
Our software is adapted to suit your requirements.	Unsere Software wird Ihren Bedürfnissen angepasst.
We manufacture high-tech shock absorbers.	Wir stellen High-Tech-Stoßdämpfer her.
Our products are designed using the latest CAD technology.	Unsere Produkte werden mit der neuesten CAD-Technologie entworfen.

Describing the job	Den Beruf beschreiben
I'm training to become a …	Ich mache eine Lehre / Ausbildung zur / zum …
I am a bricklayer / carpenter / technician / plumber / joiner.	Ich bin Maurer(in), Zimmermann / Zimmerin, Techniker(in), Klempner(in), Schreiner(in).
I work in the automotive industry.	Ich arbeite in der Automobilindustrie.
I work with automated machines.	Ich arbeite mit automatisierten Maschinen.
Describing the workplace	**Den Arbeitsplatz beschreiben**
I work on an assembly line / a machine.	Ich arbeite am Fließband / an einer Maschine.
I work in a large warehouse / factory.	Ich arbeite in einem großen Warenlager / einer großen Fabrik.
I work in a garage / workshop.	Ich arbeite in einer Autowerkstatt / Werkstatt.
I work on a building site.	Ich arbeite auf einer Baustelle.
Talking about tasks and responsibilities	**Über Aufgaben und Zuständigkeiten sprechen**
I am responsible for programming the machines.	Ich bin für die Programmierung der Maschinen zuständig.
I report to the foreman.	Ich bin dem Meister / Vorarbeiter unterstellt.
I work shifts.	Ich mache Schichtarbeit.
I often have to do overtime.	Ich muss oft Überstunden machen.
I repair electrical devices.	Ich repariere elektrische Geräte.

C | Telephoning

1. Answering the phone	Sich am Telefon melden
Introducing yourself	**Sich vorstellen**
Smart EDV GmbH, good morning. Hendrik Klopp speaking.	Smart EDV GmbH, guten Morgen. Hendrik Klopp am Apparat.
Offering help	**Hilfe anbieten**
How may I help you? / Can I help you?	(Wie) kann ich Ihnen helfen?
What can I do for you?	Was kann ich für Sie tun?
Asking for details	**Nach Details fragen**
Who's calling, please?	Wer ist am Apparat, bitte?
May I / Can I ask who's calling, please?	Darf ich fragen, wer anruft?
May I / can I take your name, please?	Könnten Sie mir bitte Ihren Namen nennen?
Could you spell that please?	Könnten Sie das bitte buchstabieren?

Connecting	Verbinden
One moment, please. I'm putting you through now.	Einen Moment bitte, ich verbinde Sie.
Shall I put you through to …?	Soll ich Sie mit … verbinden?
Hold the line, please. I'll put you through.	Bitte bleiben Sie am Apparat. Ich verbinde.
Your boss is not available	**Der / die Vorgesetzte ist nicht zu sprechen**
I'm afraid Mr Deschler is not in the office at the moment.	Es tut mir leid, Herr Deschler ist z. Zt. leider nicht in seinem Büro.
… He is on a building site.	… Er ist auf einer Baustelle.
… He has a visitor with him.	… Er hat Besuch.
… He is out at lunch	… Er ist in der Mittagspause.
Offering to call back	**Einen Rückruf anbieten**
Shall I ask her to call you back?	Soll ich sie bitten, Sie zurückzurufen?
Can she call you back this afternoon?	Kann sie Sie heute Nachmittag zurückrufen?
Does he have your telephone number?	Hat er Ihre Telefonnummer?
Can I just confirm your number?	Kann ich Ihre Nummer nochmals überprüfen?
I'll just repeat that.	Ich wiederhole.
Taking a message	**Eine Nachricht aufnehmen**
Can I take a message?	Kann ich etwas ausrichten?
Can I give him a message?	Kann ich ihm etwas ausrichten?
Would you like to leave a message?	Möchten Sie eine Nachricht hinterlassen?
Can I just confirm that?	Kann ich das kurz überprüfen?
So that's twenty-four square metres, isn't it?	Das sind also vierundzwanzig Quadratmeter, oder?
I'll make sure he gets the message.	Ich werde mich darum kümmern, dass er die Nachricht bekommt.
I'll tell her as soon as she comes back.	Ich sage ihr Bescheid, sobald sie zurückkommt.
Problems	**Probleme**
Sorry, I didn't quite catch that. Could you repeat it more slowly, please?	Es tut mir leid, das habe ich nicht verstanden. Könnten Sie es bitte etwas langsamer wiederholen?
I'm afraid I didn't catch the telephone number. Could you repeat it, please?	Leider habe ich die Telefonnummer nicht mitbekommen. Würden Sie sie bitte wiederholen?
I'm sorry, but we are having a bad connection. Could you repeat that, please?	Es tut mir leid, aber die Verbindung ist schlecht. Könnten Sie das bitte nochmals wiederholen?
Ending the call	**Das Telefongespräch beenden**
You're welcome.	Bitteschön. / Gern geschehen.
Thanks for calling.	Vielen Dank für Ihren Anruf.
Goodbye.	Auf Wiederhören.

2. Making a call	Jemanden anrufen
Introducing yourself	**Sich vorstellen**
This is … from Fertighaus Henke.	Hier spricht … von Fertighaus Henke.
My name's … I'm calling from Smart EDV.	Mein Name ist … . Ich rufe von der Firma Smart EDV an.
Asking to speak to somebody	**Nach jemandem fragen**
Could I speak to Ms Sheringham, please?	Könnte ich bitte Frau Sheringham sprechen?
Could you put me through to Mr Ferguson?	Könnten Sie mich mit Herrn Ferguson verbinden?
Could you give me his / her extension number, please?	Könnten Sie mir bitte seine / ihre Durchwahl geben?
I'd like to speak to someone from the production planning department.	Ich möchte mit jemandem in der Fertigungsplanung sprechen.
Spelling your name	**Den Namen buchstabieren**
It's S-C-H-N-E-I-D-E-R. Schneider.	Das ist S-C-H-N-E-I-D-E-R. Schneider.
Giving your phone number	**Die Telefonnummer nennen**
It's 0049 for Germany, then 0391 458 547.	Das ist die 0049 für Deutschland, dann 0391 458 547.
It's 0391 458 547.	Das ist die 0391 458 547.
Leaving a message	**Eine Nachricht hinterlassen**
Yes, please. Could you tell him that …?	Ja bitte. Könnten Sie ihm ausrichten, dass …?
Thank you. I'll ring back later.	Danke sehr. Ich rufe später zurück.
I'm afraid I won't be in the workshop this afternoon. I'll give you my mobile number.	Leider bin ich heute Nachmittag nicht in der Werkstatt. Ich gebe Ihnen meine Handynummer.
Ending the call	**Das Telefongespräch beenden**
Thank you very much for your help.	Vielen Dank für Ihre Hilfe.
Goodbye.	Auf Wiederhören.

D | Written communication

Salutation	Anrede
Dear Sir or Madam	Sehr geehrte Damen und Herren
Dear Mr … / Dear Ms …	Lieber Herr … / Liebe Frau …
Dear Peter	Lieber Peter
Complimentary close	**Schlussformel**
Yours sincerely / Yours faithfully (rarely used)	Mit freundlichen Grüßen / Hochachtungsvoll (selten benutzt)
Best regards / Kind regards / Best wishes	Schöne Grüße / Herzliche Grüße

Enquiries	Anfragen
We have visited your website and …	Wir haben Ihre Webseite besucht und …
Your services have been recommended to us by …	Ihre Dienstleistungen wurden uns von … empfohlen.
We are a well-established manufacturer of …	Wir sind ein gut etablierter Hersteller von …
Our firm is a leading importer of …	Unsere Firma ist ein führender Importeur von …
Could you please let us have a brochure and a price list?	Wir bitten um einen Prospekt und eine Preisliste.
Please send us a quotation for …	Bitte machen Sie uns ein Angebot über …
Please quote your lowest prices for …	Bitte nennen Sie uns Ihre günstigsten Preise für …
We would be grateful for information on your terms of payment and delivery.	Wir bitten um nähere Angaben zu Ihren Liefer- und Zahlungsbedingungen.
A visit by your representative would be appreciated.	Wir wären dankbar für einen Besuch Ihres Vertreters.
We look forward to hearing from you.	Wir freuen uns darauf, bald von Ihnen zu hören.
Offers	**Angebote**
Many thanks for your enquiry of 30 May about our new range of …	Wir danken Ihnen vielmals für Ihre Anfrage vom 30. Mai wegen unseres neuen Sortiments von …
As requested, we are sending you enclosed our latest catalogue and price list.	Wie gewünscht fügen wir unseren neuesten Katalog und unsere Preisliste bei.
We can offer a 10% quantity discount on orders of at least 500 units.	Für Aufträge über mindestens 500 Stück wird 10% Mengenrabatt gewährt.
We take pleasure in submitting the following cost estimate:	Wir freuen uns, Ihnen folgenden Kostenvoranschlag zu unterbreiten:
Our usual terms of payment are: - cash with order - cash on delivery - 30 days net, 10 days 2% - by irrevocable letter of credit	Unsere üblichen Zahlungsbedingungen lauten: - Barzahlung bei Auftragserteilung - Barzahlung bei Lieferung - 30 Tage netto, 10 Tage 2% Skonto - durch unwiderrufliches und bestätigtes Akkreditiv
The delivery period is 6 weeks.	Die Lieferzeit beträgt 6 Wochen.
We look forward to welcoming you as our customers.	Wir freuen uns darauf, Sie als Kunden begrüßen zu dürfen.
Orders	**Bestellungen**
Please supply the following items on the terms stated below:	Bitte liefern Sie uns folgende Positionen zu den unten genannten Bedingungen:
As agreed, we will effect payment by bank transfer 30 days from date of invoice.	Wie vereinbart werden wir die Zahlung 30 Tage nach Rechnungsdatum per Banküberweisung vornehmen lassen.
Please note that the goods must reach us by 1 March at the latest.	Wir weisen darauf hin, dass die Ware bis spätestens 1. März hier eintreffen muss.
Please acknowledge this order promptly.	Bitte bestätigen Sie diesen Auftrag umgehend.
We look forward to receiving the goods in time and to doing further business with you.	Wir freuen uns, die Ware rechtzeitig entgegennehmen und weitere Geschäfte mit Ihnen machen zu können.

E | Applications

Mentioning the source of the advertisement	Die Quelle der Anzeige nennen
I would like to apply for the job / work placement which you advertised in the … of … / on the … website.	Ich möchte mich auf die in der … vom … / auf der … Website ausgeschriebenen Stelle / Praktikumsstelle bewerben.
I saw your advertisement for a … (job / work placement) in the … of … / on the … website and would like to apply for the position.	Ich habe Ihre Anzeige für eine Stelle / Praktikumsstelle in der … vom … / auf der … Website gesehen und möchte mich auf die Stelle bewerben.
I am writing in response to your advertisement of … in the … / on the … website for a … (job / work placement).	Ich melde mich auf Ihre Anzeige vom … in der … / auf der … Website für eine Stelle / Praktikumsstelle.
Introducing yourself	**Sich vorstellen**
I am particularly attracted to this position as …	Ich bin an dieser Stelle besonders interessiert, weil …
I am currently doing a one-year / two-year … apprenticeship at a vocational college in … (town), Germany.	Ich mache zurzeit eine ein-/zweijährige … Ausbildung an einer berufsbildenden Schule in …, Deutschland.
I am in the second year of an apprenticeship in …	Ich bin im zweiten Jahr einer Ausbildung als …
At present I am working as a … with … (company).	Zurzeit arbeite ich als … bei der Firma …
After completing my apprenticeship / At the end of the apprenticeship I will be a qualified (job title).	Nachdem ich meine Ausbildung beendet habe / Mit Abschluss meiner Ausbildung bin ich eine qualifizierte / ein qualifizierter (Berufsbezeichnung).
Talking about yourself and saying why you are a good applicant	**Über sich sprechen und begründen, warum man ein guter Bewerber / eine gute Bewerberin ist**
As you will see from my CV …	Wie aus meinem Lebenslauf zu ersehen ist, …
I have a good knowledge of …	Ich verfüge über gute Kenntnisse in …
I am motivated / reliable / hard-working / keen to learn / friendly / open / a good communicator.	Ich bin motiviert / zuverlässig / sehr fleißig / lernwillig / freundlich / aufgeschlossen / ein kommunikativer Mensch.
I have previous work experience as …	Ich verfüge bereits über Berufserfahrung als …
I have a wide range of interests including …	Ich bin vielseitig interessiert, u. a. an …
I am familiar with this kind of work, because …	Mit dieser Tätigkeit bin ich vertraut, da …
I would very much welcome the opportunity to work in …	Über die Möglichkeit, in … zu arbeiten, würde ich mich sehr freuen.
I believe that I would be a valuable / enthusiastic employee.	Ich bin überzeugt, dass ich ein(e) nützliche(r) / engagierte(r) Mitarbeiter(in) wäre.

Finishing the letter	Den Brief beenden
I hope that you will consider my application.	Ich hoffe, dass Sie meine Bewerbung in Betracht ziehen werden.
Thank you in advance for considering my application.	Ich danke Ihnen im Voraus, dass Sie meine Bewerbung in Betracht ziehen.
I look forward to hearing from you (soon).	Ich freue mich auf eine (baldige) Antwort.

F | Socialising

Ice breakers	Eisbrecher
How was your weekend? Good, thanks. How about yours?	Wie war dein / Ihr Wochenende? – Gut, danke. Und bei dir / Ihnen?
Did you see the game last night? – Of course! It was unbelievable. What did you think about the red card / winning goal?	Hast du / Haben Sie das Spiel gestern abend gesehen? – Natürlich! Es war unglaublich. Was halten Sie von der roten Karte / vom Siegtor?
Quite cold / warm today, isn't it?	Ziemlich kalt / warm heute, oder?
I really like your watch. Where did you get it?	Ihre / deine Uhr gefällt mir wirklich gut. Woher haben Sie / hast du sie?
Did you read the story about … in the newspaper this morning?	Haben Sie heute Morgen den Bericht über … in der Zeitung gelesen?
Ah! I see you are also in need of a coffee / cup of tea.	Ah! Wie ich sehe brauchen Sie / brauchst du auch einen Kaffee / eine Tasse Tee.
Is this your first time in Germany?	Sind Sie / Bist du zum ersten Mal in Deutschland?
The food is pretty good here, isn't it? – You can say that again!	Das Essen hier ist ziemlich gut, oder? – Das können Sie / kannst du laut sagen.
Keeping the conversation going	**Das Gespräch in Gang halten**
Really? Is that right? You're joking!	Wirklich? Ist das wahr? Sie machen / du machst Scherze!
That's brilliant / hilarious / fascinating!	Das ist brilliant / sehr lustig / faszinierend!
And what happened then?	Und was passierte dann?
No, unfortunately I missed it. What happened?	Nein, leider habe ich es verpasst. Was ist passiert?
It's interesting you should say that, because …	Interessant, dass Sie das sagen, weil …
Talking about food, have you already tried the new Italian restaurant in the city centre?	Wo wir gerade über Essen sprechen: Haben Sie schon den neuen Italiener in der Innenstadt ausprobiert?
Changing the subject	**Das Thema wechseln**
I think it's best if we don't talk about politics.	Ich denke, es ist das Beste, wenn wir nicht über Politik sprechen.
If you don't mind, I'd rather not talk about that.	Wenn es Ihnen nichts ausmacht, würde ich lieber nicht darüber sprechen.
Yes … By the way, have you read …	Ja … Übrigens, haben Sie … gelesen?

Ending the conversation politely	Die Unterhaltung höflich beenden
Well, it's been good talking to you.	Nun, es war schön, mit Ihnen zu sprechen.
I suppose it's time to get back to work. See you around.	Ich denke, dass es Zeit ist, zur Arbeit zurückzukehren. Man sieht sich!
Excuse me, but I have just seen someone I need to speak to. It was nice talking to you.	Entschuldigen Sie, aber ich habe jemanden gesehen, mit dem ich sprechen muss. Es war nett, mit Ihnen zu reden.
Eating out	**Essen gehen**
Talking about preferences	**Über Vorlieben sprechen**
Do you eat meat / seafood / fish?	Essen Sie Fleisch / Meeresfrüchte / Fisch?
Do you like spicy food?	Mögen Sie scharfes Essen?
I'm a vegetarian / vegan.	Ich bin Vegetarier / Veganer.
I'm allergic to nuts.	Ich bin allergisch gegen Nüsse.
I'd prefer something light; I'm on a diet.	Ich würde etwas Leichtes bevorzugen – ich bin auf Diät.
I don't drink alcohol.	Ich trinke keinen Alkohol.
Talking about the menu	**Über die Speisekarte sprechen**
It's sweet / savoury / sour.	Es ist süß / herzhaft / sauer.
It's a starter / main dish / dessert.	Es ist ein(e) Vorspeise / Hauptgericht / Dessert.
What's in it?	Was ist da drin?
It's made of …	Es wird aus … gemacht.
It's boiled / fried / baked / roasted / filled with …	Es ist gekocht / gebraten/gebacken / geröstet / gefüllt mit …
Ordering	**Bestellen**
Are you ready to order?	Sind Sie bereit zum Bestellen?
As a starter, I'll take the … and then …	Als Vorspeise nehme ich …, und dann …
I'd like a side order of rice, please.	Ich hätte gerne (eine Portion) Reis als Beilage.
Shall we share a bottle of wine?	Sollen wir uns eine Flasche Wein teilen?
How do you like your steak? – Rare / medium / well-done, please.	Wie möchten Sie Ihr Steak? – Englisch / medium / durch, bitte.
What kind of wine / beer do you have?	Welche Weine / Biersorten haben Sie?
Talking about the food	**Über das Essen sprechen**
Enjoy your meal.	Guten Appetit!
How's your meal?	Wie ist Ihr Essen?
What's your … like?	Wie ist Ihr …?
The meat is very tender / a little tough.	Das Fleisch ist sehr zart / etwas zäh.
It's not as sweet as I expected.	Es ist nicht so süß, wie ich gedacht habe.
Excuse me, but my soup is cold.	Entschuldigen Sie, aber meine Suppe ist kalt.

Asking for the bill	Nach der Rechnung fragen
Excuse me, could we have the bill, please?	Entschuldigen Sie, könnten wir bitte die Rechnung haben?
Do you accept credit cards?	Akzeptieren Sie Kreditkarten?
This one's on me!	Das geht auf mich!
Shall we split the bill 50-50?	Sollen wir die Rechnung 50-50 teilen?

G | Presentations

Beginning the presentation	Die Präsentation beginnen
I should like to start by telling you about my company.	Zunächst möchte ich Ihnen etwas über meine Firma sagen.
My presentation will deal with …	Meine Präsentation behandelt …
I intend to keep my presentation as brief as possible.	Ich möchte meine Präsentation so kurz wie möglich halten.
I would welcome any questions at the end of my presentation.	Ich wäre gern bereit, etwaige Fragen am Ende meiner Präsentation zu beantworten.
The handout summarises the main points and gives an overview of the relevant figures and statistics.	Das Handout enthält die Hauptpunkte und gibt einen Überblick über die entsprechenden Zahlen und Statistiken.
Structuring the main part of your presentation	**Den Hauptteil der Präsentation strukturieren**
Now my second point is …	Ich komme nun zu Punkt 2 …
Thirdly, let me give you some basic statistics.	Drittens darf ich Ihnen ein paar grundlegende Statistiken zeigen.
I should now like to move on to the next topic.	Ich möchte nun gern zum nächsten Thema übergehen.
An excellent example of this is …	Ein hervorragendes Beispiel dafür ist …
I should like to give you an example to illustrate this point.	Ich möchte diesen Punkt mit einem Beispiel erläutern.
Concluding your presentation	**Die Präsentation beenden**
To sum up we can say that …	Zusammenfassend kann man sagen, dass …
I should like to finish by saying / thanking the organisers / pointing out …	Ich möchte schließen mit der Bemerkung / dem Dank an die Organisatoren / dem Hinweis …
Are there any questions?	Gibt es Fragen?
Thank you for your attention.	Vielen Dank für Ihre Aufmerksamkeit.

H | Dealing with customers

Making a complaint	Eine Beschwerde / Reklamation vorbringen
We are writing with reference to our order no. …	Wir nehmen Bezug auf unseren Auftrag Nr. …
On unpacking the cases our Incoming Goods Control discovered that 15 items are missing.	Beim Auspacken der Kisten stellte unsere Warenannahme fest, dass 15 Positionen fehlen.
We are afraid that several units are - seriously damaged / defective. - broken / badly scratched / stained.	Leider sind mehrere Teile - schwer beschädigt / schadhaft. - zerbrochen / stark zerkratzt / verschmutzt.
We are sorry to point out that the repair work has been poorly executed.	Wir müssen leider darauf hinweisen, dass die Reparatur schlecht ausgeführt wurde.
We believe the damage may be due to rough handling in transit.	Wir glauben, dass der Schaden auf unsachgemäße Behandlung beim Transport zurückzuführen ist.
This is very inconvenient for us because …	Dies kommt uns sehr ungelegen, da …
We would ask you to - replace the faulty goods at your expense. - grant us a price reduction of 10%. - cut the price to €550.	Wir möchten Sie bitten, - die mangelhafte Ware auf Ihre Kosten zu ersetzen. - uns einen Preisnachlass von 10% zu gewähren. - den Preis auf €550 zu senken.
We will keep the damaged goods until we hear from you.	Wir werden die beschädigten Waren behalten, bis wir von Ihnen hören.
Responding to a complaint	**Auf eine Beschwerde / Reklamation antworten**
Thank you for your email drawing a serious problem to our attention.	Danke für Ihre E-Mail, mit der Sie uns auf ein ernstes Problem aufmerksam gemacht haben.
We wish to apologise for this mistake.	Wir bitten für diesen Fehler um Entschuldigung.
We are extremely sorry for the poor service you have received.	Es tut uns außerordentlich leid, dass Sie einen unzureichenden Service erhalten haben.
We will investigate the matter thoroughly and inform you of the steps taken.	Wir werden die Angelegenheit gründlich untersuchen und Sie über die Schritte informieren, die wir unternommen haben.
Please return the faulty items at our expense.	Bitte senden Sie die mangelhaften Artikel auf unsere Kosten zurück.
We are prepared to reduce the price by 10% if you decide to keep the goods.	Wir sind bereit, den Preis um 10% zu senken, wenn Sie sich entschließen, die Ware zu behalten.
We hope that this proposal will find your approval.	Wir hoffen, dieser Vorschlag findet Ihre Zustimmung.

Audioscripts

⊙ A 2.12 Module 1 The general workshop, A 1, 2

Andreas: Well, Dave, this is the general workshop. Our apprentices are trained here in mechanical engineering. You can see a lot of the machine tools that you normally find on the shop floor. The apprentices work at those work benches with the bench vices in the centre of the shop.

Dave: And I can see a column drill between those windows over there. Is that a centre lathe next to the green door?

Andreas: Yes, that's right. And that's a milling machine opposite the lathe. Some of the apprentices' training units include basic machine skills. They get their first chance to use the machine tools that they'll operate later when they are skilled workers.

Dave: I see. Oh, and what's behind that green door?

Andreas: That's our CNC shop. The apprentices do training on the CNC machines in their third year.

Dave: Before you can operate sophisticated CNC machines you need a lot of good basic skills.

Andreas: Exactly! I guess the training at your company is structured in a similar way.

Dave: Yes, it is. You'll see it when you visit us next month. Oh, I've got a cut on my hand from one of the vices. Do you think I could get a plaster before we go on?

Andreas: Certainly. The first-aid kit is on the wall beside the emergency exit. Just go back past the work benches. You'll see it on the right if you follow the signs.

⊙ A 1.1 Module A Meeting people, A 1, 2

Dialogue 1

Mr Neureuther: Neureuther, good morning.

Ms Hornbach: Good morning, Mr Neureuther.

Mr Neureuther: Good morning, Ms Hornbach.

Ms Hornbach: Mr Neureuther, the young man you were expecting from Denmark is here.

Mr Neureuther: Ah yes, please send him in. And Ms Hornbach, give Mr Dachs a call, will you please?

Ms Hornbach: I've already called him.

Christian: Hello, my name is Christian Eriksen. I come from Fanö in Denmark, and, uh, I'd like to work here as an intern for the next three months.

Mr Neureuther: Felix Neureuther. I'm the manager of the company.

Christian: Nice to meet you, Mr Neureuther.

Mr Neureuther: Nice to meet you too, Christian. I hope you had a pleasant trip.

Christian: Yes, it was fine, thank you. It's not far from Fanö to Kiel.

Mr Neureuther: Fine. Now, let me see, I guess you've handed all the necessary papers over to my secretary, Ms Hornbach?

Christian: Yes, I have.

Mr Neureuther: Oh good, Mr Dachs. I don't believe you've met Christian Eriksen. He'll be our new intern for the next three months. Christian, this is Mr Dachs, our personnel manager.

Mr Dachs: Nice to meet you Christian.

Christian: Nice to meet you too, Mr Dachs.

Mr Neureuther: Christian, Mr Dachs will take you to your team, so you can get to know them all. See you later, Christian.

Christian: See you later, Mr Neureuther.

Dialogue 2:

Mr Dachs: Morning, everybody.

All of them: Good morning, Mr Dachs.

Mr Dachs: I'd like you to meet our new colleague. He'll be working with us for the next three months. He's in his second year of training. Christian, would you like to introduce yourself?

Christian: Hello, my name is Christian Eriksen. I come from Fanö, that's an island off the coast of Denmark. The company I work for is a bit smaller than yours; there's just the boss, a skilled worker and two trainees.

Silke: Hi Christian, nice to meet you. My name is Silke, and I'm also in my second year of training.

Christian: Nice to meet you too, Silke. I'm glad you speak English, because my German is not so fluent. But I'm doing my best to improve.

Silke: No problem, we'll manage.

Josef: Hello Christian, I'm Josef, but everybody calls me Joe. I'm your foreman. My English is not perfect, but Silke can always help. I've been here for quite a long time. Isn't that right, Mr Dachs?

Mr Dachs: Yes, Joe has been with us for over 20 years now. I think for the first few weeks you'll work with him. Well, let's get back to work now. If you have any questions, you can ask Joe, but you can always come to my office, too.

Christian: Thank you, Mr Dachs.

◎ A 2.13 Module 2 Hand and power tools, C 2, 3

Shop assistant: Hello, how can I help you?

Customer: Hello, I'm interested in buying a cordless impact drill. What have you got?

Shop assistant: We have a number of models. This one has not been on the market very long. It's a reversible, cordless screwdriver drill with some very interesting features. All of the new cordless drills are ultra-light but really powerful. This one has got a compact angle gear and a pneumatic hammer mechanism. It also comes with a powerful electric motor for a longer life and a higher torque. And here if you want to hold the drill for a moment, you can see the soft grip makes it really comfortable to handle.

Customer: You're right. It does. What about the service life of the battery?

Shop assistant: That's a very important question for cordless models. This one comes with a new-generation, compact battery which guarantees a long service life. Oh yes, another useful feature when you're working in a dark corner is the LED light here at the front just below the chuck.

Customer: What do I do with empty batteries that cannot be recharged any more?

Shop assistant: That's no problem. We can dispose of them for you in an environmentally friendly way.

Customer: When it comes to charging the battery, how long are we talking about?

Shop assistant: The drill comes with a one-hour charger with auto shut-off. The battery is an 18-V- LI compact battery.

Customer: Great. What about safety features?

Shop assistant: That's another improvement on older models. This model locks out the power when it isn't in operation.

Customer: That's useful. Does the case have enough space for drill bits?

Shop assistant: Yes, of course. It has separate compartments for the bits, the battery cartridge and the charger.

Customer: That sounds good. I think that it could be what I'm looking for.

◎ A 1.2 Module B Your company, A 4

Herr Kirchner: OK, so we've covered human resources, accounting, sales and marketing, and purchasing. Now we come to the more technical side of the company, and – of course – the area where you will be spending your time. OK, do you have any questions before we continue?

Sean: Yes, just a general question really. How old is the company?

Herr Kirchner: Older than you, Sean, that's for sure! Krone Elektronik was founded by Dr Florian Krone in 1954, and is still a family-owned company to this day.

Sean: And is this the headquarters here in Bochum?

Herr Kirchner: Yes, it is. Krone has nine manufacturing plants and sales offices across Europe, but this is the largest. In fact, we also have two in the USA – in Chicago and Baltimore.

Sean: Are there any plants in Great Britain?

Herr Kirchner: No, there aren't. But we are opening a new factory in South Korea next year.

Sean: And how many people work for Krone Elektronik?

Herr Kirchner: That's a good question, Sean. I don't know the exact number, but it is at least 10,000, if you include the USA. OK, let's go on with the tour, shall we? The building to your right is our research and development department. They are currently working on a new braking system for a major German car company.

Sean: And what goes on in the large building next to it?

Herr Kirchner: This is our main building, which has three functions. Firstly, it is where the production planners work – and this is where you will spend most of your time. Their job is to optimize the manufacturing process by keeping production times and costs down. Secondly, as you can see, here are also the production halls, where you will start your internship.

Sean: You mentioned three functions. So what else happens over there? It's a really big place.

Herr Kirchner: Yes, it's over 6,000 square metres. Those people you can see over there are responsible for quality control. They test all of the components and devices before they go to the customer.

Sean: How many components are made here in Bochum?

Herr Kirchner: Well, one of the main components we produce here are the cylinder heads, and we make thousands of them every year. And each and every one of them must be inspected by the guys in quality control.

Sean: I guess that's an important job. I'm really looking forward to getting to work.

Herr Kirchner: That's great. I will introduce you to the foreman this afternoon. OK, finally, behind this building we have the IT department. At the moment, they are very busy dealing with the problems caused by our new operating system.

Sean: Oh, that doesn't sound too good. What exactly is the problem?

Herr Kirchner: I'm not sure exactly, some kind of interface difficulties, I think. OK, let's go into the canteen and have some lunch, shall we? Then I can answer some more of your questions.

◎ A 2.14 Module 3 Cutting processes with hand and power tools, B 2, 3

Alexander: Hello Sally. Are you ready to make the base plates of the bench vice?

Sally: Hi Alexander. Of course. What can I do?

Alexander: Well, I've just shortened three flat steel bars to a length of approximately 1200 mm. The material is now 200 mm wide.

Sally: Oh great. What tool did you use?

Alexander: I used the electric hacksaw in the storeroom.

Sally: You were quick. Now for the two base plates … I'll just look at the technical drawing. OK, we have to make two different plates: one is 280 mm long and 180 mm wide.

Alexander: Let's see. The other one is 240 mm long and 160 mm wide.

Sally: OK, then I can do the first one. I think I'll use a hacksaw to cut it to an approximate length of 300 mm. Then it will be easier to finish it with the different files and get the precise dimensions.

Alexander: I wouldn't use the hacksaw, Sally. It's easier with the angle grinder.

Sally: Why is that?

Alexander: I just mean that the angle grinder is driven by electric power and you don't need so much physical strength.

Sally: Okay, that's true. And how do you want to cut the second bar? Do you want the angle grinder when I've finished with it?

Alexander: No. I'll use the circular saw while you're working with the grinder.

Sally: Good, so that's clear then. Before we start, we have to clamp the stock in the bench vice, don't we?

Alexander: Yes, and we need to wear goggles. There will be a lot of chips flying around during the cutting process.

◎ A 1.3 Module C Telephoning, B 5, 6

Alex: Fertighaus Henke, Alex Bauder.

Caller: Yes, hello. Do you speak English?

Alex: Er, yes, a little. How can I help you?

Caller: Well, my name is Matthew Reid and your company is currently building my house. I'm a little confused. I thought this was Mr Deschler's telephone number. He is the construction manager, isn't he?

Alex: Yes, he is, but unfortunately he is off sick today, so all of his calls are being diverted to me. Can I help you with something?

Caller: Well, I was calling to give Mr Deschler some changes to our house.

Alex: OK, and what was your name again, please?

Caller: Reid, Matthew Reid.

Alex: Could you possibly spell that please?

Caller: Certainly. It's R-E-I-D.

Alex: R-I-E-D.

Caller: No, R-E for England, I for India, D.

Alex: Sorry, R-E-I-D. OK, Mr Reid, and what is the address of the house?

Caller: Well, so far it is only a foundation pit, but it is Ringstrasse 26 in Lernsdorf.

Alex: Ringstrasse 26, Lernsdorf. Ah, yes, I know the site. We are scheduled to begin on your cellar next week, I think. OK, if you give me the information, I will pass it on to Mr Deschler. Let me just find a piece of paper … OK, I'm ready.

Caller: First of all, in the kitchen we need to move the extractor fan twenty centimetres to the left, so that it is directly over the hob. And the hole needs to have a diameter of one hundred and eighty-four millimetres, and we also need …

Alex: Sorry Mr Reid, but I am afraid any changes to your kitchen need to be discussed with the kitchen fitters. Are there any changes to the plans for any other part of the house?

Caller: Er, just a moment. Let me look at my list. OK, we need to change the height of the toilets in the bathroom. At the moment they are planned to be forty-five centimetres and we would like them to be fifty. Plus, we need to add another two hundred and twenty volt socket to the right of the bathroom mirror for my electric razor.

Alex: OK, anything else?

Caller: Yes, my wife and I have decided that we will need a larger carport. I have spoken to a friend and he says we should make it eight metres by six metres by three metres. Can you find out how much extra this would cost, please?

Alex: Of course. Let me just confirm, eight metres long by six metres wide. And how high should it be?

Caller: Three metres high. Of course, this means that we will have a smaller garden, but I think a carport is very useful. You can also ask Mr Deschler how big our garden will be with the new carport. It is currently one hundred and thirty-five square metres.

Alex: OK, I will ask him to adjust the plan and get in touch with you as soon as he is back in the office.

Caller: That's great. Oh, just one more thing. My wife wants to put larger windows in the living room. At the moment, the windows in the plan are one hundred and forty-eight centimetres by one hundred and eleven. She would like them to be one hundred and eighty-six by two hundred and twenty-two.

Alex: One eight six by two two two. OK Mr Reid, I will pass this information on to Mr Deschler and ask him to give you a call. Does he have your telephone number?

Caller: Yes, I think so, but let me give you my work number, too. It is 0391 587660…. Thank you for your help Mr Bauder. Goodbye.

Alex: You're welcome Mr Reid. Goodbye.

◎ A 2.15 Module 4 Machine tools, B 1, 2

Brian: Look here, Sven. I've got a brochure with some infomation about machine tools. They talk about the typical parts of machine tools. For example, a lathe has a base and it is equipped with a saddle, a headstock, a three-jaw chuck and a toolpost. The headstock houses the gears that drive the main spindle with the chuck. The main spindle then rotates the workpiece which is held by the chuck.

Sven: What do they say about the saddle and cross-slide?

Brian: Let me see. Yes, the saddle and cross-slide feeds the cutting tool. The cutting tool itself is mounted to the toolpost.

Sven: Look what it says here. The rotation of the main spindle can be performed either clockwise or anticlockwise. You just set the motor-reversing switch in the corresponding position.

Brian: That is interesting. Did you pick up a brochure about milling machines?

Sven: Yes I did. Ah, here it is. This brochure has information about milling and grinding machines. A milling machine has three main parts: a column mounted on a base, an overarm with the spindle and a vertical slide for the machine table. The table supports a machine vice which clamps the workpiece in the position you want it to have.

Brian: That grinding machine on the second page seems to have similar parts to a milling machine. Both machine tools have a base and a column. However, the grinding machine also has a table traverse to feed the material to the grinding wheel. This model has room in the base table to store the grinding wheels.

Sven: That's a good idea. Then the wheels are always ready to use.

◎ A 2.16 Module 5 Cutting processes with machine tools, A 1, 2

Volker: Hi Philip.

Philip: Hi Volker. What are you doing?

Volker: I have to do a job on the centre lathe. Can you help me? How do I start the headstock again?

Philip: You can switch on the motor here. Then the power is transmitted to the headstock or the spindles.

Volker: I see. The headstock drives the main spindle which rotates the workpiece, right?

Philip: That's it. And you can rotate the workpiece either clockwise or anticlockwise.

Volker: Oh, OK. I want to set the revolution speed of the spindle. Where do I...?

Philip: Here is the speed selection lever. You can use that.

Volker: Thanks, I remember now. What is the function of the slideways again?

Sally: Normally the slideways are used to control the feeds of either the cutting tool or the workpiece.

Volker: The slideways have a different function to the saddle and cross-slide then.

Philip: Yes, as far as I can remember the saddle and cross-slide feeds the cutting tool to the workpiece, which is clamped in the chuck.

Volker: That's quite complicated. Can we go through the process again?

⦾ A 1.4 Module E Applications, C 1

Andrea: Hi David, how are you doing?

David: Hi Andrea. I'm fine thanks. How are you?

Andrea: Yeah, I'm OK. Busy, but fine.

David: I heard that you were thinking about applying for a three-month internship in the Northampton branch. Is that true?

Andrea: Yes, that's right. I really want to spend some time in England. I guess it was the same with you and coming to Germany.

David: Exactly. I wanted to see how things worked over here. So, you want to spend some time with my old colleagues, eh? That's great.

Andrea: Well actually, I wanted to ask you for a bit of advice if that's OK with you?

David: Sure, what can I help you with?

Andrea: Well, I have to officially apply for the internship, which means a letter and a CV.

David: OK, would you like me to read your letter?

Andrea: Yes, that would be great. I am going to finish it this weekend, and then I will bring it to work on Monday. Thanks. But where I really need your advice is with the CV. I was wondering if you had any tips for me. I know there are some differences between German and English CVs.

David: Yes, there are, you're right. Hmm ... tips ... let me see. OK, the first thing to remember is that your CV should be no longer than two pages.

Andrea: Two pages, OK.

David: Also, make sure you use good-quality paper and never send your CV without a covering letter.

Andrea: OK ...

David: And don't forget to highlight your strengths and achievements. And when you talk about your work experience, start with your most recent job.

Andrea: Do I need to include a picture?

David: In England, a CV does not have a picture, but you can have one if you like. What is important is that you include the name and contact details of two references. These could be a supervisor or maybe a teacher.

Andrea: OK, great. Anything else?

David: Yeah, make sure that everything you write in your CV is the truth. If you are asked to explain something during the interview and you can't, then it could be pretty embarrassing. Be confident and sell yourself, but don't lie. Er ... once you have finished the CV, read through it and check the spelling and the grammar. The best thing to do is to give it to a friend. And, when you send it, keep a copy for yourself to read before the interview.

Andrea: Thanks a lot for the advice, David. I'm really grateful.

David: Don't mention it, Andrea. Let me know if there is anything else I can do.

Andrea: Well ... you did say somebody should read over it and check everything – and who'd be better than a native speaker ...?

⦾ A 2.17 Module 6 Engineering materials, B 3, 4

Darren: Hello Herr Zimmermann.

Sebastian: Hello Darren.

Darren: Oh, do you remember Bill Lewis? He was here in March. I've just got an email from him.

Sebastian: Yes, I remember Bill very well. How is he doing?

Darren: He's fine. College is very busy. He's making a machine vice at the moment.

Sebastian: That's funny. We had the same task last month. What materials is he going to use?

Darren: He wants to use mild steel for the clamping jaws.

Sebastian: Good idea. That should be hard enough to clamp the components while they are machined.

Darren: The vice will be rigid then, too. Aluminium or a metal like that would be too light. It couldn't hold the workpiece securely during drilling and boring processes.

Sebastian: That's true. What about the control spindle? Is Bill going to use the same kind of steel for that?

Darren: Yes, mild steel is hard enough. The metal in the control spindle has to be malleable as well as Bill has to machine a thread in the spindle.

Sebastian: So how is he going to cut a thread in the spindle?

Darren: Bill wants to use a threading tool made of tungsten carbide steel. That's definitely hard enough to cut a good thread in a spindle made of mild steel.

Sebastian: Problem solved then!

◎ A 1.5 Module F Socialising, A 1

Fabian: Hi, I'm Fabian.

Jan: Hello Fabian, my name's Jan. I'm with the group from Warsaw, Poland.

Fabian: Welcome to our company. Is this your first visit to Germany?

Jan: Actually, I've been here before. But my German isn't very good.

Fabian: Don't worry, we can talk in English. I should really practice more anyway. How was your trip? Was it a long journey?

Jan: No, not really. We took the plane from Warsaw to Stuttgart. Then someone from your company met us at the airport.

Fabian: Jan, would you like something to drink: coffee, juice, lemonade?

Jan: Sure, a lemonade would be good.

Fabian: OK, let's go to our canteen and sit down for a while.

Fabian: Here we go; I hope it's cold enough.

Jan: Thanks. So, I guess that you are also a trainee. What year are you in?

Fabian: I'm in my third year. What about you?

Jan: I've just started. How many trainees are there in your company?

Fabian: Er ... about ten, I think.

Jan: That's quite a lot. There are only three trainees in our company, all in metal engineering. I think your company is much bigger than ours.

Fabian: Yeah, we even have our own football team. We don't play in a league; it's just for fun.

Jan: That sounds great! You should visit us in Poland one day. Maybe we could arrange a match.

Fabian: That's a good idea. Are you a football fan?

Jan: Yeah. I don't play myself, but I like to watch.

Fabian: Which team do you like?

Jan: Manchester United.

Fabian: Really? They're my favourite team, too! Well, apart from VFB Stuttgart, of course.

Jan: Do you live in Stuttgart?

Fabian: No, I live in a small town nearby. I have to take the bus every morning. But when the weather's good, I can take my motorbike.

Jan: Cool! Unfortunately I don't have a motorbike. I get a lift from a colleague who works in the same department as me.

Fabian: What do you do in your free time?

Jan: I like going to clubs, and sometimes I go fishing with my friends. What about you? Playing football, I suppose.

Fabian: Yeah, football and riding my motorbike.

◎ A 2.18 Module 7 Material testing, A 3, 4

Luke: Hello Nina, hi Carsten.

Nina: Hello Luke. How are you?

Luke: Fine thanks. I am just having some trouble writing up my notes about the properties of metals.

Nina: Yes, we were just talking about that. The details were confusing. Just think about steel. Of course it's hard, but I didn't know that it's tensile, too.

Carsten: And it's even elastic to a certain extent.

Luke: If you think about it, it makes sense to test the properties of a material before you use it for a specific purpose, doesn't it?

Nina: Yes, it does. If you want to build a bridge or an aeroplane, the metal you use needs good tensile strength.

Luke: Tensile strength is also an important property when you build cars. In a crash situation you don't want the metal in the car body to fail immediately.

Nina: Okay, so these potential forces are tested before the sheet steel is used in car production. That's the function of the tensile test.

Carsten: All materials including metals have a ductility limit. And the tensile test tells you how far a material can be stretched before the ductility limit is reached.

Luke: But how is the tensile test carried out?

Nina: Well, this is what I noted last week: You put two gauge marks on the specimen, one on either side of where it will break in the test. Then you get the original gauge length by measuring between the two marks.

Carsten: When do you put the specimen in the tester?

Luke: That's the next step, I think. Then you start the test. One end is pulled until the specimen breaks at the fracture point.

Nina: Yes, and before it breaks, the metal achieves the maximum stress.

Carsten: And after the specimen breaks, you measure the distance between the gauge marks again.

Nina: Well, modern testers are computerized so the computer measures the distance for you. It can work out the percentage of elongation of the metal specimen.

Luke: Now my notes make more sense. Thanks!

⊚ A 1.6 Module G Presentations, C 1

Good morning ladies and gentlemen. Today I would like to present our new range of wooden furniture, *Simply Wood*. The range, which is shown here on the first slide, includes chairs, a large table, a lounger, and benches. I would like to start by talking about the materials used in the furniture. All of the *Simply Wood* range is made from single softwood timber and has been hand-crafted by our highly-skilled carpenters and joiners. If you look at this picture, you can see that the benches and the seats are designed with a low back, deep seats and long arms to offer a great deal of comfort and convenience. Thanks to a special varnish, the furniture is 100 % weatherproof and will not suffer from discolouring. As you can see from this final slide, the furniture is also available in white, to give it a classic, timeless look. And do not worry, we have used a durable, white polyurethane coating that is suitable for every environment. On your handout you will see more details about each piece, including measurements. Thank you for your attention this morning. Are there any questions? Yes …

⊚ A 2.19 Module 8 Measuring and gauging, A 3, 4

Claus: Hi, Sharon. Am I glad to see you. Could you help me for a minute?

Sharon: Hello, Claus. What's the problem?

Claus: I've got to measure this piece of tube and I can't find a suitable measuring instrument.

Sharon: Which parts of the tube do you want to measure, the length or the thickness?

Claus: Oh, sorry for not mentioning it. I'd like to check the internal and external diameters of the tube.

Sharon: Okay. And what about the internal thread?

Claus: Let me see. No, I'm lucky, the worksheet doesn't say anything about gauging the thread. Oh but it says I have to measure the length of the tube, too.

Sharon: Well, in that case I suggest you use a vernier calliper. It's ideal for the job. It has a pair of fixed measuring jaws and a pair of movable measuring jaws.

Claus: Yes, I remember now. You can measure the width or thickness of a component with the jaws for external measurement.

Sharon: Or you can measure the diameter of a round workpiece such as your tube.

Claus: You're right. And the other pair of jaws is used for internal measurement, isn't it?

Sharon: Yes, they can be used to measure the inside diameter of your tube.

Claus: What about this third part of the instrument?

Sharon: I can't remember what it's called. It's useful for measuring the depth of hollow objects.

Claus: How do I fix the movable jaws so that I can read the measure on the scale?

Sharon: That's easy, just turn the clamp screw at the bottom of the movable external jaw.

Claus: Alright, let me see. The reading for the external diameter is, 54.6 mm, no, sorry it's 54.2 mm.

Sharon: Can I do the internal diameter? Okay, the main scale and nonius say it is 50.2 mm.

Claus: Now for the length of the tube. It's exactly 6 cm long.

Sharon: Let me check. Sorry, it's longer. It's 6.01 cm.

Claus: Oh, you're right. Thanks for your help, Sharon.

⊚ A 1.7 Module H Dealing with customers, A 4

Answering machine: *Guten Tag. Sie sind mit Stefan Bauder verbunden. Leider bin ich im Moment nicht erreichbar. Bitte hinterlassen Sie eine Nachricht nach dem Ton. Danke!*

Brian: Hello Mr Bauder, this is Brian Jenkins calling from New Wave Marketing in Hamburg. I am calling about the new IT network that your technicians set up last week. Unfortunately, we have been experiencing some problems. Since your technicians were here, some employees have had difficulty connecting to the Internet, and others have no access to our network at all and cannot even log on to their computers! However, the worst thing is that some important files and documents seem to have been lost as a result of the migration to the new software. One of these files was a presentation for a very important client. This is a particular problem for us because we have a meeting with this client on Monday, and we need the presentation and do not have enough time to redo it. Could you please look into this problem for us urgently as time is running out? If we do not hear from you by the end of today, we will have to look elsewhere. I will be in meetings this afternoon, but you can contact me per email under B dot Jenkins at NWM…de. Thank you.

⊚ A 2.20 Module 9 Joining and assembly, C 2, 3

Stefan Hinz: We've learnt a lot about different joining and assembling methods. Today we want to fold a seam on two pieces of sheet metal. You probably remember what to do first before we start, don't you?

Harry: I think so. First we scribe the lines for the edges based on the drawing.

Stefan Hinz: That's right. Timo, please clamp the first sheet in the bench vice. Thank you. Now we can follow the marker line to make the seam. Next let's tap the edge to a 90 degree angle on this side first.

Harry: Mr Hinz, is it okay if I do the same with the other sheet?

Stefan Hinz: Yes, of course. Now we carefully bend the edges by nearly 180 degrees.

Harry: Can I do this with some pliers?

Stefan Hinz: Well, we don't want to scratch the sheet so a rubber mallet would be better.

Timo: How do we fit the sheets?

Stefan Hinz: We hook the edges together and tap them down.

Timo: Okay. Would you like me to do that?

Stefan Hinz: That's a good idea, go ahead.

⊚ A 2.21 Module 10 Welding and soldering, A 1, 2

Amélie: You know, I haven't done any welding yet in my training programme. I have no idea how all the welding equipment works.

Oli: No, me neither. Can you start from the beginning, Herr Staiger?

Mr Staiger: Well, it's difficult to explain welding in a short time. We will start with the equipment today. Does anyone know what this welding gear is called? Bernd?

Bernd: I don't know the word in English.

Mr Staiger: This is oxyacetylene welding gear. Both oxygen and acetylene are used in the welding process.

Oli: The red cylinder contains oxygen. That's mixed with acetylene from the grey cylinder to increase the temperature of the flame. That part on top of each cylinder is a valve and beside it is the regulator with two gauges for each cylinder.

Bernd: Yes, one gauge is for the pressure in the cylinder and the other is for the working pressure of the torch.

Mr Staiger: That's right. The flame comes here out of the torch. You adjust the flame to reach the right temperature. Sometimes you need it to be more than 3,000 degrees Celsius.

Amélie: Can we try out the gear?

Mr Staiger: Of course, that's why we're here. Bernd and Oli, would you please get the flip-front helmets over there? We'll need them in a minute.

Amélie: Sorry, Herr Staiger. I have a question. Is electric arc welding gear similar to gas welding gear?

Mr Staiger: We'll try out the arc welding gear next week but to answer your question, no, we need different equipment for electric arc welding.

Bernd: What's the difference?

Mr Staiger: Well, look at the arc welding equipment here.

Amélie: I see. It runs on electric power. It looks rather small, doesn't it?

Oli: Yes, it's easy to carry so it can be used in different places to weld thin metals such as car body parts.

Mr Staiger: That's right, Oli. Here you see the contact tips and the ground clamp. The clamp is clamped to the material while you are welding.

Bernd: And what are these buttons on the power station?

Mr Staiger: One button controls the wire speed and the other button sets four different heat positions.

Oli: Sounds interesting. I'm looking forward to hearing more about it next week.

A 2.22 Module 11 CAD-CAM and CNC, A 1, 2

Interviewer: Mr Taylor, why has CAD technology become so important?

Mr Taylor: Well, before the introduction of CAD technology, engineers had to build prototypes or models of a product they wanted to manufacture later on. Development took a long time especially if you didn't get the prototype right the first time. We can now use computer simulations or design three-dimensional digital mock-ups to determine the loads and stresses a material can bear before breaking, for example.

Interviewer: In what other ways has CAD changed development in industry?

Mr Taylor: Well, with the implementation of CAD, development costs have also been reduced enormously.

Interviewer: You mentioned 'mock-ups' just now. Could you explain what is meant by a mock-up?

Mr Taylor: Of course. A digital mock-up is a model that you design on your computer monitor with CAD. The model has got all of the simulated functions of a prototype.

Interviewer: I see. Where does CAM come in then?

Mr Taylor: CAM is computer aided manufacturing. Nowadays a single computer with a CAM system can control many robotic machine tools, such as milling machines, lathes and welding machines, on the factory floor.

Interviewer: That must make production easier to monitor.

Mr Taylor: Yes, it does. You can alter a set program and implement changes in design quickly and easily. You don't have to reprogram each robot individually, which would greatly increase production times.

Interviewer: Thank you very much for taking the time to talk to me, Mr Taylor.

Mr Taylor: No problem, thank you.

A 2.23 Module 12 Maintenance and troubleshooting, A 2, 3

Lukas: What's the problem, Chris? Are you having trouble with the machine?

Chris: Hi Lukas. Yes, it won't start for me, and I don't know why.

Lukas: Did you check whether the main switch is on or off?

Chris: Yes, that's the first thing I checked, and then the safety button.

Lukas: Well, let's see. Look here, Chris. The safety button is still locked in. To release it, you must turn it a bit to the right and then pull it out. Okay?

Chris: Oops, thank you. I thought I had checked it properly. Could you please check whether I've set the machine correctly?

Lukas: Well, the cutter is clamped properly in the toolpost, and the material is nice and tight in the three-jaw chuck. What is the revolution speed of the main spindle?

Chris: Well, as the material I'm using is mild steel, I set the speed to 2,500 revolutions per minute.

Lukas: OK. Is that the speed in the table on the front of the machine gear box?

Chris: Yes, it is. I remembered to check that.

Lukas: Did you remember to set the feed of the cutter so that the material isn't cut with too much stress?

Chris: Oh no. I didn't think of that. I'll check that in a minute. I set the rotation of the spindle for longitudinal turning so that it is clockwise. Is that right?

Lukas: Yes, it is. That's all. Once you've set the feed of the cutter, the machine should work OK. If you have any more problems, just come over to the milling shop as I'm working there today.

Chris: Great, I will. And thanks again!

Grammar overview

Present Tense (Gegenwart)

Bildung: Present Tense (simple)		
Merke: Bei der 3. Person Einzahl *(he / she / it)* wird ein *s* an die Endung des Verbs angehängt.	I like / you like / he (she / it) likes we like / you like / they like	computer games.

Verwendung: Present Tense (simple)	
– bei allgemein bekannten Tatsachen und Aussagen	– Most cars run on petrol.
– bei regelmäßigen Handlungen: Schlüsselwörter: *usually, normally, always, never, sometimes, often …*	– I usually start work at 7 o'clock.
– bei Gewohnheiten	– He doesn't smoke.
– bei Fahrplänen, Öffnungszeiten etc. für die Zukunft	– My train leaves at 10 o'clock tomorrow morning.

Bildung: Present Tense (progressive)		
am / are / is + Infinitiv mit Endung *-ing*	I **am** / you **are** / he / she / it / **is** we **are** / you **are** / they **are**	work**ing** on a new project.

Verwendung: Present Tense (progressive)	
– bei Handlungen im Augenblick des Sprechens	– I am reading a manual at the moment.
– bei vorübergehenden Handlungen	– I'm staying at the Royal Excelsior Hotel.
– bei (fest) geplanten Handlungen in der Zukunft	– I'm meeting Ms Winter next week.
– bei gefühlsbetonten Aussagen mit *always* (negativ besetzt)	– He is always complaining about his boss.

Past Tense (Vergangenheit)

Bildung: Past Simple	
ed-Endung bei regelmäßigen Verben	I work**ed** in Munich last year.
2. Form bei unregelmäßigen Verben *(1. meet / **2. met** / 3. met)*	He **met** Mr Miller yesterday.

Verwendung: Past Simple		
bei Vorgängen, die in der Vergangenheit abgeschlossen wurden; oft mit Zeitangabe. Signalwörter u. a.: *yesterday, in (1990), two weeks ago, last year, last month, last week.*	I finished my studies	in 2008. 3 years ago. last week.

Present Perfect (Vollendete Gegenwart)

Bildung: Present Perfect (simple)		
have oder *has* + *ed*-Endung (bei regelmäßigen Verben)	I / you / we / they **have** work**ed** He / she **has** work**ed**	as a trainee.
	It **has** work**ed** well for us.	
3. Form bei unregelmäßigen Verben *(1. see / 2. saw / **3. seen**)*	I have **seen** the new car.	

Bildung: Present Perfect (progressive)			
have / has + *been* + Infinitiv mit *-ing*	I / you / we / they He / she	**have** **has**	**been** living in Munich for 5 years.

Verwendung: Present Perfect (simple and progressive)	
– bei Handlungen in der Vergangenheit **ohne Zeitangabe**	– I have written three letters.
– bei noch andauernden Zeitbestimmungen	– We haven't had any complaints so far / today …
– bei Handlungen, die in der Vergangenheit begonnen haben, aber noch nicht abgeschlossen sind, wobei ***for*** bei Zeiträumen *(two hours / three weeks)* und ***since*** bei Zeitpunkten *(2001 / January)* benutzt wird	– I have been living in Stuttgart **for** 20 years. – I have been living in Stuttgart **since** 1982.
– Einige Verben werden in der Regel nicht in der Verlaufsform verwendet.	– I have **had** the car for five years. – I have **known** the company since 2010.

Future (Zukunft)

Bildung und Verwendung	
Shall / will drückt äußere Umstände aus.	Most of this year's teleworking jobs **will** be offered in autumn.
Will drückt die Bereitschaft oder Entschlossenheit aus, etwas zu tun, sowie Versprechungen. ***Will*** wird auch benutzt für eine spontane Entscheidung.	I'**ll** do my best to get the job. Wait a minute, I'**ll** help you!
Going to wird verwendet, um persönliche Planungen und Vorhaben auszudrücken. ***Going to*** wird auch verwendet, wenn bereits Anzeichen dafür da sind, dass etwas eintreten wird.	I **am going to** apply for a job in teleworking. *(Ich habe vor…)* Look at those clouds! It'**s going to** rain.
Present continuous wird verwendet um eine feste Vereinbarung (gewöhnlich mit Zeitangabe) mitzuteilen.	Jennifer is **meeting** her colleague this evening.
Present simple wird für die Zukuft verwendet in Verbindung mit Fahrplänen, Öffnungszeiten usw.	Jim's train **arrives** at 4.30 p.m. Our office **opens** at 9 o'clock tomorrow morning.

Comparison of adjectives (Steigerung des Adjektivs)

Bildung	
Einsilbige und zweisilbige Adjektive werden durch Anhängen von *-er* und *-est* (germanische Steigerung) gesteigert.	fast – faster – fastest
Aus **y** wird ***i***.	easy – easier – easiest
Ein einzelner Endkonsonant wird nach einfachem betonten Vokal verdoppelt.	hot – hotter – hottest
Für die zweisilbigen gibt es keine eindeutigen Regeln. Gewöhnlich werden zweisilbige Adjektive, die auf *-y, -le, -er* oder *-ow* enden germanisch gesteigert, aber dies ist keine bindende Regel.	clever – cleverer – cleverest noble – nobler – noblest narrow – narrower – narrowest
Ebenfalls germanisch gesteigert werden zweisilbige Adjektive, wenn sie ihre Betonung auf der zweiten Silbe haben. Auch diese Regel ist nicht bindend. Daneben gibt es aber z. B. auch folgende Formen: *more / the most clever* oder *more / the most polite.*	polite – politer – politest sincere – sincerer – sincerest
Andere zweisilbige Adjektive werden in der Regel romanisch gesteigert.	nervous – more nervous – most nervous splendid – more splendid – most splendid
Alle drei- und mehrsilbigen Adjektive steigert man mit ***more*** und ***the most*** (romanische Steigerung).	expensive – more expensive – the most expensive beautiful – more beautiful – the most beautiful
Es gibt auch eine Reihe von unregelmäßigen Adjektiven.	good – better – the best bad – worse – the worst much / many – more – the most little – less – the least old – elder – the eldest (bei Familienangehörigen)

Verwendung	
Gleichheiten mit *as … as*	He is **as** skilful **as** I. (so geschickt / fachmännisch wie ich)
Komparative mit *than*	Mike is **less** helpful **than** Tim. (weniger … als)
Je … desto…	**The** more I work with this machine **the** better I like it.
Superlativ beim Vergleich von mehr als 2 Objekten	The new electric drill is **the most** expensive tool in the brochure.

Adverbs (Adverbien)

Das Umstandswort (Adverb) dient zur näheren Beschreibung eines Eigenschaftswortes (Adjektives) oder eines Zeitwortes (Verbs).

Bildung	
Von der Wortbildung her unterscheidet man zwei Arten von Adverbien:	
1. ursprüngliche und durch Zusammensetzung gebildete Adverbien	often, quite, here, soon always, already, yesterday
2. durch Ableitung gebildete Abverbien: Hier wird an das Adjektiv ein *-ly* angehängt.	clear**ly**, usual**ly**, quick**ly**, easi**ly**, bad**ly**
Manche Adjektive und Adverbien sind	
– gleichlautend oder	daily, weekly, monthly, yearly, early, fast
– unterschiedlich.	good – **well**
Die Steigerung des Adverbs ist der Steigerung des Adjektivs vergleichbar.	carefully – more carefully – most carefully fast – faster – the fastest
Unregelmäßige Formen der Steigerung	well – better – best badly – worse – worst
y wird zu ***i***	happy + -ly = happily
stummes *e* fällt weg	true + -ly = truly
Verdoppelung des Endkonsonanten	beautiful + -ly = beautiful**l**y

Verwendung	
Hier wird das Verb näher beschrieben.	The new machine **works well**.
Hier wird das Adjektiv *clear* näher beschrieben.	The small printer makes **remarkably clear** printouts.
Hier wird ein anderes Adverb *(quickly)* näher beschrieben.	Our new machine works **extremely quickly**.

Questions (Fragen)

Bildung: Alternative questions (Entscheidungsfragen)	
Entscheidungsfragen, die mit ja oder nein beantwortet werden können, werden im Englischen immer mit einem Hilfsverb oder einer Form von *to do* eingeleitet.	**Do** you smoke? **Did** you see Mr Miller yesterday?
Erstes Hilfsverb steht vor dem Subjekt.	**Have** you met Mr Miller?

Verwendung: Alternative questions (Entscheidungsfragen)	
Does Sally speak French?	Yes, she **does.** / No, she **doesn't.**
Can these tools be used in milling as well as in turning?	Yes, they **can.** / No, they **can't.**
Is the lathe set properly for this job?	Yes, it **is.** / No, it **isn't.**
Did he meet the chief executive at the fair?	Yes, he **did.** / No, he **didn't.**
Will you finish this job by Friday?	Yes, I **will.** / No, I **won't.**

Bildung: Questions with interrogatives (Fragen mit Fragefürwörtern)	
Die Fragen werden mit dem Fragefürwort eingeleitet. Vor dem Subjekt steht die Form von *to do (do / does; did)*, nach dem Subjekt steht das Vollverb im Infinitiv.	**How** do you **go** to work? **What** does she **do**?
Wird nach dem Subjekt oder einem Teil des Subjekts gefragt *(who, what, which, whose)*, so wird die Form von 'to do' nicht verwendet.	**What** is his job?

Verwendung: Questions with interrogatives (Fragen mit Fragefürwörtern)	
Fragewort ist Subjekt.	Who operates this machine? Which tools do you need for this job?
Fragewort ist nicht Subjekt.	Who / Whom did he meet at the exhibition? Which tool have you chosen for this job?

Word order (Wortstellung)

Bildung	
Die Wortstellung folgt im englischen Aussagesatz der Regel S – P – O: *Subject [They] – Predicate [have repaired] – Object [the broken tools]*	They have repaired the broken tools.
Dies gilt auch im Nebensatz (im Deutschen steht ja im Nebensatz das Prädikat am Ende).	I was told that they had repaired the broken tools.
Zeitbestimmungen stehen in der Regel entweder am Anfang oder am Ende des Satzes.	Yesterday they repaired the broken tools. They repaired the broken tools a week ago.
Mehrere Umstandsbestimmungen folgen gewöhnlich folgender Reihenfolge: *Manner – Place – Time* (Art und Weise – Ort – Zeit)	The mechanic repaired the tools in the shop yesterday. The mechanic repaired the tools quite skilfully in the shop last night.
Adverbien der Häufigkeit *(frequency)* können auch vor dem Hauptverb stehen: *always, ever, never, often, regularly, generally, rarely, seldom, occasionally.* Diese Adverbien stehen aber nach dem Verb *to be.* Bei Hilfsverben stehen die Adverbien der Häufigkeit zwischen dem Hilfsverb und dem Vollverb, bzw. nach dem Hilfsverb.	The service people **always** come on time. The service people **never** come without calling ahead. The service people **usually** check the machine in May. They are **generally** very reliable. The machine has **sometimes** had problems. With old machines you can **never** tell.

Defining relative clauses (Notwendige Relativsätze)

Ein Relativsatz ist notwendig, wenn die darin gegebene Information nötig ist, um deutlich zu machen, welche Person oder Sache gemeint ist.

Verwendung	
bei Personen ***who*** oder ***that***	The man **who / that** is operating the CNC machine usually works at the training centre.
bei Sachen ***which*** oder ***that***	The machine element **which / that** is moving the tool is the main spindle.
im Genitiv wird **whose** verwendet	Tom is an engineer **whose** skills are highly praised.
Das Relativpronomen als Satzobjekt kann weggelassen werden.	They called the technician (**who**) they saw standing at the milling machine. Sally read the operation plan (**which**) she had filled in this morning.

Non-defining relative clauses (Nicht notwendige Relativsätze)

Ein Relativsatz ist nicht notwendig, wenn die darin gegebene Information nicht nötig ist, um deutlich zu machen, welche Person oder Sache gemeint ist.

Verwendung	
Ein Relativsatz ist nicht notwendig, wenn die darin enthaltene Information nicht nötig ist, um zu erkennen, welche Person oder Sache gemeint ist.	**Sally's friend**, who is a skilled worker, **is doing his final exams this summer**. **The machine**, which is DEG's latest model, **works perfectly**.
Relativpronomen als Satzobjekt	**The three German apprentices**, who Sally met at the training centre, **are in their last year of training.**

Reported speech (Indirekte Rede)

Die indirekte Rede wird benutzt, wenn berichtet wird oder wurde, was jemand sagt oder sagte, bzw. macht oder machte (**Aussage**), wenn jemandem gesagt wird oder wurde, was geschehen soll (**Aufforderung**), oder wenn gefragt wird oder wurde, was geschieht oder geschah (**Frage**).

Bildung / Verwendung	
Steht das Wort, welches die indirekte Rede einleitet, in der Gegenwart, so ändern sich die Zeitformen der direkten Rede nicht.	"We **are measuring** this machined component." → Sally explains that they are measuring the machined component.
Steht das Wort, welches die indirekte Rede einleitet, in der Vergangenheit, so ändern sich die Zeitformen der direkten Rede wie folgt.	
Simple past und *present perfect* werden zu *past perfect.*	Sally **explained that they were measuring** the machined component. "The trainee **forgot** to set the revolution speed." → The master **noticed that the trainee had forgotten** to check the revolution speed.
Will wird zu *would.*	"The drilling operation **will** have to be prepared by marking out and centring." → Oliver **remembered** that the drilling operation **would** have to be prepared by marking out and centring.
Pronomen werden angepasst.	"**I can't** find the measuring equipment." → **Sally told** me that she **couldn't find** the measuring equipment.
Orts- und Zeitbestimmungen werden angepasst.	"**We** are seeing the other students **tomorrow**." → Oliver **added** that **they** were seeing the other students **the next day**. "I programmed the CNC machine **two days ago**." → He said that he had programmed the CNC machine **two days earlier**.
Aufforderungen werden in der indirekten Rede im Infinitiv wiedergegeben.	"**Use** HSS twist drills to drill metal stock." → The instructor **advised** Sally **to use** HSS twist drills to drill metal stock.
Bei Fragen wird die Wortstellung wie im Aussagesatz verwendet, d.h. am Anfang steht das Fragewort, dann folgen Subjekt, Prädikat und Objekt.	"Why has Oliver used the impact drilling function?" → The master **wanted to know why Oliver had used** the impact drilling function. "When did you sharpen the drill?" → He asked **when he had sharpened** the drill.
Die Umschreibung mit 'to do' wird nur bei Verneinungen angewendet.	"Why **don't** you call the salesman?" → She **asked** Sally why she **didn't call** the salesman.

Passive voice (Passiv)

Bildung	
Form von *to be* + *ed*-Endung (wie bei *simple past*) bei regelmäßigen Verben Form von *to be* + 3. Form bei unregelmäßigen Verben (*1. take / 2. took / 3.* ***taken***. Siehe Liste der unregelmäßigen Verben.)	The machine is equipp**ed** with an emergency stop. He **is taken** to hospital.

Aktiv:	We *Subjekt*	recharge *Prädikat*	the batteries. *Objekt*
Passiv:	*Subjekt* The batteries	*Prädikat* are recharged	*Objekt (by-agent)* (by us).

Formen	
Present Tense (Simple)	The goods are transported every day.
Present Tense (Progressive)	The goods are being transported at the moment.
Past Tense (Simple)	The goods were transported yesterday.
Past Tense (Progressive)	The goods were being transported when the truck crashed.
Future 1 (will)	The goods will be transported next Monday, I promise.
Future 1 (going to)	The goods are going to be transported next month.
Present Perfect	The goods have already been transported.
Past Perfect	The goods had been transported before the order arrived.

Verwendung	
Das Passiv wird hauptsächlich verwendet, wenn der Ausführende (*by-agent*) unwichtig oder unbekannt ist oder nicht genannt werden soll. Deshalb wird der *by-agent* nur bei besonderer Betonung genannt.	The batteries **are recharged** (**by us**) when they are empty. A few years ago the first cars **were equipped** with airbags (**by the manufacturers**).
Die Passivkonstruktion wird besonders bei technischen Beschreibungen, Anweisungen in Handbüchern usw. verwendet. Bei der Umwandlung von Aktiv in Passiv wird das Objekt des Aktivsatzes zum Subjekt des Passivsatzes.	Aktiv: We recharge **the batteries**. Passiv: **The batteries** are recharged (by us).
Im Gegensatz zum Deutschen können bestimmte Verben im Englischen im Passiv verwendet werden. Die Übersetzung ins Deutsche erfolgt durch eine Konstruktion mit 'man'.	The fuel cell is considered to be a very promising invention. *(Man hält die Brennstoffzelle für eine sehr zukunftsweisende Erfindung.)*
Die Verlaufsform ist im Passiv nur im *Present Tense* und *Past Tense* gebräuchlich.	He **is being** taken to hospital. *(Er wird gerade ins Krankenhaus gebracht.)* He **was being** taken to hospital. *(Er wurde gerade ins Krankenhaus gebracht.)*

Gerund (Gerundium)

Wie im Deutschen kann man auch im Englischen aus einem Verb ein Substantiv machen. Beispiel: Durch häufiges **Messen** können Fehler vermieden werden.

Bildung		
Anhängen von *-ing* an den Infinitiv (Grundform) des Verbs	check + ing = checking drill + ing = drilling	
Verdoppelung eines Endkonsonanten (Mitlaut) nach einem Vokal (Selbstlaut)	put – putting control – controlling	travel – travelling refuel – refuelling
Stummes *e* fällt weg: aber: *agree – agreeing; see – seeing*	file – filing measure – measuring	

Verwendung	
Ein *gerund* kann Subjekt (Satzgegenstand) sein. Ebenso kann es die Funktion eines Objekts (Satzergänzung) haben.	**Filing** is rarely done by hand. He began **cleaning** the machine.
Nach Präpositionen (Verhältniswörtern) oder präpositionalen Ausdrücken steht ebenfalls das *gerund*.	He was afraid of **setting** the lever to a higher speed. They objected **to trying** the new software **without having** made a backup of the hard drive. The manager apologised **for being** late. They prevented the visitors **from entering** the production area without a hard hat. He was tired **of hearing** the same complaint.
Nach bestimmten Verben (Zeitwörtern) steht das *gerund*.	Try to **avoid overheating** the machine. The trainer **recommended turning** the machine off. We cannot **risk losing** this customer. Phillip **suggested using** a different production method.
Weitere Verben, die ein *gerund* nach sich haben.	enjoy, like, dislike, remember, stop He enjoys working in Italy.

Prepositions (Verhältniswörter)

Präpositionen geben das Verhältnis von Personen oder Dingen zueinander an (z. B. räumlich oder zeitlich).

Räumliche Präpositionen			
above	oberhalb	**into**	in … hinein
across	durch, quer durch	**off**	von … herunter, von … weg
at	neben, bei	**on, upon**	auf
opposite	gegenüber		

Räumliche Präpositionen			
behind	hinter	**out, out of**	aus, heraus
below	unter, unterhalb	**through**	durch
beneath	unter, unterhalb	**to**	zu, nach, in Richtung auf
beside	neben	**towards**	auf … zu (Richtung)
between	zwischen	**under**	unter
in	in	**within**	innerhalb

Zeitliche Präpositionen			
at	an, in	**from**	von
before	vor	**in**	am, im (Jahre)
between	zwischen	**on**	an, am
by	bis, bis spätestens	**since**	seit (Zeitpunkt)
during	während	**until, till**	bis
for	seit (Zeitraum)		

Modale Präpositionen und Präpositionen des Grundes			
according to	entsprechend, gemäß	**despite, in spite of**	trotz
because of	wegen	**with**	mit
besides	außer	**without**	ohne

Verwendung	
Laut Gebrauchsanweisung sollte **das Auswechseln** der Werkzeuge kein Problem darstellen.	**According to** the manual, there should be no problem **with** changing the tools.
… **hinten** im Raum … **unten** auf jeder Seite … **am** Eingang	The machine is **at** the back of the room. You'll find the number of the module **at** the bottom of every page. They were waiting **at** the entrance when it happened.
… ist **gegenüber / auf der anderen Seite** … rannte quer **über** die Straße	The printer is **across** the hall. The dog ran **across** the road.
… **zwischen** zwei Aktenmappen (räumlich) … **zwischen** 9 und 10 Uhr (zeitlich)	He found the letter **between** two folders. Why don't we meet **between** nine and ten?
… nur **während**	Smoking is allowed **during** the lunch break only!
… **von** … **bis**	He worked in Cardiff **from** December **until** January.
… **auf** der Straße	You should not park your car **in** the street.
… **bis** (spätestens)	You must be back **by** six o'clock at the latest.

Modal auxiliaries (Modale Hilfsverben)

Die modalen Hilfsverben werden im Englischen oft auch *defective* (d.h. unvollständige) *auxiliaries* genannt, denn sie können in der Regel nur das Präsens bilden. Für die übrigen Zeiten müssen Ersatzformen verwendet werden.

Bildung		
Hilfsverb	**Ersatzform**	**deutsche Bedeutung**
can	to be able to	können, fähig sein, in der Lage sein
can	to be allowed to	dürfen, die Erlaubnis haben
may	to be allowed to	dürfen, die Erlaubnis haben
must	to have to	müssen
mustn't	not to be allowed to	nicht dürfen
needn't	not to have to	nicht brauchen, nicht müssen

Verwendung	
Present Tense: You **must** read the installation instructions very carefully. After the installation is completed you **needn't reboot** your system.	**Simple past:** Yesterday he **had to** read the installation instructions twice because they were badly translated. I **didn't have to** reboot my system when I installed the screensaver the other day.
Present Tense: He **can** handle software problems quite well.	**Present perfect:** Up to now he **has been able** to handle software problems quite well.
Present Tense: You **must not smoke** in the office.	**Future:** You **will not be allowed** to smoke in the office.

Participles (Partizipien)

Bildung	
Present Participle Infinitiv + *-ing*	Wind turbines are a **promising** option.
Past Participle 3. Stammform: ***damaged*** (*ed*-Endung wie bei *simple past*); (3. Form bei unregelmäßigen Verben: *1. know/2. knew/**3. known***. Siehe Liste der unregelmäßigen Verben.)	After the storm we had to replace three **damaged** solar panels.

Verwendung	
als Adjektiv	It is a **known** fact that solar power can be used as an alternative energy.
Partizipialkonstruktionen dienen zur **Verkürzung** von:	
1. adverbialen Nebensätzen mit Konjunktion *(when, although, as, while,…)*	When **planning** to build a home, you should consider using solar energy to heat your water.
2. adverbialen Nebensätzen ohne Konjunktion	**Unlocking** the warehouse door, he smelled gas.
3. Relativsätzen	Wind farms **built** along the coast are most efficient.
Partizipialkonstruktionen zur **Verknüpfung** von zwei Hauptsätzen.	The guide led us through the factory. He warned us to stay away from the machines. The guide led us through the factory **warning** us to stay away from the machines.

If-clauses (Bedingungssätze)

Man unterscheidet drei Arten von Bedingungen:
1. erfüllbare Bedingungen
2. Bedingungen, deren Erfüllung unwahrscheinlich ist
3. Bedingungen, die überhaupt nicht mehr erfüllt werden können.

Zusätzlich zu den drei Typen gibt es noch einen weiteren Typ, der Regeln und Naturgesetze ausdrückt.

Bildung und Verwendung	
Type I (probable condition)	If you **lubricate** this machine regularly, it **will run** smoothly for a long time. *(Wenn man die Maschine regelmäßig ölt, läuft sie lange Zeit problemlos.)*
Type II (improbable condition)	If you **lubricated** this machine regularly, **it would** run smoothly for a long time. *(Wenn man diese Maschine regelmäßig ölen würde, würde sie für lange Zeit problemlos laufen.)*
Type III (impossible condition)	If you **had lubricated** this machine regularly, it **would have run** smoothly for a long time. *(Wenn man die Maschine regelmäßig geölt hätte, wäre sie lange Zeit problemlos gelaufen (jetzt läuft sie aber offensichtlich nicht mehr).*
Rules and laws of nature Hier handelt es sich im eigentlichen Sinne nicht mehr um eine Bedingung, sondern um ein Naturgesetz. Deshalb steht im Hauptsatz auch kein Futur, sondern ebenfalls das Präsens.	If you **heat** ice, it **melts**. *(Wenn man Eis erhitzt, schmilzt es.)*
Besonderheit bei Formen von *to be*	If I **were** you, I wouldn't use a combination spanner here.

Chronological word list

🌐 Videotraining: Englische Aussprache

Perfekte englische Aussprache leicht gemacht: Mit dem Lernprogramm zur englischen Lautschrift können Sie alle Laute einüben. Wählen Sie einfach in der Navigation rechts den entsprechenden Reiter (*Vowels* oder *Consonants*) aus und klicken Sie dann auf das gewünschte phonetische Symbol. Sprechen Sie die Wörter laut nach.

Unter www.klett.de geben Sie bitte den Code unter der Abbildung rechts ein.

🌐 n633sn

Abkürzungen und Zeichen

etw. = etwas
Pl. = Plural
jmdn., jmdm. = jemanden, jemandem
sb. = somebody
sth. = something
BE = britisches Englisch
AE = amerikanisches Englisch
◎ = Vokabeln zu den Hörtexten

Module 1 The general workshop

general workshop [ˌdʒənrl ˈwɜːkʃɒp] Grundwerkstatt
apprentice [əˈprentɪs] Auszubildende(r)
machine tool [məˈʃiːn ˌtuːl] Werkzeugmaschine
state-of-the-art [ˌsteɪt‿əv ðiˈɑːt] neuester, neueste, neuestes
to manufacture [ˌmænjəˈfæktʃə] herstellen, produzieren
mechanical engineering [mɪˌkænɪkl‿endʒɪˈnɪərɪŋ] Maschinenbau
skill [skɪl] Fähigkeit, Fertigkeit
hand tool [ˈhænd ˌtuːl] Handwerkzeug
work bench [ˈwɜːk ˌbenʃ] Werkbank
bench vice [ˈbenʃ ˌvaɪs] Bankschraubstock
column drill [ˈkɒləm ˌdrɪl] Ständerbohrmaschine
to operate [ˈɒpreɪt] bearbeiten
centre lathe [ˈsentə ˌleɪð] Drehbank, Drehmaschine
milling machine [ˈmɪlɪŋ məˌʃiːn] Fräsmaschine

A | A visit to a machine-tool company

chief executive [ˌtʃiːf‿ɪgˈzekjətɪv] geschäftsführender Direktor
shop floor [ˌʃɒp ˈflɔː] Fabrikhalle, Produktionshalle
well-equipped [ˌwelɪˈkwɪpt] gut ausgestattet
CNC (computerized numerical control) [ˌsiːenˈsiː kəmˌpjuːtraɪzd njuːˌmerɪkl kənˈtrəʊl] computergesteuert
advanced [ədˈvɑːnst] fortgeschritten

◎
skilled worker [ˌskɪld ˈwɜːkə] Facharbeiter(in)
plaster [ˈplɑːstə] Pflaster
first-aid kit [ˌfɜːstˈeɪd ˌkɪt] Erste-Hilfe-Kasten

to receive [rɪˈsiːv] erhalten
sophisticated [səˈfɪstɪkeɪtɪd] hochentwickelt, anspruchsvoll
in relation to [ɪn rɪˈleɪʃn tə] im Verhältnis zu
to draw [drɔː] zeichnen
to label [ˈleɪbl] benennen, bezeichnen

B | Protective clothing in the workshop

protective [prə'tektɪv] Schutz-
to damage ['dæmɪdʒ] beschädigen
to injure ['ɪndʒə] verletzen
machinist [mə'ʃi:nɪst] Maschinist(in), Maschinenarbeiter(in)
safety boots ['seɪfti ˌbu:ts] Arbeitsschuhe
goggles ['gɒglz] Schutzbrille
protection [prə'tekʃn] Schutz
helmet ['helmɪt] Helm
to avoid [ə'vɔɪd] vermeiden
accident ['æksɪdnt] Unfall
metal stock [ˌmetl 'stɒk] Metall-, Eisenmaterial
milling shop ['mɪlɪŋ ˌʃɒp] Fräserei
hole [həʊl] Loch
metal plate [ˌmetl 'pleɪt] Metallplatte
to grind [graɪnd] schleifen
surface ['sɜ:fɪs] Oberfläche
to weld [weld] schweißen
bar [bɑ:] (Metall-)Stange
hand shield ['hænd ˌʃi:ld] Schutzschild
gangway ['gæŋweɪ] Gang
necessary ['nesəsri] notwendig, nötig
design [dɪ'zaɪn] Konstruktion

C | Safety signs in the workshop

safety sign ['seɪfti ˌsaɪn] Sicherheitsschild, -hinweis
emergency [ɪ'mɜ:dʒnsi] Notfall
high voltage [ˌhaɪ 'vəʊltɪdʒ] Hochspannung, Starkstrom
toxic ['tɒksɪk] giftig

Module A Meeting people

confident ['kɒnfɪdənt] sicher, selbstbewusst
appropriate [ə'prəʊpriət] angemessen, passend

A | Saying "hello" and "goodbye" and giving your name

existing [ɪg'zɪstɪŋ] bestehend
trade fair ['treɪd ˌfeə] Messe
job fair ['dʒɒb ˌfeə] Jobmesse

B | Intercultural awareness

politeness [pə'laɪtnəs] Höflichkeit
pleasantry ['plezntri] höfliche Floskel
profitability [ˌprɒfɪtəbɪləti] Rentabilität
to chat [tʃæt] sich unterhalten
health [helθ] Gesundheit
pleasant ['pleznt] angenehm
to waste time [ˌweɪst 'taɪm] Zeit verschwenden
impression [ɪm'preʃn] Eindruck
conference ['kɒnfrəns] Tagung
minutes ['mɪnɪts] Protokoll
polite [pə'laɪt] höflich
usual ['ju:ʒl] gewöhnlich, üblich, normal
upset [ʌp'set] verärgert
stranger ['streɪndʒə] Unbekannte(r)
on the other hand [ɒn ði‿'ʌðə ˌhænd] andererseits
in charge of [ɪn 'tʃɑ:dʒ‿əv] verantwortlich für
cash register ['kæʃ ˌredʒɪstə] Kasse
given name [ˌgɪvn 'neɪm] Vorname
family name [ˌfæmli 'neɪm] Nachname
to intend [ɪn'tend] beabsichtigen

Module 2 Hand and power tools

power tool ['paʊə ˌtu:l] Elektrowerkzeug
hammer ['hæmə] Hammer
screwdriver ['skru:ˌdraɪvə] Schraubendreher
pliers ['plaɪəz] Zange
DIY-enthusiast [ˌdi:aɪwaɪ‿ɪn'θju:ziæst] Heimwerker(in)
toolbox ['tu:lbɒks] Werkzeugkasten
vernier calliper [ˌvɜ:nɪə 'kælɪpə] Messschieber, Schieblehre
spanner ['spænə] Schraubenschlüssel
bit [bɪt] -aufsatz, Bit
hacksaw ['hæksɔ:] Bügelsäge
riveting tongs ['rɪvɪtɪŋ ˌtɒŋz] Nietenzange
file [faɪl] Feile
steel brush [ˌsti:l 'brʌʃ] Stahlbürste
round nose pliers [ˌraʊndnəʊz 'plaɪəz] Kneifzange, Rundzange
vice [vaɪs] Schraubstock
Allen key ['ælən ˌki:] Inbusschlüssel, Innensechskantschlüssel
adjustable wrench [əˌdʒʌstəbl 'renʃ] verstellbarer Schraubenschlüssel, Engländer
square [skweə] Winkel

A | Discussing hand tools

manual ['mænjuəl] Hand-
to bend [bend] biegen
wire [waɪə] Draht

to clamp [klæmp] klemmen, einspannen
to debur [ˌdi:'bɜ:] entgraten
edge [edʒ] Kante
to join [dʒɔɪn] fügen, verbinden
to bore [bɔ:] bohren (ins Volle)
to screw [skru:] schrauben
to tighten ['taɪtn] fest-, anziehen
to loosen ['lu:sn] lösen
to drill [drɪl] aufbohren
to drive [draɪv] treiben, hinein-
to counter ['kaʊntə] kontern
hole [həʊl] Loch
bench vice ['benʃ ˌvaɪs] Schraubstock
hexagonal head bolt [hekˌsægnl 'hed ˌbəʊlt] Innensechskant-Schraubenbolzen
nut [nʌt] Schraubenmutter
metal bar [ˌmetl 'bɑ:] Eisenstange
bolt [bəʊlt] Bolzen, Schraubenbolzen
tin sheet [ˌtɪn 'ʃi:t] Metallblech
bubble ['bʌbl] Blase
to damage ['dæmɪdʒ] beschädigen

B | Power tools

electric power [ɪˌlektrɪk 'paʊə] (elektrischer) Strom
socket ['sɒkɪt] Steckdose
cordless ['kɔ:dləs] schnurlos
light-duty drill [ˌlaɪtdju:ti 'drɪl] Leichtbohrer
impact drill ['ɪmpækt ˌdrɪl] Schlagbohrer
angle grinder ['æŋgl ˌgraɪndə] Winkelschleifer
jigsaw ['dʒɪgsɔ:] Stichsäge
sander ['sændə] Schleifer, Schleifmaschine
concrete ['kɒŋkri:t] Beton
accessory [ək'sesri] Zubehör
to mount [maʊnt] montieren
nut [nʌt] Mutter, Schraubenmutter
assembly [ə'sembli] Versammlung
to improve [ɪm'pru:v] verbessern
instructor [ɪn'strʌktə] Ausbilder(in)

C | Sales talk

sales talk ['seɪlz ˌtɔ:k] Verkaufsgespräch
LI, Lithium ['lɪθiəm] Lithium
pneumatic [nju:'mætɪk] pneumatisch
hammer mechanism ['hæmə ˌmekənɪzm] Schlag-mechanismus
angle gear ['æŋgl ˌgɪə] Umlenkgetriebe
toolfitter ['tu:lˌfɪtə] Werkzeugaufnahme
insulated ['ɪnsjəleɪtɪd] isoliert
gearbox ['gɪəbɒks] Getriebegehäuse
battery cartridge ['bætri ˌkɑ:trɪdʒ] Batterieladegerät
diameter [daɪ'æmɪtə] Durchmesser
to recommend [ˌrekə'mend] empfehlen

reversible [rɪ'vɜ:səbl] mit Rechts-Linkslauf
driver drill ['draɪvə ˌdrɪl] Bohrschrauber
feature ['fi:tʃə] Funktion
torque [tɔ:rk] Drehmoment
chuck [tʃʌk] Spannfutter
to dispose [dɪ'spəʊz] entsorgen
to charge [tʃɑ:dʒ] (auf-)laden
charger ['tʃɑ:dʒə] Ladegerät
auto shut-off [ˌɔ:təʊ 'ʃʌtɒf] automatischer Abschalter
to lock out [ˌlɒk‿'aʊt] abschalten
compartment [kəm'pɑ:tmənt] Fach

Module B Your company

regardless of [rɪ'gɑ:dləs‿əv] ungeachtet, unabhängig von
furniture ['fɜ:nɪtʃə] Möbel
likely ['laɪkli] wahrscheinlich
supplier [sə'plaɪə] Lieferant
skill [skɪl] Fähigkeit, Fertigkeit
to express [ɪk'spres] zum Ausdruck bringen
grease [gri:s] Fett
ratchet ['rætʃɪt] Knarre
tool [tu:l] Werkzeug

A | The company and its departments

department [dɪ'pɑ:tmənt] Abteilung
to distribute [dɪ'strɪbju:t] vertreiben, verteilen
damaged ['dæmɪdʒd] beschädigt
employee [ɪm'plɔɪi:] Beschäftigte(r), Angestellte(r)
accounts [ə'kaʊnts] Buchhaltung
raw materials [ˌrɔ: mə'tɪəriəlz] Rohstoffe
human resources [ˌhju:mən 'ri:zɔ:sɪz] Personal-abteilung
to recruit [rɪ'kru:t] rekrutieren, anstellen
purchasing (department) ['pɜ:tʃəsɪŋ dɪˌpɑ:tmənt)] Einkauf(-sabteilung)
to maintain [meɪn'teɪn] warten, in Stand halten
R&D (Research and Development) [rɪˌsɜ:tʃ‿ən dɪ'veləpmənt] Forschungs- und Entwicklungsabteilung
to develop [dɪ'veləp] entwickeln
in charge of [ɪn 'tʃɑ:dʒ‿əv] zuständig für

to cover ['kʌvə] abdecken, bedecken
headquarters [ˌhed'kwɔ:təz] Hauptsitz
to found [faʊnd] gründen
family-owned [ˌfæmli'əʊnd] in Familienbesitz
manufacturing plant [ˌmænjə'fæktʃərɪŋ ˌplɑ:nt] Produktionsbetrieb
currently ['kʌrəntli] derzeit, zurzeit, momentan
braking system ['breɪkɪŋ ˌsɪstəm] Bremsanlage
internship (AE) ['ɪntɜ:rnʃɪp] Praktikum
device [dɪ'vaɪs] Gerät
cylinder head ['sɪlɪndə ˌhed] Zylinderkopf
to inspect [ɪn'spekt] prüfen
operating system ['ɒpəreɪtɪŋ ˌsɪstəm] Betriebssystem
interface ['ɪntəfeɪs] Schnittstelle, Interface

B | Tasks and responsibilities

task [tɑ:sk] Aufgabe
responsibility [rɪˌspɒnsə'bɪləti] Verantwortung
to manufacture [ˌmænjə'fæktʃə] herstellen
to occur [ə'kɜ:] vorkommen
apprenticeship [ə'prentɪsʃɪp] Ausbildung, Lehre
branch [brɑ:nʃ] Niederlassung
precision [prɪ'sɪʒn] Genauigkeit
essential [ɪ'senʃl] wesentlich, unbedingt erforderlich
to drill [drɪl] bohren
to shape [ʃeɪp] formen, fräsen
to polish ['pɒlɪʃ] abschleifen, polieren
to intervene [ˌɪntə'vi:n] einschreiten
to vibrate [vaɪ'breɪt] vibrieren
workpiece ['wɜ:kpi:s] Werkstück
to monitor ['mɒnɪtə] überwachen, kontrollieren, beobachten
to measure ['meʒə] messen
dimension [daɪ'menʃn] Maß, Abmessung
lubricated ['lu:brɪkeɪtɪd] geölt
lubricating oil ['lu:brɪkeɪtɪŋ‿ɔɪl] Schmieröl
generally ['dʒenrəli] normalerweise, im Allgemeinen
shift [ʃɪft] Schicht
to prefer [prɪ'fɜ:] bevorzugen
rarely ['reəli] selten
accuracy ['ækjərəsi] Genauigkeit
to include [ɪn'klu:d] einbeziehen, einschließen
to swap [swɒp] tauschen

C | Organisational structure

to employ [ɪm'plɔɪ] beschäftigen
to support [sə'pɔ:t] unterstützen
to split [splɪt] aufteilen
core area [ˌkɔ: 'eəriə] Kernbereich
to report to [rɪ'pɔ:t tu:] unterstehen
to belong to [bɪ'lɒŋ tu:] gehören zu
experienced [ɪk'spɪəriənst] erfahren
capable ['keɪpəbl] fähig
closely ['kləʊsli] eng

Module 3 Cutting processes with hand and power tools

cutting process ['kʌtɪŋ ˌprəʊses] spanabhebende Verfahren, Zerspanungsverfahren, -prozess
to involve [ɪn'vɒlv] mit sich bringen
to remove [rɪ'mu:v] entfernen
chip [tʃɪp] Span
swarf [swɔ:f] Span
file [faɪl] Feile
to require [rɪ'kwaɪə] erfordern
precision [prɪ'sɪʒn] Genauigkeit
machining job [mə'ʃi:nɪŋ ˌdʒɒb] maschinelle Bearbeitung
lathe [leɪð] Drehmaschine, Drehbank
roughly ['rʌfli] grob
hacksaw ['hæksɔ:] Bügelsäge
angle grinder ['æŋgl ˌgraɪndə] Winkelschleifer
power cutter ['paʊə ˌkʌtə] Trennschleifer
chipping process ['tʃɪpɪŋ ˌprəʊses] Zerspanungs-prozess

A | Cutting metal with hand tools

metal bar [ˌmetl 'bɑ:] Metallstab, -stange
base plate ['beɪs ˌpleɪt] Grundplatte
metal plate [ˌmetl 'pleɪt] Flachmaterial
angle ['æŋgl] Winkel
to debur [ˌdi:'bɜ:] entgraten
roughing file ['rʌfɪŋ ˌfaɪl] Schruppfeile
finishing file ['fɪnɪʃɪŋ ˌfaɪl] Schlichtfeile
square [skweə] Winkel (rechtwinkliges Messgerät)
scriber ['skraɪbə] Anreissnadel
to mark [mɑ:k] anreißen, markieren
diameter [daɪ'æmɪtə] Durchmesser
to centre punch [ˌsentə 'pʌnʃ] körnern
mark [mɑ:k] Markierung
centre punch ['sentə ˌpʌnʃ] Körner
to bore [bɔ:] (auf-)bohren, (in die Vollen) bohren
twist drill ['twɪst ˌdrɪl] Spiralbohrer

B | Cutting metal with power tools

garage ['gærɑ:ʒ] Autowerkstatt
circular saw [ˌsɜ:kjələ 'sɔ:] (Metall-)Kreissäge
building site ['bɪldɪŋ ˌsaɪt] Baustelle
approximate [əprɒksɪmət] ungefähr
vice [vaɪs] Schraubstock

to build [bɪld] herstellen, produzieren
steel bar [ˌsti:l 'bɑ:] Stahleisen, Stabstahl
storeroom ['stɔ:rʊm] Lager, Materiallager
to drive [draɪv] antreiben
to clamp [klæmp] einspannen
stock [stɒk] Material, Rohmaterial

goggles ['gɒglz] Schutzbrille(n)
accessory [ək'sesri] Zubehör
grinding disc ['graɪndɪŋ ˌdɪsk] Schleifscheibe
cutting-off job [ˌkʌtɪŋ'ɒf ˌdʒɒb] Trennschleifen
surface ['sɜ:fɪs] Oberfläche

C | An advertisement for hand tools and power tools

variety [və'raɪəti] Auswahl
second-cut file [ˌsekndkʌt 'faɪl] Doppelschlichtfeile
workpiece ['wɜ:kpi:s] Werkstück

Module C Telephoning

line [laɪn] *(hier:)* Branche
to fix [fɪks] reparieren
leak [li:k] undichte Stelle
to install [ɪn'stɔ:l] installieren, montieren, anschließen
complaint [kəm'pleɪnt] Beschwerde, Reklamation
order ['ɔ:də] Bestellung, Auftrag
necessary ['nesəsri] nötig, notwendig
delay [dɪ'leɪ] Verspätung, Verzögerung
breakdown ['breɪkdaʊn] Panne, Störung
solution [sə'lu:ʃn] Lösung
confused [kən'fju:zd] verwirrt
crash [kræʃ] Absturz

A | Making and receiving a phone call

meeting ['mi:tɪŋ] Sitzung, Besprechung
country code ['kʌntri ˌkəʊd] Ländervorwahl
area code ['eəriə ˌkəʊd] Vorwahl
extension number [ɪk'stenʃn ˌnʌmbə] Durchwahl
suitable ['su:təbl] geeignet, passend
polite [pə'laɪt] höflich
although [ɔ:l'ðəʊ] obwohl
to remain [rɪ'meɪn] bleiben
request [rɪ'kwest] Bitte
grateful ['greɪtfl] dankbar
whereas [weə'ræz] während
impolite [ˌɪmpə'laɪt] unhöflich

B | Giving information over the phone

valuable ['væljuəbl] *(hier:)* wichtig
figures ['fɪgəz] Nummern, Daten
clearly ['klɪəli] deutlich, klar

confused [kən'fju:zd] verwirrt
to divert [daɪ'vɜ:t] weiterleiten
extractor fan [ik'stræktəfæn] Dunstabzug
hob [hɒb] Kochfeld
diameter [daɪ'æmɪtə] Durchmesser
socket ['sɒkɪt] Steckdose

Module 4 Machine tools

lathe [leɪð] Drehmaschine, Drehbank
milling machine ['mɪlɪŋ məˌʃi:n] Fräsmaschine
grinding machine ['graɪndɪŋ məˌʃi:n] Schleifmaschine
in common [ɪn 'kɒmən] gemeinsam
main switch [ˌmeɪn 'swɪtʃ] Hauptschalter
emergency stop [ɪˌmɜ:dʒnsi 'stɒp] Notaus(-schalter)
machine frame [mə'ʃi:n ˌfreɪm] Maschinengestell, rahmen
slide [slaɪd] Schlitten, Support
turner ['tɜ:nə] Dreher(in)
to feed [fi:d] zustellen
lathe cutter ['leɪð ˌkʌtə] Drehmeißel
chuck [tʃʌk] Spannfutter, Backenfutter
machine bed [mə'ʃi:n ˌbed] Maschinenbett, Fundament
clamping element ['klæmpɪŋ ˌelɪmənt] Spannelement

A | Machine tools and their parts

to remove [rɪ'mu:v] entfernen
main spindle [ˌmeɪn 'spɪndl] Hauptspindel
gear and control unit [ˌgɪər ən kən'trəʊl ˌju:nɪt] Steuerungseinheit

feed [fi:d] (Vor-)Schub, Zustellung
revolution speed [ˌrevə'lu:ʃn ˌspi:d] Drehgeschwindigkeit
headstock ['hedstɒk] Spindelkasten
gearbox ['gɪəbɒks] Getriebeblock
toolpost ['tu:lpəʊst] Werkzeughalter
saddle ['sædl] Schlitten
cross slide ['krɒs ˌslaɪd] Querschlitten, Support
handwheel control ['hændwi:l kənˌtrəʊl] Radsteuerung
tool quick exchange [ˌtu:l ˌkwɪk‿ɪks'tʃeɪndʒ] Werkzeugschnellwechsler
tailstock ['teɪlstɒk] Reitstock
control rod [kən'trəʊl ˌrɒd] Steuerstange
column ['kɒləm] Ständer, Säule
vertical slide [ˌvɜ:tɪkl 'slaɪd] Senkrechtschlitten
overarm ['əʊvərɑ:m] Führungsarm
control panel [kən'trəʊl ˌpænl] Bedienungs-, Steuerpult
machine table [mə'ʃi:n ˌteɪbl] Maschinentisch
knee [ni:] Winkeltisch
base [beɪs] Sockel, Fundament
table traverse ['teɪbl ˌtrævəs] beweglicher Schleiftisch, Zustelltisch
table hand feed ['teɪbl ˌhændfi:d] Handvorschub-Tisch
grinding disc ['graɪndɪŋ ˌdɪsk] Schleifscheibe
start and stop switch [ˌstɑ:t‿ən 'stɒp ˌswɪtʃ] Anlass- und Ausschalter

B | The function of machine tool components

component [kəm'pəʊnənt] Maschinenbauteil
to be mounted [bi 'maʊntɪd] befestigt sein, festgeschraubt sein
horizontally [ˌhɒrɪ'zɒntli] horizontal
magnetically [mæg'netɪkli] magnetisch

equipped with [ɪ'kwɪpt wɪð] ausgestattet mit
three-jaw chuck [ˌθri:dʒɔ: 'tʃʌk] Dreibackenfutter
to perform [pə'fɔ:m] durchführen
clockwise ['klɒkwaɪz] im Uhrzeigersinn
anticlockwise [ˌæntɪ'klɒkwaɪz] gegen den Uhrzeigersinn
corresponding [ˌkɒrɪ'spɒndɪŋ] entsprechend

to house [haʊz] innewohnen, unterbringen
gears [gɪəz] Getriebe

cutting tool ['kʌtɪŋ ˌtu:l] Schneid-, Zerspanungswerkzeug
grinding wheel ['graɪndɪŋ ˌwi:l] Schleifscheibe
to drive [draɪv] antreiben
cross-feed ['krɒsfi:d] Quervorschub
longitudinal [ˌlɒndʒɪ'tju:dɪnl] Längs-
large-scale-manufacturing [ˌlɑ:dʒskeɪl ˌmænjə'fæktʃrɪŋ] Massenfertigung

Module D Written communication

essential [ɪ'senʃl] sehr wichtig
workshop ['wɜ:kʃɒp] Werkstatt
efficiently [ɪ'fɪʃntli] effizient
necessary ['nesəsri] nötig, notwendig
enquiry [ɪn'kwaɪəri] Anfrage
promptly ['prɒmtli] sofort
offer ['ɒfə] Angebot
order ['ɔ:də] Bestellung
to replace [rɪ'pleɪs] ersetzen
lesser ['lesə] geringer
advantage [əd'vɑ:ntɪdʒ] Vorteil
disadvantage [ˌdɪsəd'vɑ:ntɪdʒ] Nachteil
confidential [ˌkɒnfɪ'denʃl] vertraulich
time-consuming ['taɪmkənˌsju:mɪŋ] zeitraubend
reliable [rɪ'laɪəbl] zuverlässig
misunderstanding [ˌmɪsʌndə'stændɪŋ] Missverständnis

A | Enquiries

enquiry [ɪn'kwaɪəri] Anfrage
car mechanic ['kɑ: mɪˌkænɪk] Automechaniker(in)
appropriate [ə'prəʊpriət] angemessen, passend
salutation [ˌsæljə'teɪʃn] (Brief:) Anrede
supplier [sə'plaɪə] Lieferant, Zulieferer
subject line ['sʌbdʒɪkt ˌlaɪn] (Brief:) Betreffzeile
bonnet (BE) ['bɒnɪt] Motorhaube
family-run [ˌfæmli'rʌn] in Familienbesitz, familiengeführt
to expand [ɪk'spænd] erweitern, vergrößern
catalogue ['kætəlɒg] Katalog
discount ['dɪskaʊnt] Rabatt, Preisnachlass
terms of payment [ˌtɜ:mz‿əv 'peɪmənt] Zahlungsbedingungen
delivery times [dɪ'lɪvri ˌtaɪmz] Lieferzeiten
sample ['sæmpl] Muster
closing phrase ['kləʊzɪŋ ˌfreɪz] Schlussworte

complimentary close [ˌkɒmplɪmentri ˈkləʊz] Grußformel (am Briefende)
to recommend [ˌrekəˈmend] empfehlen
cost estimate [ˈkɒst‿estɪmət] Kostenvoranschlag
configure [kənˈfɪgə] konfigurieren
to appreciate [əˈpriːʃieɪt] etw. (wert-)schätzen
supply from stock [səˌplaɪ frəm ˈstɒk] ab Lager liefern

B | Offers

bank transfer [ˈbæŋk ˌtrænsfɜː] Banküberweisung
working day [ˌwɜːkɪŋ ˈdeɪ] Werktag
attachment [əˈtætʃmənt] Anhang
stock [stɒk] Bestand, Vorrat
to require [rɪˈkwaɪə] benötigen
ratchet [ˈrætʃɪt] Knarre, Ratsche
socket [ˈsɒkɪt] Stecknuss
(adjustable) wrench [əˌdʒʌstəbl ˈrenʃ] (verstellbarer) Schraubenschlüssel
screwdriver [ˈskruːˌdraɪvə] Schraubendreher
to dispatch [dɪˈspætʃ] versenden, verschicken
DIY (Do-it-yourself) [ˌdiːaɪˈwaɪ] Heimwerken

C | Orders

sum [sʌm] Betrag
consignment [kənˈsaɪnmənt] Lieferung, Sendung
torque wrench [ˈtɔːk ˌrenʃ] Drehmomentschlüssel

Module 5 Cutting processes with machine tools

process [ˈprəʊsəs] maschinelle Bearbeitung
machine tool [məˈʃiːn ˌtuːl] Werkzeugmaschine
conventional [kənˈvenʃnl] herkömmlich
centre lathe [ˈsentə ˌleɪð] Drehmaschine
milling machine [ˈmɪlɪŋ məˌʃiːn] Fräsmaschine
grinding machine [ˈgraɪndɪŋ məˌʃiːn] Schleifmaschine
cutting process [ˈkʌtɪŋ ˌprəʊsəs] Zerspanungsprozess, spanabhebendes Verfahren
large-scale [ˌlɑːdʒˈskeɪl] Groß-, Massen-
shape [ʃeɪp] Form
workpiece [ˈwɜːkpiːs] Werkstück
to mill [mɪl] fräsen
to sharpen [ˈʃɑːpn] schärfen
to smoothen [ˈsmuːðn] glätten
surface [ˈsɜːfɪs] Oberfläche
machinist [məˈʃiːnɪst] Maschinist(in)

stud bolt [ˈstʌd ˌbəʊlt] Gewindebolzen
threaded [ˈθredɪd] mit einem Gewinde versehen
shaft [ʃɑːft] Schaft
steel [stiːl] Stahl
groove [gruːv] Nut
to process [ˈprəʊses] (maschinell) bearbeiten

A | Working with machine tools

to turn [tɜːn] drehen (auf der Drehbank)

headstock [ˈhedstɒk] Spindelkasten
to transmit [trænzˈmɪt] übermitteln
main spindle [ˌmeɪn ˈspɪndl] Hauptspindel
to rotate [rəˈteɪt] drehen (um eine feste Achse)
clockwise [ˈklɒkwaɪz] im Uhrzeigersinn
anticlockwise [ˌæntɪˈklɒkwaɪz] gegen den Uhrzeigersinn
revolution speed [ˌrevəˈluːʃn ˌspiːd] Drehzahlgeschwindigkeit
speed selection lever [ˌspiːd səˈlekʃn ˌliːvə] Geschwindigkeitsregler
slideway [ˈslaɪdweɪ] Führungsbahn
feed [fiːd] Schub, Vorschub
saddle [ˈsædl] Schlitten
cross-slide [ˈkrɒsslaɪd] Querschlitten
to clamp [klæmp] einspannen, aufspannen
chuck [tʃʌk] Spannfutter

three-jaw chuck [ˌθriːdʒɔː ˈtʃʌk] Dreibackenfutter
gear unit [ˈgɪə ˌjuːnɪt] Getriebeblock
control unit [kənˈtrəʊl ˌjuːnɪt] Steuerungseinheit
motor-reversing switch [ˌməʊtə rɪˈvɜːsɪŋ ˌswɪtʃ] Motorumschalter

B | Setting up a milling machine

to set up [ˌset‿ˈʌp] (eine Maschine) aufrüsten
process plan [ˈprəʊses ˌplæn] Arbeitsplan
technical drawing [ˌteknɪkl ˈdrɔːɪŋ] technische Zeichnung
rectangle [ˈrektæŋgl] Rechteck
dimension [daɪˈmenʃn] Maß
to specify [ˈspesɪfaɪ] bestimmen
to adjust [əˈdʒʌst] ausrichten, justieren
various [ˈveəriəs] verschieden
working axis, (Pl.) axes [ˌwɜːkɪŋ‿ˈæksɪs, ˈæksiːz] Arbeitsachse, Messachse
right angle [ˈraɪt‿æŋgl] rechter Winkel
working spindle [ˈwɜːkɪŋ ˌspɪndl] Arbeitsspindel
machine vice [məˈʃiːn ˌvaɪs] Maschinenschraubstock

milling cutter [ˈmɪlɪŋ ˌkʌtə] Fräser
value [ˈvæljuː] (Mess-)Wert
control panel [kənˈtrəʊl ˌpænl] Steuerungspult
supplier [səˈplaɪə] Lieferant
end-mill cutter [ˈendmɪl ˌkʌtə] Walzenstirnfräser, Schaftfräser
cutting arbor [ˈkʌtɪŋ ˌɑːbə] Fräsdorn
to correspond [ˌkɒrɪˈspɒnd] entsprechen
to flee [fliː] fliehen

C | Working safely with machine tools

to ruin [ˈruːɪn] kaputt machen
machine operator [məˈʃiːn‿ɒpreɪtə] Maschinenbediener(in)
properly [ˈprɒpli] genau, richtig
to refer to [rɪˈfɜː tə] sich beziehen auf
main spindle [ˌmeɪn ˈspɪndl] Hauptspindel
emergency stop [ɪˌmɜːdʒnsi ˈstɒp] Notaus, Notschalter
guard [ɡɑːd] Schutzvorrichtung
spark [spɑːk] Funke
ambulance [ˈæmbjʊləns] Ambulanz, Krankenwagen
to unclamp [ʌnˈklæmp] abspannen, ausspannen

Module E Applications

to sign [saɪn] unterschreiben
application [ˌæplɪˈkeɪʃn] Bewerbung
opportunity [ˌɒpəˈtjuːnəti] Möglichkeit
to decide [dɪˈsaɪd] sich entscheiden
branch [brɑːnʃ] Niederlassung
advert [ˈædvɜːt] Anzeige
letter of application [ˌletər‿əv‿æplɪˈkeɪʃn] Bewerbungsschreiben
CV (curriculum vitae) [ˌsiːˈviː, kəˌrɪkjələm ˈviːtaɪ] Lebenslauf
job interview [ˈdʒɒb‿ɪntəvjuː] Vorstellungsgespräch
employment contract [ɪmˈplɔɪmənt ˌkɒntrækt] Arbeitsvertrag
to invite [ɪnˈvaɪt] einladen
skill [skɪl] Fähigkeit
industry [ˈɪndəstri] *(hier:)* Branche
hard-working [ˌhɑːdˈwɜːkɪŋ] fleißig

A | Job advertisements

recently [ˈriːsntli] kürzlich
willing to learn [ˌwɪlɪŋ tə ˈlɜːn] lernbereit, lernwillig
responsible [rɪˈspɒnsəbl] verantwortlich
punctual [ˈpʌŋktʃuəl] pünktlich
pleasant [ˈpleznt] angenehm, sympathisch
working atmosphere [ˌwɜːkɪŋ‿ˈætməsfɪə] Arbeitsklima
valid [ˈvælɪd] gültig
troubleshooting [ˈtrʌblˌʃuːtɪŋ] Fehlersuche
to maintain [meɪnˈteɪn] bewahren
leading [ˈliːdɪŋ] führend
supplier [səˈplaɪə] Lieferant, Zulieferer
vacancy [ˈveɪknsi] freie Stelle
fault [fɒlt] Fehler
assembly [əˈsembli] Montage
summary [ˈsʌmri] Zusammenfassung

B | Letter of application

internship (AE) [ˈɪntɜːrnʃɪp] Praktikum
theoretical [θɪəˈretɪkl] theoretisch
to gain [ɡeɪn] *(hier:)* sammeln
reliable [rɪˈlaɪəbl] zuverlässig
to consider [kənˈsɪdə] betrachten
to require [rɪˈkwaɪə] benötigen

C | The CV

advice [ədˈvaɪs] Rat
tip [tɪp] Tipp, Hinweis
to highlight [ˈhaɪlaɪt] betonen
strength [streŋθ] Stärke
achievement [əˈtʃiːvmənt] Leistung
supervisor [ˈsuːpəvaɪzə] Leiter(in), Kontrolleur(in)
truth [truːθ] Wahrheit
embarrassing [ɪmˈbærəsɪŋ] peinlich
to spell [spel] buchstabieren
grateful [ˈɡreɪtfl] dankbar

Module 6 Engineering materials

property [ˈprɒpəti] (Material-)Eigenschaft
dense [dens] dicht, fest
malleable [ˈmæliəbl] verformbar, schmiedbar
sheet steel [ˌʃiːt ˈstiːl] Stahlblech
to press [pres] pressen, stanzen
to roll [rəʊl] rollen, walzen
cutting tool [ˈkʌtɪŋ ˌtuːl] Schneidwerkzeug, Zerspanungswerkzeug
lathe cutter [ˈleɪð ˌkʌtə] Drehmeißel
metal carbide steel [ˌmetlˌkɑːbaɪd ˈstiːl] Hartmetall

sawing disc [ˈsɔːɪŋ ˌdɪsk] Sägeblatt
ceramic [səˈræmɪk] Keramik (als Werkstoff)
to coat [kəʊt] beschichten
industrial diamond [ɪnˌdʌstriəl ˈdaɪəmənd] Industriediamant
steel [stiːl] Stahl
diamond-tipped sawing disc [ˌdaɪəmənˌtɪpt ˈsɔːɪŋ ˌdɪsk] Diamantsägeblatt

A | Materials – an overview

ferrous [ˈferəs] Eisen-
non-ferrous [ˌnɒnˈferəs] Nichteisen-
mild steel [ˌmaɪld ˈstiːl] (Maschinen-)Baustahl
iron ore [ˈaɪən‿ɔː] Eisenerz
cast iron [ˌkɑːst‿ˈaɪən] Gusseisen
lead [led] Blei
brittle [ˈbrɪtl] brüchig
carbide-tipped [ˌkɑːbaɪdˈtɪpt] mit einem Hartmetall (-schneide-)plättchen
toxic [ˈtɒksɪk] giftig
corrosion [kəˈrəʊʒn] Korrosion
resistant [rɪˈzɪstnt] resistent, beständig
alloy [ˈælɔɪ] Legierung
copper [ˈkɒpə] Kupfer
porcelain [ˈpɔːslɪn] Porzellan
stainless [ˈsteɪnləs] rostfrei
to corrode [kəˈrəʊd] korrodieren, verrosten
carbon [ˈkɑːbn] Kohlenstoff
chromium [ˈkrəʊmiəm] Chrom
hardness [hɑːdnəs] Härte, Festigkeit
application [ˌæplɪˈkeɪʃn] Anwendung
cylinder block [ˈsɪlɪndə ˌblɒk] Zylinderblock
automotive [ˌɔːtəˈməʊtɪv] Automobil-

B | Steel

to withstand [wɪðˈstænd] widerstehen
load [ləʊd] Last
durable [ˈdjʊərəbl] haltbar, strapazierfähig
tungsten carbide steel [ˌtʌŋstənˌkɑːbaɪd ˈstiːl] Hartmetallstahl, Werkzeugmetall
reversible carbide tip [rɪˌvɜːsəbl ˌkɑːbaɪd ˈtɪp] Wendeplatte aus Hartmetall
blunt [blʌnt] stumpf
low-carbon steel [ˌləʊˌkɑːbn ˈstiːl] weicher Stahl, kohlenstoffarmer Stahl
high-carbon steel [ˌhaɪˌkɑːbn ˈstiːl] (unlegierter) Hartstahl
manganese [ˈmæŋgəniːz] Mangan
phosphorous [ˈfɒsfrəs] Phosphor
silicon [ˈsɪlɪkən] Silizium
roller [ˈrəʊlə] Walze

◎ **machine vice** [məˈʃiːn ˌvaɪs] Maschinenschraubstock
clamping jaw [ˈklæmpɪŋ ˌdʒɔː] Spannbacke
to clamp [klæmp] einspannen
securely [sɪˈkjʊəli] sicher, fest
control spindle [kənˈtrəʊl ˌspɪndl] Steuerspindel
thread [θred] Gewinde
threading tool [ˈθredɪŋ ˌtuːl] Gewindeschneidwerkzeug

C | The mechanical properties of metals

durability [ˌdjʊərəˈbɪləti] Haltbarkeit
ductility [dʌkˈtɪləti] Dehnbarkeit
elasticity [ˌɪlæsˈtɪsəti] Elastizität
malleability [ˌmæliəˈbɪləti] Verformbarkeit, Schmiedbarkeit
abrasion [əˈbreɪʒn] Abnutzung, Verschleiß
strength [streŋθ] Festigkeit
spring steel [ˌsprɪŋ ˈstiːl] Federstahl
masonry [ˈmeɪsnri] Mauerwerk

Module F Socialising

relationship [rɪˈleɪʃnʃɪp] Beziehung

A | Small talk

subsidiary [səbˈsɪdɪəri] Tochtergesellschaft
trainee [ˌtreɪˈniː] Auszubildende(r)
appropriate [əˈprəʊpriət] angemessen, passend

B | Small talk in business

to dismiss [dɪˈsmɪs] nicht beachten
common ground [ˌkɒmən ˈgraʊnd] gemeinsame Basis
trivial [ˈtrɪviəl] unwichtig
uneasiness [ʌnˈiːzinəs] Unbehagen
tension [ˈtenʃn] Spannung
to avoid [əˈvɔɪd] vermeiden
awkward [ˈɔːkwəd] peinlich, unangenehm

C | Eating out

well-done [ˌwelˈdʌn] (Steak) gut durchgebraten
pork [pɔːk] Schweinefleisch

side order ['saɪd‿ɔ:də] Beilage
bill [bɪl] Rechnung
game [geɪm] *(hier:)* Wild
dessert [dɪ'zɜ:t] Nachtisch, Nachspeise
fork [fɔ:k] Gabel
main dish [ˌmeɪn 'dɪʃ] Hauptgericht
beef [bi:f] Rindfleisch
poultry ['pəʊltri] Geflügel
starter ['stɑ:tə] Vorspeise
tip [tɪp] Trinkgeld

Module 7 Material testing

to carry out [ˌkæri‿'aʊt] durchführen, ausführen
to determine [dɪ'tɜ:mɪn] festlegen, feststellen
property ['prɒpəti] Eigenschaft
malleable ['mæliəbl] schmiedbar, hämmerbar
brittle ['brɪtl] brüchig, spröde
tensile test ['tensaɪl ˌtest] Zugversuch
to load [ləʊd] laden
tension ['tenʃn] Zugspannung
impact test ['ɪmpækt ˌtest] Schlag-, Stoßprüfung, -versuch
to hammer ['hæmə] hämmern
tensility [ten'sɪləti] Zugfestigkeit
ductility [dʌk'tɪləti] Dehnbarkeit, Verformbarkeit, Hämmerbarkeit
toughness ['tʌfnəs] Zähigkeit, Festigkeit
tensile strength [ˌtensaɪl 'streŋθ] Zugfestigkeit
to withstand [wɪð'stænd] widerstehen
stretching ['stretʃɪŋ] Dehn-
stress [stres] Belastung, Spannung
to stretch [stretʃ] dehnen, strecken
to deform [dɪ'fɔ:m] verbiegen
resistance [rɪ'zɪstns] Widerstand
impact ['ɪmpækt] Schlag, Stoß
load [ləʊd] Last

A | The tensile test

elastic limit [ɪˌlæstɪk 'lɪmɪt] Elastizitätsgrenze
to fail [feɪl] ausfallen, versagen
test specimen ['test ˌspesɪmən] Prüfstück
shoulder ['ʃəʊldə] Randteil
to neck [nek] einschnüren
fracture point ['fræktʃə ˌpɔɪnt] Bruchstelle
gauge length ['geɪdʒ ˌleŋθ] Messlänge
test equipment ['test‿ɪˌkwɪpmənt] Prüfgerät
intern ['ɪntɜ:n] Praktikant(in)
subsidiary [səb'sɪdiəri] Tochtergesellschaft

confusing [kən'fju:zɪŋ] verwirrend
to a certain extent [tu‿ə ˌsɜ:tn‿ɪk'stent] bis zu einem gewissen Grad
to make sense [ˌmeɪk 'sens] einen Sinn ergeben
purpose ['pɜ:pəs] Zweck
crash [kræʃ] Zusammenstoß, Aufprall
potential [pə'tenʃl] potentiell, möglich
sheet steel [ˌʃi:t 'sti:l] Stahlblech
gauge mark ['geɪdʒ ˌmɑ:k] Messpunkt
elongation [ˌi:lɒŋ'geɪʃn] Längung, Dehnung

B | The impact test

machine tool [mə'ʃi:n ˌtu:l] Werkzeugmaschine
to fracture ['fræktʃə] brechen
to resist [rɪ'zɪst] widerstehen, standhalten
diagram ['daɪəgræm] Zeichnung
weighted ['weɪtɪd] gewichtet, beschwert
pendulum ['pendjələm] Pendel
stationary ['steɪʃnri] fest, stationär
constant ['kɒnstənt] konstant, gleich, unverändert
to release [rɪ'li:s] loslassen
to absorb [əb'zɔ:b] aufnehmen, absorbieren
to attain [ə'teɪn] erreichen
joule [dʒu:l] Joule
tough [tʌf] fest
upward ['ʌpwəd] Aufwärts-
pointer ['pɔɪntə] Zeiger
scale [skeɪl] Skala
starting position ['stɑ:tɪŋ pəˌzɪʃn] Ausgangsposition
pendulum hammer ['pendjələm ˌhæmə] Pendelhammer
anvil ['ænvɪl] Amboss

C | Testing and measuring hardness

scratching ['skrætʃɪŋ] Kratzen
abrasion [ə'breɪʒn] Abrieb, Verschleiß
bent [bent] verbogen
penetration [ˌpenə'treɪʃn] Eindringtiefe
indentation [ˌɪnden'teɪʃn] Eindruck
shallow ['ʃæləʊ] flach
penetrator ['penətreɪtə] Prüfspitze
preload ['pri:ləʊd] Vorlast(-spannung)
minor load ['maɪnə ˌləʊd] Anfangslast
indenter [ɪn'dentə] Eindringkörper
reference position ['refrns pəˌzɪʃn] Bezugspunkt, Referenzpunkt

surface finish [ˌsɜ:fɪs ˈfɪnɪʃ] Oberflächenbeschaffenheit, -güte
total test force [ˌtəʊtl ˈtest ˌfɔ:s] Gesamtprüflast, Versuchslast, Hauptlast
to recover [rɪˈkʌvə] wiederherstellen
to convert [kənˈvɜ:t] umwandeln
diameter [daɪˈæmətə] Durchmesser

Module G Presentations

required [rɪˈkwaɪəd] erforderlich, verlangt, erwünscht
service [ˈsɜ:vɪs] Dienstleistung
positional sketch [pəˌzɪʃnl ˈsketʃ] Technologieschema
to develop [dɪˈveləp] entwickeln
to improve [ɪmˈpru:v] besser werden, sich verbessern
meeting [ˈmi:tɪŋ] Sitzung, Besprechung
graph [grɑ:f] Diagramm
chart [tʃɑ:t] Schaubild, Diagramm
preparation [ˌprepr'eɪʃn] Vorbereitung
to explain [ɪkˈspleɪn] erklären
sales pitch [ˈseɪlz ˌpɪtʃ] Verkaufspräsentation
reason [ˈri:zn] Grund

A | Preparing a presentation

audience [ˈɔ:diəns] Zuhörer (Pl.), Publikum
body language [ˈbɒdi ˌlæŋgwɪdʒ] Körpersprache
handout [ˈhændaʊt] Informationsblatt
to prepare [prɪˈpeə] vorbereiten
visual aids [ˌvɪʒuəl‿ˈeɪdz] Anschauungsmaterial, visuelle Hilfen
to describe [dɪˈskraɪb] beschreiben
summary [ˈsʌmri] Zusammenfassung
overview [ˈəʊvəvju:] Überblick
to reinforce [ˌri:ɪnˈfɔ:s] verstärken, betonen
guidelines [ˈgaɪdlaɪnz] Leitlinien

B | Describing materials and products

sturdy [ˈstɜ:di] robust
shiny [ˈʃaɪni] glänzend
robust [rəˈbʌst] stabil
state-of-the-art [ˌsteɪt‿əv ðiˈ‿ɑ:t] auf dem neuesten Stand (der Technik)
user-friendly [ju:zəˈfrendli] benutzerfreundlich
reliable [rɪˈlaɪəbl] zuverlässig
hand-crafted [ˌhænˈkrɑ:ftɪd] handgefertigt

C | Delivering a presentation

carpenter [ˈkɑ:pɪntə] Tischler(in), Zimmerer, Zimmerin
furniture [ˈfɜ:nɪtʃə] Möbel
trade show [ˈtreɪd ˌʃəʊ] Messe

lounger [ˈlaʊndʒə] Liegesessel
softwood [ˈsɒftˌwʊd] Weichholz
timber [ˈtɪmbə] Holz, Bauholz
joiner [ˈdʒɔɪnə] Tischler(in), Schreiner(in)
convenience [kənˌvi:niəns] Zweckmäßigkeit, Bequemlichkeit
varnish [ˈvɑ:nɪʃ] Lack
durable [ˈdjʊərəbl] haltbar
polyurethane coating [ˌpɒlɪˌjʊərəθeɪn ˈkəʊtɪŋ] Polyurethanbeschichtung

Module 8 Measuring and gauging

to measure [ˈmeʒə] messen
to gauge [geɪdʒ] nachprüfen
gauge [geɪdʒ] Messgerät, Eichmaß, (Prüf-)Lehre
vernier calliper [ˌvɜ:niə ˈkælɪpə] Messschieber, Messlehre
micrometer [maɪˈkrɒmɪtə] Mikrometer, Bügelmessschraube
dial gauge [ˈdaɪəl ˌgeɪdʒ] Messuhr
square [skweə] Winkel
fixed gauge [ˈfɪkst ˌgeɪdʒ] (Prüf-)Lehre
calibre [ˈkælɪbə] (Prüf-)Lehre
diameter [daɪˈæmɪtə] Durchmesser
calibrated [ˈkælɪbreɪtɪd] kalibriert, geeicht
measurement [ˈmeʒəmənt] Maß
slip gauge [ˈslɪp ˌgeɪdʒ] Parallelendmaß
gauge block [ˈgeɪdʒ ˌblɒk] Endmaß
good/no good, go/no go [gʊd, ˌnəʊ ˈgʊd, gəʊ, ˌnəʊ ˈgəʊ] geeignet/ungeeignet
bolt [bəʊlt] Bolzen, Schraubenbolzen
lathe [leɪð] Drehmaschine, Drehbank
slot [slɒt] Nut

A | Measuring with a vernier calliper

external [ɪkˈstɜ:nl] Außen-
internal [ɪnˈtɜ:nl] Innen-
depth [depθ] Tiefen-

jaw for internal measurement [ˌdʒɔ: fər‿ɪnˌtɜ:nl ˈmeʒəmənt] Backen für Innenmaße
vernier [ˈvɜ:niə] Nonius
main scale [ˌmeɪn ˈskeɪl] Hauptskala
depth gauge [ˈdepθ ˌgeɪdʒ] Tiefenmaß
fixed jaw [ˌfɪkst ˈdʒɔ:] feststehender Backen
jaw for external measurement [ˌdʒɔ: fər‿ɪkˌstɜ:nl ˈmeʒəmənt] Backen für Außenmaße
movable jaw [ˌmu:vəbl ˈdʒɔ:] beweglicher Backen
clamp screw [ˈklæmp ˌskru:] Feststellschraube
to consist of [kənˈsɪst‿əv] bestehen aus
main [meɪn] Haupt-
jaw [dʒɔ:] Backen
to adjust [əˈdʒʌst] einstellen, justieren
to fit [fɪt] passen
pipe [paɪp] Rohr, Röhrchen
auxiliary scale [ɔ:gˌzɪliəri ˈskeɪl] Hilfsskala
nonius [ˈnəʊnɪəs] Nonius

tube [tju:b] Rohr, Röhrchen
thread [θred] Gewinde
hollow [ˈhɒləʊ] hohl

value [ˈvælju:] (Mess-)Wert
to align [əˈlaɪn] übereinstimmen
reading [ˈri:dɪŋ] abgelesener Messwert

B | Gauges

according to [əˈkɔ:dɪŋ tə] gemäß, entsprechend
SI base unit [ˌesaɪ ˈbeɪs ˌju:nɪt] SI-Einheit
thread gauge [ˈθred ˌgeɪdʒ] Gewindelehre
thread ring gauge [ˈθredrɪŋ ˌgeɪdʒ] Gewindelehrring
slot [slɒt] Nut
fuel [ˈfju:əl] Treibstoff

C | The International System of Units

to refer to [rɪˈfɜ: tə] sich beziehen auf
abbreviation [əˌbri:viˈeɪʃn] Abkürzung
mass [mæs] Masse
current [ˈkʌrnt] Stromstärke
light intensity [ˈlaɪt‿ɪnˌtensəti] Lichtstärke
amount of substance [əˌmaʊnt‿əv ˈsʌbstns] Stoffmenge(-nanteil)
fitting [ˈfɪtɪŋ] Fassung

Module H Dealing with customers

to deal with [ˈdi:l wɪð] umgehen mit, sich befassen mit
customer [ˈkʌstəmə] Kunde, Kundin
success [səkˈses] Erfolg
appointment [əˈpɔɪntmənt] Termin
enquiry [ɪnˈkwaɪəri] Anfrage
complaint [kəmˈpleɪnt] Beschwerde
essential [ɪˈsenʃl] sehr wichtig
builder [ˈbɪldə] Bauunternehmer(in)
building site [ˈbɪldɪŋ ˌsaɪt] Baustelle
to explain [ɪkˈspleɪn] erklären

A | Complaints

solution [səˈlu:ʃn] Lösung
delay [dɪˈleɪ] Verzögerung, Verspätung
price reduction [ˈpraɪs rɪˌdʌkʃn] Preisnachlass
faulty [ˈfɒlti] fehlerhaft, defekt, mangelhaft
damaged [ˈdæmɪdʒd] beschädigt
unsatisfactory [ʌnˌsætɪsˈfæktri] unbefriedigend, ungenügend, unzureichend
to replace [rɪˈpleɪs] ersetzen
air freight [ˈeə ˌfreɪt] Luftfracht
surplus [ˈsɜ:pləs] überschüssig
credit note [ˈkredɪt ˌnəʊt] Gutschrift
specific [spəˈsɪfɪk] bestimmt, spezifisch

access [ˈækses] Zugang
to log on [ˌlɒg‿ˈɒn] sich anmelden, sich einwählen
migration [maɪˈgreɪʃn] *(hier:)* Umstellung
to redo [ˌri:ˈdu:] noch einmal machen
to look into sth. [ˌlʊk‿ˈɪntə] einer Sache nachgehen

technician [tekˈnɪʃn] Techniker(in)
plumbing and heating [ˌplʌmɪŋ‿ənd ˈhi:tɪŋ] Heizung und Sanitär

B | Customer service

upset [ʌpˈset] verärgert
to avoid [əˈvɔɪd] vermeiden
argument [ˈɑ:gjəmənt] Streit, Auseinandersetzung
to calm sb. [kɑ:m] jmdn. beruhigen
to reassure [ˌri:əˈʃʊə] beruhigen
patient [ˈpeɪʃnt] geduldig
to solve [sɒlv] lösen
frame of mind [ˌfreɪm‿əv ˈmaɪnd] geistige Verfassung

furious ['fjʊəriəs] wütend
to affect [ə'fekt] Einfluss nehmen auf
mood [mu:d] Laune
to blame sb./sth. for sth. [bleɪm] jmdm./etw. die Schuld an etw. geben, jmdn. verantwortlich machen
excuse [ɪk'skju:s] Ausrede

Module 9 Joining and assembly

to join [dʒɔɪn] fügen, verbinden
joining technique ['dʒɔɪnɪŋ tek,ni:k] Fügetechnik
rivet ['rɪvɪt] Niet
fitting part ['fɪtɪŋ ,pɑ:t] Passstück, Passteil
joint [dʒɔɪnt] Verbindung, Verbindungsstelle
assembly [ə'sembli] Fügen, Montage
to weld [weld] schweißen
to solder ['səʊldə] (weich-)löten
dismantling process [dɪ'smæntlɪŋ ,prəʊses] Demontage
bonding technique ['bɒndɪŋ tek,ni:k] Klebetechnik
adhesive [əd'hi:sɪv] Kleber, Klebstoff
riveting tongs ['rɪvɪtɪŋ ,tɒŋz] Nietenzange
welding torch ['weldɪŋ ,tɔ:tʃ] Schweißbrenner
screwdriver ['skru:,draɪvə] Schraubendreher
rivet gun ['rɪvɪt ,gʌn] Nietpistole
to drive [draɪv] hineintreiben

A | Choosing joining and assembling techniques

to assemble [ə'sembl] montieren, fügen
sheet metal [,ʃi:t 'metl] Blech
plumber ['plʌmə] Klempner(in), Installateur(in)
press fit ['pres ,fɪt] Presspassung
fitting groove ['fɪtɪŋ ,gru:v] Passnut
fitting strip ['fɪtɪŋ ,strɪp] Passleiste
folded joint [,fəʊldɪd 'dʒɔɪnt] Falzverbindung
to bond [bɒnd] kleben
polymer ['pɒlɪmə] Kunststoff

B | Joints with fasteners

fastener ['fɑ:snə] Verbindungselement, Fügeteil
washer ['wɔʃə] Unterlegscheibe
application [,æplɪ'keɪʃn] Anwendung
to determine [dɪ'tɜ:mɪn] bestimmen
slotted screw [,slɒtɪd 'skru:] Schlitzschraube
hexagonal headed bolt [hek,sægnl,hedɪd 'bəʊlt] Schraubbolzen mit Sechskantkopf
cross-slot screw [,krɒs,slɒt 'skru:] Kreuzschlitzschraube
to counter ['kaʊntə] kontern
hexagon nut [,heksəgən 'nʌt] Sechskantmutter
Allen screw [,ælən 'skru:] Inbusschraube
countersunk rivet [,kaʊntəsʌŋk 'rɪvɪt] Senkkopfniet
flat washer [,flæt 'wɒʃə] flache Unterlegscheibe
spring washer [,sprɪŋ 'wɒʃə] Federscheibe
slotted [slɒtɪd] geschlitzt

C | Assembly by fitting

to fit [fɪt] fügen durch Passungen
sheet steel [,ʃi:t 'sti:l] (dünnes) Stahlblech
by means of [,baɪ 'mi:nz‿əv] mittels
locking seam ['lɒkɪŋ ,si:m] Falzverbindung
seam [si:m] Falz
edge [edʒ] Kante
to tap (down) [,tæp 'daʊn] (zusammen-)klopfen
rubber mallet [,rʌbə 'mælɪt] Gummihammer
to dent [dent] verbeulen
to hook together [,hʊk tə'geðə] festhaken
to lock [lɒk] festklemmen

◎
to scribe [skraɪb] vorreißen
to clamp [klæmp] einspannen
bench vice ['benʃ ,vaɪs] Schraubstock
marker line ['mɑ:kə ,laɪn] Markierungslinie
degree [dɪ'gri:] Grad
angle ['æŋgl] Winkel
to bend [bend] biegen
pliers ['plaɪəz] Zange

Module 10 Welding and soldering

to weld [weld] schweißen
to solder ['səʊldə] löten
joint [dʒɔɪnt] Verbindungsstelle
fastener ['fɑ:snə] Verbindungselement
to dismantle [dɪ'smæntl] zerlegen, demontieren, auseinandernehmen
to reassemble [,ri:ə'sembl] wieder zusammenbauen, zusammensetzen
reversible [rɪ'vɜ:səbl] umkehrbar
to determine [dɪ'tɜ:mɪn] bestimmen, festlegen
steel girder [,sti:l 'gɜ:də] Stahlträger
automotive engineering [,ɔ:təməʊtɪv ,endʒɪ'nɪərɪŋ] Automobilbau
car body ['kɑ: ,bɒdi] Karosserie

robot ['rəʊbɒt] Roboter
weld joint ['weld ˌdʒɔɪnt] Schweißverbindung
electrical engineering [ɪˌlektrɪkl ˌendʒɪ'nɪərɪŋ] Elektrotechnik
printed circuit board (PCB) [ˌprɪntɪd 'sɜ:kɪt ˌbɔ:d, ˌpi:si:'bi:] Leiterplatte
plumbing trade ['plʌmɪŋ ˌtreɪd] Installationstechnik
pipe [paɪp] Rohr

A | Welding

gas welding ['gæs ˌweldɪŋ] Gasschweißen
electric welding [ɪ'lektrɪk ˌweldɪŋ] Elektroschweißen
oxyacetylene welding [ˌɒksiə'setli:n ˌweldɪŋ] Autogenesschweißen, Schutzgasschweißen
torch [tɔ:tʃ] Schweißbrenner
welding wire ['weldɪŋ ˌwaɪə] Schweißdraht
to melt [melt] schmelzen
valve [vælv] Ventil
gauge [geɪdʒ] Messgerät
working pressure [ˌwɜ:kɪŋ 'preʃə] Betriebsdruck
arc welding ['ɑ:k ˌweldɪŋ] Lichtbogenschweißen
to operate ['ɒpreɪt] durchführen
power [paʊə] elektrischer Strom, Spannung
contact tip ['kɒntækt ˌtɪp] Kontaktierungsklemme
ground clamp ['graʊnd ˌklæmp] Erdungsklemme
flux core ['flʌks ˌkɔ:] Fließdraht

welding process ['weldɪŋ ˌprəʊses] Schweißverfahren
to increase [ɪn'kri:s] erhöhen, steigern
to adjust [ə'dʒʌst] einstellen
gear [gɪə] Ausrüstung
flip-front helmet [ˌflɪpfrʌnt 'helmɪt] Helm mit Klappvisier
wire speed ['waɪə ˌspi:d] Drahtzufuhr

polarity plug [pə'lærəti ˌplʌg] Polaritätsstecker
changeover ['tʃeɪndʒˌəʊvə] Umstellung
thermal overload [ˌθɜ:ml‿'əʊvələʊd] Überhitzung
heat setting ['hi:t ˌsetɪŋ] Temperaturauswahl
stainless steel [ˌsteɪnləs 'sti:l] Edelstahl
aluminium [ˌæljə'mɪniəm] Aluminium
portable ['pɔ:təbl] tragfähig

B | Soldering and brazing

to braze [breɪz] hartlöten
plumbing ['plʌmɪŋ] Sanitär-
electrical engineer [ɪˌlektrɪkl ˌendʒɪ'nɪə] Elektrotechniker(in)
board [bɔ:d] Platine, Leiterplatte
plumber ['plʌmə] Klempner(in), Installateur(in)
melting point ['meltɪŋ ˌpɔɪnt] Schmelzpunkt
solder ['səʊldə] Lot, Lötmetall
soldering station ['səʊldrɪŋ ˌsteɪʃn] Lötstation
soldering iron tip ['səʊldrɪŋ‿aɪən ˌtɪp] Lötkolbenspitze
soldering piston tip ['səʊldrɪŋ ˌpɪstn ˌtɪp] Lötkolbenspitze
iron holder ['aɪən ˌhəʊldə] Lötkolbenhalter
solder paste ['səʊldə ˌpeɪst] Lötfett
solder tin ['səʊldə ˌtɪn] Lötzinn
solder wire ['səʊldə ˌwaɪə] Lötdraht
brazing torch ['breɪzɪŋ ˌtɔ:tʃ] Lötlampe
mixer ['mɪksə] Mischregler
oxygen ['ɒksɪdʒən] Sauerstoff
acetylene [ə'setɪli:n] Azetylen
brass [brɑ:s] Messing
hose [həʊz] Schlauch
regulator ['regjəleɪtə] Regler
processor-soldering station [ˌprəʊsesə 'səʊldrɪŋ ˌsteɪʃn] Prozessor Lötstation
to prolong [prə'lɒŋ] verlängern
key [ki:] Taste
operating mode ['ɒpreɪtɪŋ ˌməʊd] Betriebsmodus
preset ['pri:set] vorgegeben
feature ['fi:tʃə] (Leistungs-)Merkmal
protective gear [prəˌtektɪv 'gɪə] Schutzkleidung, -ausrüstung
button-up [ˌbʌtn‿'ʌp] hochgeknöpft
collar ['kɒlə] Kragen
helmet ['helmɪt] Helm
filtered ['fɪltəd] Filter-
lens [lenz] Brillenglas
fire-resistant ['faɪə rɪˌzɪstnt] feuerfest
apron ['eɪprən] Schürze
spark ['spɑ:k] Funke
upper body [ˌʌpə 'bɒdi] Oberkörper

Module 11 CAD-CAM and CNC

CAD (computer aided design) [ˌsi:eɪ'di:, kəmˌpju:tər‿ˌeɪdɪd dɪ'zaɪn] computergestützte Konstruktion
CAM (computer aided manufacture) [ˌsi:eɪ'em, kəmˌpju:tər‿eɪdɪd ˌmænjə'fæktʃə] computergestützte Fertigung
CNC (computerized numerical control) [ˌsi:en'si:, kəmˌpju:traɪzd nju:ˌmerɪkl kən'trəʊl] CNC Steuerung

CAE (computer aided engineering) [ˌsiːeɪ'iː, kəmˌpjuːtər‿eɪdɪd‿endʒɪ'nɪərɪn] computergestützte Bearbeitung
control [kən'trəʊl] Steuerung
machine operator [mə'ʃiːn‿ɒpreɪtə] Maschinenbediener(in)
database ['deɪtəbeɪs] Datenbank
warehouse ['weəhaʊs] Lager
manufacturing [ˌmænjə'fæktʃrɪŋ] Produktion
technical drawing [ˌteknɪkl 'drɔːɪŋ] technische Zeichnung
to create [kri'eɪt] erstellen, erschaffen
screen [skriːn] Bildschirm
to mill [mɪl] fräsen
to carry out [ˌkæri‿'aʊt] durchführen, ausführen
quality control check ['kwɒləti kənˌtrəʊl ˌtʃek] Qualitätskontrolle

A | CAD-CAM technology

area ['eəriə] Sachgebiet, Branche
automotive engineering [ˌɔːtəməʊtɪv‿endʒɪ'nɪərɪŋ] Automobiltechnik, -bau
mechanical engineering [məˌkænɪkl‿endʒɪ'nɪərɪŋ] Maschinenbau
architecture ['ɑːkɪtektʃə] Architektur
drafting tool ['drɑːftɪŋ ˌtuːl] Konstruktions-, Zeichnungswerkzeug
drawing board ['drɔːɪŋ ˌbɔːd] Zeichenbrett
three-dimensional [ˌθriːdaɪ'menʃnl] dreidimensional
model ['mɒdl] Modell
computer-simulated operation [kəmˌpjuːtə ˌsɪmjəleɪtɪd‿ɒpɪ'eɪʃn] computersimulierter Betrieb
digital mock-up [ˌdɪdʒɪtl 'mɒkʌp] virtueller CAD Prototyp

◎ **prototype** ['prəʊtətaɪp] Prototyp
implementation [ˌɪmplɪmen'teɪʃn] Einführung, Implementierung
load [ləʊd] Last, Belastung
stress [stres] Spannung, Belastung
to bear [beə] aushalten
on the factory floor [ɒn ðə ˌfæktri 'flɔː] in der Fabrikhalle
to alter ['ɔːltə] verändern

tactile sensor [ˌtæktaɪl 'sensə] Berührungssensor
assembly line [ə'sembli ˌlaɪn] Montagestraße, Fließbandfertigung
sensory device [ˌsensri dɪ'vaɪs] Sensorgerät
spray painting ['spreɪ ˌpeɪntɪŋ] Sprühlackierung

component [kəm'pəʊnənt] Bauteil
to mount [maʊnt] montieren, anbauen
multitasking system [ˌmʌlti'tɑːskɪŋ ˌsɪstəm] Mehrprogrammbetrieb
feature ['fiːtʃə] Leistungsmerkmal

B | CNC technology in industry

CNC machine tool [ˌsiːensiː mə'ʃiːn ˌtuːl] CNC Werkzeugmaschine
control panel [kən'trəʊl ˌpænl] Bedienungs-, Steuerpult
command [kə'mɑːnd] Befehl, Eingabe
to monitor ['mɒnɪtə] überwachen
milling operation ['mɪlɪŋ‿ɒprˌeɪʃn] Fräsarbeit
drilling operation ['drɪlɪŋ‿ɒprˌeɪʃn] Bohrarbeit
cutting operation ['kʌtɪŋ‿ɒprˌeɪʃn] Zerspanungsarbeit
operation motion [ɒprˌeɪʃn 'məʊʃn] Betriebs-, Funktionsbewegung
axis, (Pl.) axes ['æksɪs, 'æksiːz] (Funktions-)Achse(n)
linear axis [ˌlɪniər‿'æksɪs] Linearachse
rotary axis [ˌrəʊtri‿'æksɪs] Drehachse
motion path ['məʊʃn ˌpɑːθ] Funktions-, Arbeitsweg
motion control ['məʊʃn kənˌtrəʊl] Strecken-, Bahnsteuerung
length of travel [ˌleŋθ‿əv 'trævl] (Arbeits-)Weglänge
feed rate ['fiːd ˌreɪt] Vorschubgeschwindigkeit
three-jaw chuck [ˌθriːdʒɔː 'tʃʌk] Dreibackenfutter
to counter ['kaʊntə] kontern
tailstock ['teɪlstɒk] Reitstock
turret ['tʌrɪt] (Werkzeug-)Revolverkopf
drive motor ['draɪv ˌməʊtə] Antriebsmotor
ball screw ['bɔːl ˌskruː] Kugelrollspindel
feedback device ['fiːdbæk dɪˌvaɪs] Messwertgeber
to perform [pə'fɔːm] durch-, ausführen
safety guard ['seɪfti ˌgɑːd] Schutzvorrichtung
appropriate [ə'prəʊpriət] passend
emergency shut-off [ɪˌmɜːdʒnsi 'ʃʌtɒf] Notaus(-schalter), (-knopf)
visibility [ˌvɪzə'bɪləti] Sicht, Sichtbarkeit

Module 12 Maintenance and troubleshooting

maintenance ['meɪntnəns] Instandhaltung, Wartung
troubleshooting ['trʌblˌʃuːtɪŋ] Fehler-, Problemsuche und -lösung
to maintain [meɪn'teɪn] warten, instand halten

operator ['ɒpreɪtə] Bediener(in)
warranty ['wɒrnti] Garantie
to claim [kleɪm] beanspruchen
to neglect [nɪ'glekt] vernachlässigen
to treat [tri:t] behandeln
to lie idle [ˌlaɪ‿'aɪdl] (wegen einer Störung) nicht in Betrieb sein
breakdown ['breɪkdaʊn] Panne, Störung
to service ['sɜ:vɪs] warten, instand halten
fault [fɔ:lt] Fehler, Fehlfunktion, Störung
appropriate [ə'prəʊpriət] passend, geeignet
control panel [kən'trəʊl ˌpænl] Steuerpult
coolant ['ku:lənt] Kühlmittel
to check ['tʃek] kontrollieren, prüfen
revolution speed [ˌrevə'lu:ʃn ˌspi:d] Drehgeschwindigkeit, -zahl
sharpness ['ʃɑ:pnəs] Schärfe

A | Troubleshooting

to perform [pə'fɔ:m] ausführen, verrichten, leisten
required [rɪ'kwaɪəd] erforderlich, gewünscht
main spindle [ˌmeɪn 'spɪndl] Hauptspindel
feed [fi:d] Vorschub
lathe cutter ['leɪð ˌkʌtə] Drehmeißel, -stahl
blunt [blʌnt] stumpf
to release [rɪ'li:s] lösen
to set [set] einstellen
anticlockwise [ˌæntɪ'klɒkwaɪz] gegen den Uhrzeigersinn
to clamp [klæmp] einspannen
safety button ['seɪfti ˌbʌtn] Notaus, Sicherheits-, Notschalter
toolpost ['tu:lpəʊst] Werkzeughalter
table ['teɪbl] Tabelle
gear box ['gɪəbɒks] Getriebe
main switch [ˌmeɪn 'swɪtʃ] Hauptschalter
rotation [rə'teɪʃn] Umdrehung

to lock in [ˌlɒk‿'ɪn] arretieren, sperren
three-jaw chuck [ˌθri:dʒɔ: 'tʃʌk] Dreibackenfutter
mild steel [ˌmaɪld 'sti:l] (Maschinen-)Baustahl
revolution [ˌrevə'lu:ʃn] Umdrehung
ratio ['reɪʃiəʊ] Verhältnis
diameter [daɪ'æmɪtə] Durchmesser
stress [stres] Last, Belastung
longitudinal turning [ˌlɒndʒɪˌtju:dɪnl 'tɜ:nɪŋ] Längsdrehen
clockwise ['klɒkwaɪz] im Uhrzeigersinn
milling shop ['mɪlɪŋ ʃɒp] Fräserei

scratch [skrætʃ] Kratzer, Riefe
grinding ['graɪndɪŋ] Schleif-
slot [slɒt] Schlitz, Rille, Nut
to mill [mɪl] fräsen
twist drill ['twɪst ˌdrɪl] Spiralbohrer
column drill ['kɒləm ˌdrɪl] Ständerbohrmaschine
abrasive [ə'breɪsɪv] Schleifmittel, -korn
to wear out [ˌweər‿'aʊt] sich abnutzen, verschleißen

B | Maintenance

power tool ['paʊə tu:l] Elektrowerkzeug
drill [drɪl] Bohrer, Bohrmaschine
angle grinder ['æŋgl ˌgraɪndə] Winkelschleifer
saw [sɔ:] Säge
manual ['mænjʊəl] Gebrauchsanweisung, Handbuch
to be unfamiliar with [bi‿ʌnfə'mɪljə wɪð] nicht vertraut sein mit
to arise [ə'raɪz] entstehen
operating instructions ['ɒpreɪtɪŋ‿ɪnˌstrʌkʃnz] Bedienungsanleitung
masonry ['meɪsnri] Mauerwerk
concrete ['kɒŋkri:t] Beton
to vary ['veəri] variieren
drill bit ['drɪl ˌbɪt] Bohreinsatz
brad point ['bræd ˌpɔɪnt] Zentrierspitze
high-speed steel (HSS) [ˌhaɪspi:d 'sti:l, ˌeɪtʃes'es] Hochgeschwindigkeitsstahl
tungsten carbide [ˌtʌŋstən 'kɑ:baɪd] Hartmetall
drilling speed ['drɪlɪŋ ˌspi:d] Bohrgeschwindigkeit
to state [steɪt] sagen
multi-purpose drill [ˌmʌltipɜ:pəs 'drɪl] Mehrzweckbohrer
to cope with ['kəʊp wɪð] bewältigen, meistern, fertig werden mit
impact drill ['ɪmpækt ˌdrɪl] Schlagbohrer, Bohrhammer
screwdriver bit ['skru:ˌdraɪvə ˌbɪt] Schraubendrehereinsatz
to centre-punch ['sentəˌpʌnʃ] zentrieren
hard metal tip [ˌhɑ:dmetl 'tɪp] Hartmetallspitze
to pre-drill [ˌpri:'drɪl] vorbohren
to deform [dɪ'fɔ:m] verbiegen
vice [vaɪs] Schraubstock
shape [ʃeɪp] Form
marble ['mɑ:bl] Marmor
to solder ['səʊldə] löten
sheet metal [ˌʃi:t 'metl] Blech
to mark [mɑ:k] markieren

to rotate [rə'teɪt] rotieren, sich drehen
ventilation slot [ˌventɪ'leɪʃn ˌslɒt] Lüftungsschlitz
chuck [tʃʌk] Spannfutter
impact drilling ['ɪmpækt ˌdrɪlɪŋ] Schlagbohren
cleaning spray ['kli:nɪŋ ˌspreɪ] Reinigungsspray
clamping jaws ['klæmpɪŋ ˌdʒɔ:z] Spannbacken
boring ['bɔ:rɪŋ] Bohrung
spare part [ˌspeə 'pɑ:t] Ersatzteil
accessories [ək'sesriz] Zubehör
exploded view [ɪkˌspləʊdɪd 'vju:] Explosionszeichnung
to unplug [ʌn'plʌg] ausstecken
chip [tʃɪp] Span
goggles ['gɒglz] Schutzbrille
mask [mɑ:sk] Schutzmaske
connection cable [kə'nekʃn ˌkeɪbl] Verbindungskabel
working range [ˌwɜ:kɪŋ 'reɪndʒ] Arbeits-, Wirkungsbereich
toxic ['tɒksɪk] giftig
residual current device (RCD) [rɪˌzɪdjuəl 'kʌrnt dɪˌvaɪs, ˌɑ:si:'di:] Fehlstromschutzschalter

Alphabetical word list

A

abbreviation Abkürzung 67
abrasion Abrieb, Verschleiß 58
abrasive Schleifmittel, -korn 85
to absorb aufnehmen, absorbieren 58
access Zugang 69
accessory Zubehör 26, 87
accident Unfall 10
according to gemäß, entsprechend 66
accounts Buchhaltung 21
accuracy Genauigkeit 23
to a certain extent bis zu einem gewissen Grad 57
acetylene Azetylen 78
achievement Leistung 47
adhesive Kleber, Klebstoff 72
to adjust einstellen 77
adjustable wrench verstellbarer Schraubenschlüssel, Engländer 16
advanced fortgeschritten 9
advantage Vorteil 36
advert Anzeige 44
advice Rat 47
to affect Einfluss nehmen auf 71
air freight Luftfracht 69
to align übereinstimmen 66
Allen key Inbusschlüssel, Innensechskantschlüssel 16
Allen screw Inbusschraube 74
alloy Legierung 49
to alter verändern 81
although obwohl 30
aluminium Aluminium 77
ambulance Ambulanz, Krankenwagen 43
amount of substance Stoffmenge(-nanteil) 67
angle Winkel 25
angle gear Umlenkgetriebe 19
angle grinder Winkelschleifer 24
anticlockwise gegen den Uhrzeigersinn 85
anvil Amboss 58
application Bewerbung 44
appointment Termin 68
to appreciate etw. (wert-)schätzen 37
apprentice Auszbildende(r) 8
apprenticeship Ausbildung, Lehre 22
appropriate passend, geeignet 12, 83
approximate ungefähr 26
apron Schürze 79
architecture Architektur 81
arc welding Lichtbogenschweißen 77
area Sachgebiet, Branche 81
area code Vorwahl 29
argument Streit, Auseinandersetzung 71
to arise entstehen 86
to assemble montieren, fügen 73
assembly Fügen, Montage 72
assembly line Montagestraße, Fließbandfertigung 81
attachment Anhang 38
to attain erreichen 58
audience Zuhörer (Pl.), Publikum 61
automotive Automobil- 49
automotive engineering Automobiltechnik, -bau 76, 81
auto shut-off automatischer Abschalter 19
auxiliary scale Hilfsskala 65
to avoid vermeiden 71
awkward peinlich, unangenehm 54
axis, (Pl.) axes (Funktions-)Achse(n) 82

B

ball screw Kugelrollspindel 82
bank transfer Banküberweisung 38
bar (Metall-)Stange 10
base Sockel, Fundament 33
base plate Grundplatte 25
battery cartridge Batterieladegerät 19
to bear aushalten 81
beef Rindfleisch 55
to belong to gehören zu 23
to be mounted befestigt sein, festgeschraubt sein 34
bench vice Bankschraubstock 8
to bend biegen 17, 75
bent verbogen 58
to be unfamiliar with nicht vertraut sein mit 86
bill Rechnung 55
bit -aufsatz, Bit 16
to blame sb. / sth. for sth. jmdm. / etw. die Schuld an etw. geben, jmdn. verantwortlich machen 71
blunt stumpf 85
board Platine, Leiterplatte 78
body language Körpersprache 61
bolt Bolzen, Schraubenbolzen 64
to bond kleben 73
bonding technique Klebetechnik 72
bonnet (BE) Motorhaube 37
to bore (auf-)bohren, (in die Vollen) bohren 25
boring Bohrung 87
brad point Zentrierspitze 86
braking system Bremsanlage 21
branch Niederlassung 44
brass Messing 78
to braze hartlöten 78
brazing torch Lötlampe 78
breakdown Panne, Störung 84
brittle brüchig, spröde 49, 56
bubble Blase 17
to build herstellen, produzieren 26
builder Bauunternehmer(in) 68
building site Baustelle 68
button-up hochgeknöpft 79
by means of mittels 75

C

CAD (computer aided design) computergestützte Konstruktion 80
CAE (computer aided engineering) computergestützte Bearbeitung 80
calibrated kalibriert, geeicht 64

D

E

F

G

H

I

J

K

L

M

N

O

P

Q

R

S

saddle Schlitten 41
safety boots Arbeitsschuhe 10
safety button Notaus, Sicherheits-, Notschalter 85
safety guard Schutzvorrichtung 82
safety sign Sicherheitsschild, -hinweis 11
sales pitch Verkaufspräsentation 60
sales talk Verkaufsgespräch 19
salutation (Brief:) Anrede 37
sample Muster 37
sander Schleifer, Schleifmaschine 18
saw Säge 86
sawing disc Sägeblatt 48
scale Skala 58
scratch Kratzer, Riefe 85
scratching Kratzen 58
screen Bildschirm 80
to screw schrauben 17
screwdriver Schraubendreher 72
screwdriver bit Schraubendreher-einsatz 86
to scribe vorreißen 75
scriber Anreissnadel 25
seam Falz 75
second-cut file Doppelschlichtfeile 27
securely sicher, fest 50
sensory device Sensorgerät 81
service Dienstleistung 60
to service warten, instand halten 84
to set einstellen 85
to set up (eine Maschine) aufrüsten 41
shaft Schaft 40
shallow flach 58
shape Form 40
to shape formen, fräsen 22
to sharpen schärfen 40
sharpness Schärfe 84
sheet metal Blech 73
sheet steel Stahlblech 48
shift Schicht 22
shiny glänzend 62
shop floor Fabrikhalle, Produktionshalle 9
shoulder Randteil 57
SI base unit SI-Einheit 66
side order Beilage 55
to sign unterschreiben 44
silicon Silizium 50
skill Fähigkeit 44
skilled worker Facharbeiter(in) 9
slide Schlitten, Support 32
slideway Führungsbahn 41
slip gauge Parallelendmaß 64
slot Nut 64
slotted geschlitzt 74
slotted screw Schlitzschraube 74
to smoothen glätten 40
socket Stecknuss 38
softwood Weichholz 63
solder Lot, Lötmetall 78
to solder löten 76
soldering iron tip Lötkolbenspitze 78
soldering piston tip Lötkolbenspitze 78
soldering station Lötstation 78
solder paste Lötfett 78
solder tin Lötzinn 78
solder wire Lötdraht 78
solution Lösung 28
to solve lösen 71
sophisticated hochentwickelt, anspruchsvoll 9
spanner Schraubenschlüssel 16
spare part Ersatzteil 87
spark Funke 43, 79
specific bestimmt, spezifisch 69
to specify bestimmen 41
speed selection lever Geschwindig-keitsregler 41
to spell buchstabieren 47
to split aufteilen 23
spray painting Sprühlackierung 81
spring steel Federstahl 51
spring washer Federscheibe 74
square Winkel 64
stainless rostfrei 49
stainless steel Edelstahl 77
start and stop switch Anlass- und Ausschalter 34
starter Vorspeise 55
starting position Ausgangsposition 58
to state sagen 86
state-of-the-art neuester, neueste, neuestes; auf dem neuesten Stand (der Technik) 8, 62
stationary fest, stationär 58
steel Stahl 48
steel bar Stahleisen, Stabstahl 26
steel brush Stahlbürste 16
steel girder Stahlträger 76
stock Bestand, Vorrat 38
storeroom Lager, Materiallager 26
stranger Unbekannte(r) 15
strength Stärke, Festigkeit 47, 51
stress Belastung, Spannung, Last 56, 85
to stretch dehnen, strecken 56
stretching Dehn- 56
stud bolt Gewindebolzen 40
sturdy robust 62
subject line (Brief:) Betreffzeile 37
subsidiary Tochtergesellschaft 53, 57
success Erfolg 68
suitable geeignet, passend 30
sum Betrag 39
summary Zusammenfassung 61
supervisor Leiter(in), Kontrolleur(in) 47
supplier Lieferant 20
supply from stock ab Lager liefern 37
to support unterstützen 23
surface Oberfläche 40
surface finish Oberflächenbeschaffen-heit, -güte 59
surplus überschüssig 69
to swap tauschen 23
swarf Span 24

T

table Tabelle 85
table hand feed Handvorschub-Tisch 34
table traverse beweglicher Schleiftisch, Zustelltisch 34
tactile sensor Berührungssensor 81
tailstock Reitstock 33, 82
to tap (down) (zusammen-) klopfen 75
task Aufgabe 22
technical drawing technische Zeichnung 80
technician Techniker(in) 69
tensile strength Zugfestigkeit 56

U

V

W

Bildquellenverzeichnis

4 Thinkstock (Hemera), München; **4** iStockphoto (David Jones), Calgary, Alberta; **5** iStockphoto (Artush), Calgary, Alberta; **5** BigStockPhoto.com (starfotograf), Davis, CA; **6** LinguaTV GmbH, Berlin; **6** Video(s) supplied by BBC Motion Gallery, London; **6** ZDF, Mainz; **6** ZDF Enterprises GmbH, Mainz; **8** iStockphoto (GYI NSEA), Calgary, Alberta; **10** Thinkstock (Hemera), München; **11** Fotolia.com (yobidaba), New York; **11** Thinkstock (iStockphoto), München; **12** iStockphoto (daniel rodriguez), Calgary, Alberta; **12** Thinkstock (Stockbyte), München; **12** iStockphoto (David Jones), Calgary, Alberta; **12** iStockphoto (Helder Almeida), Calgary, Alberta; **14** iStockphoto (Dean Mitchell), Calgary, Alberta; **15** iStockphoto (4x6), Calgary, Alberta; **16** BigStockPhoto.com (Gresei), Davis, CA; **18** iStockphoto (Tor Lindqvist), Calgary, Alberta; **18** iStockphoto (druvo), Calgary, Alberta; **18** iStockphoto (tuja66), Calgary, Alberta; **18** Thinkstock (iStockphoto), München; **19** iStockphoto (Daniel Loiselle), Calgary, Alberta; **20** shutterstock (Dmitry Kalinovsky), New York, NY; **20** Thinkstock (BananaStock), München; **20** iStockphoto (sturti), Calgary, Alberta; **20** Thinkstock (iStockphoto), München; **22** shutterstock (Dmitry Kalinovsky), New York, NY; **23** iStockphoto (mediaphotos), Calgary, Alberta; **24** iStockphoto (Joe Gough), Calgary, Alberta; **24** PantherMedia GmbH (gualtiero boffi), München; **24** shutterstock (yuyangc), New York, NY; **24** shutterstock (Dan70), New York, NY; **26** iStockphoto (Andris Daugovich), Calgary, Alberta; **27** Fotolia.com (BG), New York; **28** iStockphoto (diego cervo), Calgary, Alberta; **28** iStockphoto (nolimitpictures), Calgary, Alberta; **28** Thinkstock (Wavebreak Media), München; **28** PantherMedia GmbH (Benis Arapovic), München; **30** iStockphoto (PeskyMonkey), Calgary, Alberta; **32** iStockphoto (Hakan Caglav), Calgary, Alberta; **33** PantherMedia GmbH (Dainis Derics), München; **33** iStockphoto (clu), Calgary, Alberta; **34** CC-BY-SA-3.0 (Glenn McKechnie), siehe *3; **36** iStockphoto (David Jones), Calgary, Alberta; **36** iStockphoto (Warwick Lister-Kaye), Calgary, Alberta; **36** shutterstock (Stephen Coburn), New York, NY; **36** shutterstock (rangizzz), New York, NY; **40** Robert Bosch GmbH, Stuttgart; **41** iStockphoto (Prill Mediendesign & Fotografie), Calgary, Alberta; **43** iStockphoto (Joerg Reimann), Calgary, Alberta; **44** shutterstock (Minerva Studio), New York, NY; **44** iStockphoto (Brian Jackson), Calgary, Alberta; **44** shutterstock (StockLite), New York, NY; **44** iStockphoto (Willie B. Thomas), Calgary, Alberta; **46** shutterstock (Goodluz), New York, NY; **48** shutterstock (Dainis Derics), New York, NY; **48** iStockphoto (Konstantin Kulikov), Calgary, Alberta; **48** iStockphoto (hsihsiang Liu), Calgary, Alberta; **48** iStockphoto (pic4you), Calgary, Alberta; **50** Thinkstock (Photos.com), München; **51** iStockphoto (Chris Fertnig), Calgary, Alberta; **52** iStockphoto (fatihhoca), Calgary, Alberta; **52** iStockphoto (Clerkenwell_Images), Calgary, Alberta; **52** Thinkstock (Purestock), München; **52** iStockphoto (Chris Schmidt), Calgary, Alberta; **53** Thinkstock (BananaStock), München; **54** Thinkstock (Stockbyte), München; **55** iStockphoto (kristian sekulic), Calgary, Alberta; **56** Picture-Alliance (dpa - Report/ZB), Frankfurt; **57** PantherMedia GmbH (Uwe Moser), München; **59** ITW Test & Measurement GmbH, Esslingen; **60** iStockphoto (Clerkenwell_Images), Calgary, Alberta; **60** shutterstock (wavebreakmedia ltd), New York, NY; **60** Thinkstock (Purestock), München; **60** iStockphoto (Oleg Prikhodko), Calgary, Alberta; **61** iStockphoto (bluecinema), Calgary, Alberta; **63** iStockphoto (Joshua Hodge Photography), Calgary, Alberta; **64** iStockphoto (Chris Fertnig), Calgary, Alberta; **64** iStockphoto (Frank Wright), Calgary, Alberta; **64** iStockphoto (Artush), Calgary, Alberta; **64** iStockphoto (Joerg Reimann), Calgary, Alberta; **64** iStockphoto (t_kimura), Calgary, Alberta; **66** iStockphoto (Ivan Majtán), Calgary, Alberta; **66** Hommel Hercules Werkzeughandel GmbH & Co. KG, Viernheim; **66** shutterstock (alterfalter), New York, NY; **67** iStockphoto (JazzIRT), Calgary, Alberta; **67** Fotolia.com (KvinOz), New York; **67** shutterstock (Josef Bosak), New York, NY; **68** iStockphoto (YanLev), Calgary, Alberta; **68** iStockphoto (Steve Debenport), Calgary, Alberta; **68** iStockphoto (Sean Locke), Calgary, Alberta; **68** iStockphoto (Louis-Paul St-Onge), Calgary, Alberta; **69** iStockphoto (Sean Locke), Calgary, Alberta; **72** PantherMedia GmbH (Dusan Kostic), München; **72** iStockphoto (Srdjan Stefanovic), Calgary, Alberta; **72** BigStockPhoto.com (pixpax), Davis, CA; **72** iStockphoto (zilli), Calgary, Alberta; **74** BigStockPhoto.com (phil holmes), Davis, CA; **76** Thinkstock (Hemera), München; **76** BigStockPhoto.com (lisafx), Davis, CA; **76** BigStockPhoto.com (Otna Ydur), Davis, CA; **76** BigStockPhoto.com (laurentiu iordache), Davis, CA; **77** Rothenberger Werkzeuge GmbH, Kelkheim; **77** BigStockPhoto.com (prill), Davis, CA; **78** PantherMedia GmbH (Bernd Jürgens), München; **78** Rothenberger Werkzeuge GmbH, Kelkheim; **79** BigStockPhoto.com (starfotograf), Davis, CA; **80** BigStockPhoto.com (ragsac), Davis, CA; **81** Picture-Alliance (dpa/Rainer Jensen), Frankfurt; **81** BigStockPhoto.com (Nataliya Hora), Davis, CA; **81** Thinkstock (iStockphoto), München; **82** BigStockPhoto.com (buketbariskan), Davis, CA; **82** PantherMedia GmbH (Dmitry Kalinovsky), München; **84** shutterstock (Dmitry Kalinovsky), New York, NY; **86** shutterstock (Dan70), New York, NY; **86** Fotolia.com (Arpad Nagy-Bagoly), New York; **87** shutterstock (Jaroslaw Grudzinski), New York, NY; **88** LinguaTV GmbH, Berlin; **89** LinguaTV GmbH, Berlin; **90** ZDF Enterprises GmbH, Mainz; **91** ZDF Enterprises GmbH, Mainz; **92** ZDF, Mainz; **92** ZDF Enterprises GmbH, Mainz; **93** Video(s) supplied by BBC Motion Gallery, London; **COVER** iStockphoto (Louis Aguinaldo), Calgary, Alberta; **COVER** Corbis (Nathan Griffith), Düsseldorf

***3 Lizenzbestimmungen zu CC-BY-SA-3.0 siehe: http://creativecommons.org/licenses/by-sa/3.0/de/**

Sollte es in einem Einzelfall nicht gelungen sein, den korrekten Rechteinhaber ausfindig zu machen, so werden berechtigte Ansprüche selbstverständlich im Rahmen der üblichen Regelungen abgegolten.

Textquellenverzeichnis

97/98 Source: Powered Hand Tools - Pneumatic Tools - Basic Safety, http://www.ccohs.ca/oshanswers/safety_haz/power_tools/pneumat.html, Canadian Centre of Occupational Health and Safety (CCOHS), year of publication. Reproduced with the permission of CCOHS, 2012.

Grafik

25 Rainer Hilbert, Hardheim-Gerichtsstetten.